DATE DUE			
~~Apr 8 '74~~			
~~Dec 21 '80~~			
Dec 11 '84			

GAYLORD M-2   PRINTED IN U.S.A.

THE
PURSUIT OF DEATH

THE
PURSUIT OF
DEATH

A Study of Shelley's Poetry

By

BENJAMIN P. KURTZ

WITH A NEW PREFACE BY

JAMES D. HART

" The true disciple of philosophy is likely to be misunderstood by other men; they do not perceive that he is ever pursuing death and dying."
SOCRATES (*Phædo*, 64)

1970

OCTAGON BOOKS

New York

CAROLO MILLS GAYLEY
PRAESTANTI ET SINGVLARI INGENIO
NEC VERO NON CORDE

CONTENTS

PREFACE TO THE OCTAGON EDITION

Benjamin Putnam Kurtz was born in Hawaii in 1878 but as a youth he moved to Oakland, California, and the rest of his life was spent there and in the nearby Berkeley, to whose University of California he was devoted.

As a brilliant student at the state university, young Kurtz attracted the attention of Professor Charles Mills Gayley, the Chairman of the Department of English, who became his mentor. Under Gayley's direction he moved from the A.B. directly on to graduate work, selecting studies in the marvellous as his dissertation topic. In 1906 Kurtz became the first man to be awarded a doctorate in English by the University of California.

Three years before he earned the Ph.D., Kurtz was appointed an Instructor in the Department of English. All told he was an active member of that Department for forty-six years, a tenure longer than anybody has had before or since, or is likely to have again in these days when the profession is marked by mobility and when retirement comes earlier. Even though he was a quiet and a modest man, Benjamin Kurtz was happy to assist his much admired "Chief" in the business of running the Department. Gayley remained in the chairmanship until 1923 and Kurtz played a part in shaping the policies and the program of the Department which for many years he served as Secretary, when that position was one of real significance, and for some time too as Chairman of its Committee on Graduate Studies. Professor Kurtz liked all sorts of people and they liked him, and so it is understandable that he preferred the classroom to the activities of administration.

Although Professor Kurtz enjoyed teaching at every level, from the freshman to that of adults who attended his University Extension lectures, he was particularly devoted to graduate students, whom he aided both academically and personally. He loved the literature that brought him together with these young scholars, but he was fond of them as persons too. Always a compassionate man, Kurtz was happy not only to assist others to appreciate and to analyze great writings but also to aid them in their development from raw young men into developed scholars and teachers. One of his former students, later a member of the faculty at Berkeley, wrote of him: "I remember with immense gratitude his profound understanding of youth's problems, his sympathy and tolerance. . . . His gift was to evoke a love of the subject in all the students. To those who wanted to go on in the teaching profession he was particularly helpful, setting a high standard for scholarship, but counselling them to safeguard the flame of creative imagination and not permit it to be smothered by over-critical analysis and pedantry."

Professor Kurtz was himself an active, enthusiastic and humane scholar. He interested himself in a tremendous variety of subjects and he treated them on a diversity of levels. He saw nothing odd about publishing within one year an article on "English Versification" in *Modern Language Notes* and another on "Poetry at the University" in the popular regional journal, *Sunset Magazine*. His first book was *Studies in the Marvellous*, published in 1909 as a revision of the dissertation he had finished three years earlier. His next two books were, naturally enough, collaborations with Gayley: *English Poetry: Its Principles and Progress* and a second volume of Gayley's *Methods and Materials of Literary Criticism*, treating lyric, epic, and allied forms of poetry. The first work was a standard text for some years and Sir A. W. Ward, Master of Peterhouse, found the second to be possessed "of incomparable fulness and a balance equally rare," a judgment shared by others. His association with and admiration for Gayley in course of time led Kurtz to write a biography of his master, published in 1943 by the University of California Press.

Professor Kurtz also had his own scholarly interests, separate from those of Gayley, and he developed them not only in courses but in writings. Several of his publications in scholarly journals dealt with Occleve's "Lerne to Dye," and to the University's own publications in modern philology he contributed "From St. Antony to St. Guthlac, A Study in Biography." The range of Kurtz's interest is further indicated by other short publications: "Twelve Andamanese Songs," "Gifer the Worm: An Essay Toward the History of an Idea," "William Caxton: A Biographical Essay," and "Coleridge and Swedenborg." Even more striking is the variety among his complete, though brief books. One, written with a collaborator, edited four newly discovered letters by Mary Wollstonecraft and Helen M. Williams, and another is a biography that paid tribute to Joseph Cummings Rowell, the University of California's first librarian.

Perhaps the most significant of his works is this study of Shelley's poetry, *The Pursuit of Death*, issued in 1933, the same year that he published his highly regarded edition of *Shelley's Complete Poems*. The critical book was recognized immediately as an outstanding work of scholarship. At the time of publication, a review in the *New York Times* declared: "Professor Kurtz's book is the most comprehensive study yet printed of Shelley's thought and of the personal trials and intellectual rationalizations the poet struggled through in order to declare his prophetic message. The author is that unusual combination, a fine scholar and a very excellent interpreter of the poetic sensibility. His study of Shelley's unique treatment of the theme of death, related as it was to all the poet's other themes, is a book that no student of the creative imagination can neglect." This view was not just one of the moment. In 1934 the Commonwealth Club presented Professor Kurtz with its sole gold medal of the year, awarded to him "for the most outstanding literary achievement published by a resident of California." His book continues to be appreciated. In 1956 when Professor Bennett Weaver of the University of Michigan surveyed Shelley scholarship for *The English Romantic Poets: A Review of Research,* published by the Modern Language Association of America, he wrote: "Benjamin Putnam Kurtz, in *The Pursuit of Death* (1933), writes a richly informed study: he knows philosophy and he knows Shelley, and he recognizes Shelley as a developing intelligence, ... In the work of Kurtz we have come close to the center of Shelley's maturest thinking."

Professor Kurtz died in 1950 but what he stood for is well remembered. His Department annually awards a Benjamin Putnam Kurtz Prize to that graduate student who, in the estimation of a panel of judges, has written the best paper in a seminar or other course during that academic year. Thus his influence upon and his aid to graduate students continues indefinitely. The republication of *The Pursuit of Death* helps to achieve the same ends in other ways.

James D. Hart

INTRODUCTION

Around death the human being gathers his records of life. The prehistoric dwellers in the world's great river-valleys deposited samples of their culture in the graves of their dead, a few feet underground. To-day, the artist places in a poem concerning death his understanding of reality. As from ancient graves archaeologists have learned much of the ways of thinking of races long since extinct, so in what a poet says about death critics may discover much of his attitude toward life.

If philosophy is the attempt to understand being, death is its great instigator; for death, having more than anything else made men aware of life, has especially forced them to ask, What is being? or reality? Realists, nominalists, intuitionists, dualists, monists, idealists, naturalists, pragmatists, mystics: all have been stimulated by death to try to answer this question. Some have endeavoured by looking beneath appearances, and beyond common sense, to conceive some otherness that is reality, or some synthesis of life and death that is being. Others, building upon common sense, while distrusting the absolute, have reinterpreted ' reality ' as relative to belief and practicableness; death leaves them stoical or mournful — in any case, wondering what may lie beyond their common sense. Socrates said: " The true disciple of philosophy . . . is ever pursuing death and dying."

The poets, too, have pursued death; but with a difference. The philosopher has employed concepts and skilful reasoning; his endeavour has been to achieve clear and precise statement. And he has entrusted his thought primarily to words, or to words alone; and particularly to one phase of words —

their denotation. Moreover, he has depended upon abstract words and definitive meaning in spite of the acknowledged fact that all words, and especially abstract words, are by their very nature tricky phantoms — indefinite and ambiguous. But the poet, instinctively distrusting mere denotations and logical argument, in his pursuit has made use of every possible extension of word-meaning — the richness, the infinite variety, of connotation; the incommensurable suggestion of verbal music; the incalculable stimulus of poetic imagery; the unfathomable qualities of emotional appeal: without altogether losing the intellectual, or critical, means of definite demonstration, but avoiding the endless challenge to disagreement and debate that arises from a too exclusive use of that means.

What have been the findings of the poets? No such inclusive question is asked in this little essay. A more modest problem endeavours to engage attention. What was the finding of just one poet, but one who constantly pursued the subject — more constantly than any other of the major English poets?

A century ago a thoughtful man in assembling what the poets have hazarded about death would have hoped to find some inspired answers to the fearful riddle. Religious faith and metaphysical philosophy opined that great poets by inspiration have vision of hidden things. It was not considered unintelligent to believe that imagination can discover what reason cannot. But to-day many well-read men, though not those of the company of Mr. Yeats, will take pride in finding in such a compilation something very different. They may see in it only a number of phantom-ideas, vague images, and sublimated feelings, variously coalescing into mental attitudes that partially satisfy urgent emotional needs in facing death. They may detect even less — mere emotional sedatives. And, of course, matter-of-fact solution to the riddle of death there is none. The idealist's assertion that the individual mind returns into an absolute, unmoved, but all-moving mind, and the realist's contention that death is only a name for plasmic change, alike rest upon assumptions. One thinker guesses there is something incomprehensible beyond the limitations that shut in our human consciousness; another guesses there is nothing but what we know or can know with this human mind. Guesses all! Nevertheless, there persists the very deep need of taking some attitude confidently. Hence, imaginings and moods, touched whether more or less with conviction, continue to be necessary resources. It may, possibly, matter little what any poet thinks about anything. Certainly systematic thinking is not his vocation. It is his danger. But his imaginative transformations of death, and their entail of emotional balance and repose, continue to minister comfort.

The poets of the romantic revival had a great deal to say about death, and often they said it with a fervour and a strangeness that made their utterances seem prophetic. To analyze their intuitions, therefore, would be an attractive stratagem for the critic of culture. It might, indeed, be a revealing adventure, partly in disillusionment, partly in appreciation; for it was profoundly characteristic of the romanticists to love mysteries, and for them death was the greatest of mysteries. Hence, to detect and explain the changes in a given romanticist's intuitions of death, to disengage idea and enveloping mood and entrancing image and to appraise the relative power of each for comfort or for conviction, to learn the number and variety, whether great or small, of the attitudes assumed by the poet, to mark out his peculiar sagacity, and his special skill in presentation, and to survey his total accomplishment in this theme of death, is at least a significant approach in criticizing the mysteries and pretensions of romanticism.

If there be considered merely the absolute quantity of what a great variety of poets have said about death, few will be found to have written so much, either romantically or otherwise, upon the subject as did Shelley. And if the quantity be considered relatively, in proportion to the writer's utterances upon all subjects, perhaps no English poet of major importance will be found to have equalled Shelley. Counting relatively, Tennyson, probably, is closest to Shelley's record; and then, approximately in descending order, come Shakespeare, Keats, Milton, Browning, and Wordsworth, the last three being very close together and each of them reaching scarcely to one third of Shelley's achievement.

Because of this peculiar preponderance, as well as because of the amazing beauty of his most mature rendering of the theme, in the *Adonais*, Shelley has been made the centre of the present study. Other poets, notably Wordsworth and Coleridge, Keats and Byron, Tennyson and Browning, Rossetti and Swinburne, have been brought into the scheme incidentally; not in historical order, nor for exhaustive treatment, but solely for illuminating here and there Shelley's attitudes, by comparison and contrast.

Nor is it unreasonable to expect that in isolating these attitudes we may chance upon discoveries in other fields. Some special realization may be hoped for of the sequences in which Shelley's mind habitually worked; of the relative force therein of reason and sensitive mood and picturesque imaging; of the genesis of his ideas in his reading, their first and often but little considered utterance — hasty and crude — only to be carried thus as so much unrefined ore in the mind, until stress of personal experience should press out from them their true metal. Then the poet's candescent energy illumines truth with loveliness. Herein, too, some corroborative teaching may be found of how, in general, poets deal with facts and ideas — whether in the manner of the philosopher by adding abstractly to their meaning, as when Aristotle tried to purify Plato's thought of a stubborn dualism; or chiefly by investing them with human realness and exquisitely interpretative music and well-considered grace of image, as Shakespeare so often does in his sonnets, transforming the trite by his intense power of feeling the very thing itself and of adding to it words of rare greatness. For though, I suppose, more than one man has finally disposed of this subject, we nevertheless are constantly debating the relative importance in poetry of originality of idea and perfection of form. Continually in our criticism we are maintaining, yet more often assuming, that the poet's function is to contribute to the world's sum of ideas. More rarely we boldly assert his function is, rather, " in full and carrying gale," impetuously to bear the commonest and simplest of age-old experiences and ideas to the utmost of realization and beauty; or, at least, to approach the same end in a more tranquil spirit. This renewal of the deep meaning and sanctity of the commonplace, so that every bush, indeed, becomes a burning bush, is what Shelley himself meant by that metaphor of his to the effect that poetry redeems from decay the visitations of the divine in man — turning all things, even death, to loveliness, and thereby making familiar objects be, in a way, not familiar, yet in another way, piercingly familiar.

The story, of course, can be a story of attitudes only: of habitual emotional complexes, of speculations, beliefs, and convictions — all well enough regarded as attitudes of mind. But tenuous as some of these are by their very nature or may come to be in the particular forms they assume in Shelley's poetry, they are each and all the repeated experiences of many men in many ages. Some of them are the commonplaces of universal sorrow and hope. Some belong especially to the more philosophically minded. Some can be traced through nearly all poets who have at all considered death. Some are attitudes of dejection, defeat, despair; others are of hope and victory. Some are alive with passionate love that refuses to admit annihilation. Some, very few in Shelley's case, are marked by the ruin that despair makes in the mind. But there is in Shelley's poetry no example of terror, or even fear. That characteristic threat and dread, that new shudder, that utter terror, which, as Mr. H. O. Taylor has observed, pervaded early Christian theology and poetry, and thence became a tradition, are lacking here. Nor is there very much on another subject dear to Christian poets — personal immortality. To that belief, which to Shelley seemed to lack plausible support from the observed facts of life, he was indifferent or agnostic, like so many of our contemporary poets. To his way of thinking, once the larger spiritual reality could be accepted, the smaller matter of the fate of the individual could be taken on trust. Fear of death, indeed, arises very largely from narrow contemplation of self; by consecrating our thoughts to interests beyond self, we diminish the minatory power of death. Shelley's interests were notoriously social and ideal.

If the attitudes that await discussion are so universal, the value of merely discovering them in Shelley's work can be but little: we should know with which ones he is concerned, and to what extent — a brief addition to the statistics of thought. But these attitudes are so omnipresent in Shelley's work, so intertwined with all his ideas and ideals, efforts and failures and achievements, so fundamental to his dejections and visions, that an exploration of their genesis and development, and of the ever culminating force of their presentation, becomes indeed a radical study of his special intellectual and poetic quality. In particular, the three attitudes by which he progressed to a complete victory over the arch enemy, death, are of the essence of his character both as a man and a poet. These three victories, ethical, aesthetic, and mystical, in fact far more dynamically interrelated and overlapping than any separative account necessary for the purpose of discourse can adequately picture, are the trophies of his furthest advance as poet. To study them, therefore, in their intimate relations to his thought and emotions on the one hand, and to the ever developing force and beauty of poetic presentation on the other hand, is to study pretty much all his work from one of the most significant points of view possible to be taken.

This research, then, is a narrative of a progress in both thought and emotions, as well as in power of imaginative enchantment and musical incantation. But there is no intention to reduce Shelley's poetry to a logical or illogical development of ideas. Mr. J. M. Murry, in one of his sympathetic studies of Keats, has sternly repudiated that narrow sort of critical study, and I am quite in agreement with his position. But in Shelley's poetry ideas have all the force of sensations, though they are ideas nevertheless. Shelley is a poet of ideas, and his images are the incorporation of ideas, as he himself repeatedly informed his readers. Indeed, Keats went so far as to criticize Shelley for too great abundance of thought, even at the very time he was reproaching himself with a serious paucity of ideas. Shelley's ideas, as a matter of fact, cannot be separated from his poetry. Only in his earlier work does intellect encroach upon beauty. In the rest, one cannot penetrate his imagery or hear to the full his interpretive music until he has reconceived the incarnated thought. His poetry is not a thing apart either from his spiritualistic philosophy or from his matter-of-fact existence. Swinburne remarked, " His thoughts, words, deeds, all sang together."

It is true that this philosophical tendency has made understanding his poetry difficult. As E. R. Wodehouse, M.P. used pompously to inform the " Bath Literary and Philosophical Association," Shelley's " finest verse exhales metaphysics." But, after all, Shelley believed rather than theorized; was too closely given to conviction and action to be really of the philosophical, theoretical cast of mind. To him, his poetry was not a vacant theorizing; but an idealized expression of his beliefs concerning human accomplishment and progress.

No! Shelley the poet and the man were singularly in agreement with each other, and the statements of the one are nearly always the opinions of the other. Fundamental in each was a worship of an ideal Reality, and an unbelievably deep, sincere sense of the world's wrong. He was " cradled in poetry by wrong," as he himself said. He was like Carlyle in that the world's miseries were his miseries — not mere material for literary artistry. He spent his life and his genius in trying to make a connection between ideal and commonplace reality. Browning observed that he had an intenser belief than ordinary in the possibility of harmonizing the actual and the ideal. And his ideas and his poetic presentation of them, his philosophy and his poetry, come together repeatedly in aesthetic attitudes toward the ugliness he found in society and the beauty of deed and thought he believed men capable of reaching.

He developed neither the ideal nor the common-sense reality systematically. He touched metaphysics allusively, in concretizing myths that to-day read like new myths to explain the Platonic Ideas. His poetry was a symbolic realization of his idealism, intended to wake men with a vision of a promised land. He " submitted the shadows of things to the desires of the mind." He did not build a philosophy of pessimism out of the unromantic lust and cruelty of the actual world. Nor was he content to mourn because he could not have life on his own terms. He did not use his dream of benevolence and love as a way to escape captivity to the lower reality. But he repeatedly tried to live his romantic philosophy in the matter-of-fact world. Those attempts the common-sense world has never forgiven him. For in his failures, as in too true a mirror, common sense beholds its ugliness.

What, indeed, is the outstanding, ironic fact of his life and his fame? It is that he felt human woes too strongly, that he loved mankind too well and thought too highly of it, that he made poetic attempts to alleviate its woes by setting up lovely pictures of an ideal world to entrance men, that he confused economic facts and political science with heavenly philosophy; that, in a word (J. A. Symonds's word), he " confused the border lands of the actual and the visionary."

Yet, if a list be made of these false political and economic ideas of his, it will be found that by far the greater number of them have long since, or but recently, been converted into real practice; that of the remainder, a few are now in course of agitation, and others are yet in the lap of the future. Those that have been realized are: catholic emancipation, universal suffrage, and repeal of the Union, in Ireland; in England, abolition of the rotten boroughs, enfranchisement of the large, unrepresented towns, universal suffrage, complete religious toleration, universal education at public expense, extension of the jury system, emancipation of women, prison reform, abolition of starvation, the rule of labour. Those that are at present being agitated are: abolition of tithes, disestablishment of the Church of England, economic freedom through repudiating the public debt and imposing a capital levy, confiscation of large property-holdings, internationalism. Those that possibly lie ahead are: abolition of the present form of marriage, change to a republican form of government, abolition of common law, and the application, instead, of common sense to each case, disbanding of the standing army, passive resistance as the means of revolution, anarchy. Moreover, if it be objected that Shelley's theory of social oppression as arising from the short-sightedness of a privileged governing class is contrary to political and economic fact, we have only to note the present intense, popular dissatisfaction with national governing bodies to realize that his view yet retains a large measure of pragmatic significance. Certainly his genius was not that to which Milton refused praise: " a fugitive and cloistered virtue, unexercised and unbreathed, that never sallies out and seeks her adversary, but shrinks out of the race where that immortal garland is to be run for, not without dust and shame." Finally, if it be held that his approach in theory and poetry to social questions was aesthetic rather than practical, two observations are in order. First, it should be remembered that whenever he spoke in prose of possible reformations, he advocated gradual change, always maintaining that the dream of the best possible condition should never become the enemy of an immediate change for the better. His prose tracts and his letters give ample proof of this habit of thought. Second, the aesthetic approach in his poetry is a method at least arguable in respect of its propriety. One remembers that Schiller, in the second of his *Aesthetical Letters*, justified his failure to consider the great political issues of his day, by maintaining the thesis that the proper way of solving the all-important problems of the state is through aesthetic, since it is only by the beautiful that one arrives at freedom. The aim of living, for each man, is, after all, to make his life as beautiful as he can.

But what Shelley learned from this poetizing of human facts and possibilities was, of course, what all the world's idealistic leaders learn, that " the wise want love, and those who love want wisdom," that " the children of Mammon are wiser in their generation than the children of light," but " that to be wise in one's generation is, after all, not to be wise." At last, he attained Prospero's wisdom:

> Though with their high wrongs I am struck to the quick,
> Yet with my nobler reason 'gainst my fury
> Do I take part: the rarer action is
> In virtue than in vengeance.

Now, all this poetic struggle with, and representation of, the antithesis of the actual and the ideal, culminated for Shelley in a fact and in a metaphor derived from the fact. The fact was biological death, the going down of all things, and especially beautiful things, to the grave. The metaphor derived from this fact lay in making death a symbol of all that is ugly in human affairs. Ugliness culminates in death. Nor is he at all unique in giving death this double meaning of fact and symbol, of enigmatic cessation and human sin. The poet of *Genesis* made death the punishment of sin, and Milton followed him by making Death the son of Satan and his daughter-paramour, Sin. The list could be extended almost endlessly. Death is the wages of sin: that is the orthodox Christian teaching, from St. Augustine, down. It was the heretic, Pelagius, who taught that death is only the debt of nature.

Death, therefore, as conceived in this essay, is more than physical death. Physical death becomes here, as for Shelley, the symbol of all that kills, or seems to kill, the noble, the gentle, the beautiful. Brutish selfishness, vicious ambition, all rule by fear alone, are included in it, as well as that physical mutability which carries all living things down to the grave. Death must be understood here as the destruction, or seeming destruction, of both the physical and the spiritual life, of what men hold good and beautiful.

Those deaths may be, philosophically and scientifically, in different categories. They may be united more in feeling than in fact. One may be only a metaphorical extension of the other. The connection may be only aesthetic. But the aesthetic connection is a fact, nevertheless, of poetry, to say nothing of commonplace tragic experience. It is, after all, with feeling that we are primarily concerned in this survey. We cannot expect to find out anything new about death by reading poetry. But, by following what poets have said, we can conceive more fully, feel more intensely, imagine more completely the values men have attributed to death and the attitudes they have assumed toward it. And there is deep similarity, sometimes an actual identity, in some of the values and attitudes associated with these two sorts of death; for both sorts are destructive, or seemingly destructive, of values vital to the body and the mind. The attitudes of mind, then, that conquer the shocking antithesis of life and death, are a matter of great human concern, howsoever they be achieved, on whatsoever basis, logical or illogical.

It becomes of less moment, therefore, to point out the logical inconsistencies of Shelley's poetized thought (though that, too, must be done), than to put into some sort of sympathetic narration the successive stages by which he achieved his three victories over death. How and where, and under what influences both of matter-of-fact experience and of creative reading and imagining, he reached these victories; with what increase of poetic realization he completed each victory; whether he was put off with comfortable, traditional assurances, or made tragic, original research into the mystery; where he advanced, where he fell back; how feeling bred thought and thought informed and transformed feeling; where figurative language seems to hide defective thinking, and hyperbole takes the place of literal intention; when he confuses philosophies, but attains through aesthetic experience to poetic mysticism: to follow these and other movements of his mind as revealed in his poetry, is the object of this study.

Always he desired to see the unseen, the land beyond death, the "tower beyond tragedy." He played, therefore, with ghosts, wrestled with materialism, pursued dreams, preached idealism, suffered significant disappointment in all material adventures and disillusionment in all ardent friendships and loves, created hope out of its own wreck, attained vision, and then suddenly departed into the death that had always interested him as much as, if not more than, anything else. Maeterlinck calls Bossuet "the great poet of the tomb." But Bossuet's gorgeous theistic oratory of the pomp of death and of personal resurrection lacks the human struggle and enveloping mystery of Shelley's truer poetry. Pascal spoke more rationally and poetically, and was closer to Shelley's testament: "For man is more incomprehensible without that mystery than the mystery itself is incomprehensible to man."

Introduction

The gist of Shelley's final thought on death is contained in that sentence from Pascal; or in this prose statement of his own: " The destiny of man can scarcely be so degraded, that he was born only to die."

Yet it were a mistake to assume that Shelley's thought and emotional attitudes followed a lineal evolution, with new states of mind born of the death of old states; for that assumption would belie the essential character and movement of his mind, or genius. What Mr. Yeats believes to be true of all men — that they do not change much " in their deepest thought " — is particularly true of Shelley. It would be close to the fact, I believe, to hold that in all his later poems there is scarcely an idea about death, or mood related to it, that was not present, in embryo, at least, in his mind when he wrote *Queen Mab*. From the experience of later years he reaped richer realization of the significance of those early intuitions, and ever greater power, imaginative and musical, to express them. And he never assassinated an intuition in order to perfect a thesis. He perfected the intuitions, both in conception and expression, progressively leaving behind not the core of the idea but the cruder applications of it and the less beautiful poetizing of it. Even to assume that with the truer and lovelier use of an idea, or attitude, its antithesis is expunged, is to falsify the poetical history of Shelley, if not of all highly poetic minds. For the poet remains true to the commonest and most inescapable value of human life — its emotional value — in continually passing back and forth between antithetical moods, on whatever higher, successive levels of realization. It is of the nature of men to veer from one emotion to its opposite. This alternation between the electric poles of the spirit is to be found even in the maker of a one-way philosophic system, even after the system has been completed intellectually — perhaps *then* most of all, by a fortunate law of necessary reaction or compensation. A perfect stoic, like a perfect pragmatist, would be the best illustration of the weakness of his theory. Marcus Aurelius, after philosophizing on the strong acceptance of things as they are, longed for an escape from the world; William James, after assessing reality in terms of usefulness, found refuge from dreary pragmatical routine in a reminder, borrowed from Kant, that no experiment has proved that the brain may not be an instrument to record an unbodied reality. Shelley, the poet, with greater fidelity to the emotional swing between opposite poles on successive levels of experience, avoided a symmetrical theory by giving off freely the momentary poetic coruscations of his moods, irrespective of their logical coherence.

Chapter One

PLAYING WITH GHOSTS

There is more in a ghost than meets the eye. Naïve minds attempt to see the invisible, and ghosts are born. There is a kind of genius in thus expressing our ignorance of reality, and one of the most inspired of all naïve minds, James Boswell, spoke for many a votary of romance when he remarked that tales of terror make the reader aware he has a soul, however invisible a part of the body it may be. Murder-and-ghost stories for some thousands of years have reminded fascinated audiences, young and old, sophisticated and simple, from savage to scientist, that there is something mysterious about existing — *omnia exeunt in mysterium*. The ghost is a disappearing witness to the oldest as well as the newest guess about the nature of reality: that matter and mind are products of an undiscovered, all-unifying force. Some men, by some chemistry or alchemy of their spirit, seem born especially aware of the thinness of the veil called mortality or practical reality. They are well enough typified by a twelfth century mystic, Richard of St. Victor, who all his life exercised a deep aptitude for " gazing through the veils of creatures." *Mutatis mutandis*, he is representative not only of the hundreds of millions of peasants who have seen ghosts, but of the long line of idealists from the ancient Vedantists and from Plato to Blake, Swedenborg, and Coleridge. Both phases of this dream — the naïve and the philosophical — were united in Shelley. His outstanding characteristic was his genius for the unseen. The dream, or vision, was innate and ineradicable. All his disappointments, dejections, and tragedy

1

never infected his ideals. Like Eugene O'Neill's Dion Anthony, he was born with ghosts in his eyes.

I

All his life he played and experimented with ghosts. If he and Claire Clairmont told each other tales of terror, he passed from deliberate invention to involuntary hallucination. Edward Williams in 1822 made an entry in his *Journal:* " Shelley sees spirits, and alarms the whole house." Medwin says that Shelley in his boyhood, after devouring a Gothic horror-story, would be the victim of " strange, and sometimes frightful dreams " and of " apparitions which bore all the semblance of reality." In his early teens he loved to regale himself and his young friends at Sion House Academy with stories of fairies, spirits, murderers, and ghosts. Before he was ten, more than half-believing his own incantations, he had already bewildered with monsters and spirits the gardens, attic, and cellar of the Shelley house, Field Place, and the nearby Sussex woods and hedgerows, and Warnham Pond. He invented a grey alchemist. He pranked his little sisters as demons. He even fashioned a small hell of his own and raised devils. And he by no means neglected to explore by night the traditional haunts of ghosts — ruins, caves, woods, and graveyards. For, as was long ago observed by a poet of the Elder Edda,

> . . . mightier now at night are all
> The ghosts of the dead than when day is bright.

Shelley himself tells the story. In wild and remarkably fearless hopes of " high talk with the departed dead " he would speed

> Through many a listening chamber, cave and ruin,
> And starlight wood,

calling on the " poisonous names with which our youth is fed." His parents, anxiously suspicious of these nocturnal and singularly practical experiments, thinking, probably, they led to some mischief, sent a servant to spy upon him. The servant returned and said that Master Shelley had only taken a walk.

Shelley never hesitated to conduct an experiment; the results never deterred him. Godwin preached the blasphemy of marriage. Shelley, already unhappily married, eloped with the philosopher's daughter. The philosopher was horribly offended. Someone told the poet that anyone could learn to swim by jumping into deep water. Shelley jumped forthwith into the Arno, and sank to the bottom like lead. French philosophers theorized on the rather sudden perfectibility of man. Shelley tried out the theory by practising on the Irish, and failed. Chemistry and electricity held out promises of the wonderful, if not the metaphysical. He filled his college rooms with apparatus, drank strange concoctions, and mischievously electrified solemn tutors. He was under suspicion for his experiments. He read about the calm detachment with which philosophers consider all problems. He sent his *Necessity of Atheism* to all the heads of colleges at Oxford, with a request for high and noble correspondence on the subject. He was expelled. He believed in suicide, and tried it more than once, and fortunately failed. He heard there were ghosts in churchyards. So he hied him to churchyards, for high and noble discourse with the dead. He was disappointed.

This young rapture in graveyard speculation riots in nearly all of his juvenile writing. Out of some fifty-eight compositions written before *Queen Mab*, only four poems, each very short, and three very brief fragments, fail to mention death; and in a great majority of the remaining fifty-one the subject is stressed emphatically. Although no great poet ever wrote such bad poetry in his nonage as did Shelley, yet this extraordinary preoccupation with death makes his early

3

verses, poor as they are, strangely significant. His first poem, barring an infantile vapour on a cat in tragic distress through a scarcity of mice, is a Chattertonian quatrain on an owl, a raven, and approaching death. It is followed by a Latin version of the epitaph in Gray's *Elegy*. He was by now, as he later said in his second letter to Godwin, a " votary of romance — haunted with a passion for the wildest and most extravagant romances." His last year at Eton was pretty well filled with literary accomplishment and projects. His two tales, *Zastrozzi* and *St. Irvyne*, the poems of *Victor and Cazire*, a *Dialogue between Death and a Mortal*, and a rapture upon moonbeams and midnight death, were written or published during this year, at the age of seventeen to eighteen. In all these Shelley is a juvenile Gothicist plunging into excited play with the melodramatic, but especially with horror and mystery carried into ludicrous exaggeration. In this wild mood, death and ghosts are repeatedly used as the tip-top of terror. Death is merely his stormiest, most sombre colour, and he quite improvidently outdoes Monk Lewis, Walpole, Beckford, Mrs. Radcliffe, and even Charlotte Dacre, in the frequency and extravagance of his use of this raw horror. The hero of *Zastrozzi*, after having been for over a hundred pages in continual danger of death, and daily having experienced tortures worse than death, at last commits suicide; the heroine is slashed into pieces by another lady; the villain, writhing upon a rack, in the last paragraph dies with a wild, convulsive laugh of exulting revenge; and, to fill every chink in the chapter, there is a demon's own plenty of corroding fears, crawling worms, excruciating agonies, Lethean torpors, indescribable paroxysms, resistlessly horrible ideas, glaring eyes starting from their sockets and rolling wildly around, burning fevers and sudden madness, delirious convulsions, reeking daggers, blood-stained garments, horrific spectres, and poisoned domestics. Here is an authentic sample from *St. Irvyne:*

Playing with Ghosts

It was night — all was still. Wolfstein has sped him to the chateau. He entered the vaults. He fell on a body which appeared motionless and without life! He raised it in his arms, and, taking it to the light, beheld, pallid in death, the features of Megalena. The laugh of anguish which had convulsed her expiring frame, still played around her mouth, as a smile of horror and despair; her hair was loose and wild, seemingly gathered in knots by the convulsive grasp of dissolution. She moved not; his soul was nerved by almost superhuman powers; yet the ice of despair chilled his burning brain. He dashed the body convulsively upon the earth, and, wildered by the suscitated energies of his soul almost to madness, rushed into the vaults. At midnight a bell struck, Ginotti came: his step was rapid, and his manner wild; his figure was wasted almost to a skeleton. Deeper grew the gloom of the cavern. Darkness almost visible seemed to press them round; yet did the scintillations which flashed from Ginotti's burning gaze dance on its bosom. Suddenly a flash of lightning hissed through the lengthened vaults; a burst of frightful thunder seemed to convulse the universal fabric of nature; and, borne on the pinions of hell's sulphurous whirlwind, he himself, the frightful prince of terror, stood before them. On a sudden Ginotti's frame mouldered to a gigantic skeleton, yet two pale and ghastly flames glared in his eyeless sockets. Blackened in terrible convulsions, Wolfstein expired.

So these convulsive six-penny dreadfuls of a subfreshman carry on the dance of death with verdant lightheartedness. The ghosts in his eyes are rather healthy ghosts, after all. Between the lines one may hear the pleased, half-raucous chortling of the youthful enthusiast. Presently, as soon as he outgrows it, this romantic nonsense will seem to him immature and bizarre, even dull and stupefactive; and he will resuscitate it only to play at " frightful creatures " with Leigh Hunt's eldest boy, whose susceptibility to " grim " impressions greatly delighted Shelley. But the boy's chortling is unmistakable in the following letter of April 23, 1810, written jointly by Shelley and his sister Elizabeth, to Edward Fergus Graham:

> My dear Graham: At half after twelve do you be walking up and down the avenue of trees near Clapham Church, and when you see a Post Chaise stop at Mrs. Fenning's door, do you advance towards it, and without observing who are inside of it speak to them — An eventful and terrific mystery hangs over it — you are to change your name from Edward Fergus Graham to William Grove — prepare therefore for something extraordinary. There is more in a cucumber than you are aware of — in two cucumbers indeed; they are now almost 2s. 6d. a piece — reflect well upon that!!! — All this is to be done on Tuesday [April 24], neither Elisbh. or myself cares what else you have to do.
>
> > If Satan had never fallen
> > Hell had been made for thee! . . .
>
> N.B. — The avenue is composed of vegetable substances moulded in the form of trees called by the multitude Elm trees. Elisabeth calls them so, but they all lean as if the wind had given them a box on the ear, you therefore will know them — Stalk along the road towards them — and mind and keep yourself concealed as my Mother brings a blood-stained stiletto which she purposes to make you bathe in the life-blood of her enemy. Never mind the Death-demons, and skeletons dripping with the putrefaction of the grave, that occasionally may blast your straining eyeball. — Persevere even though Hell and destruction should yawn beneath your feet. Think of all this at the frightful hour of midnight, when the Hell-demon leans over your sleeping form and inspires those thoughts which eventually will lead you to the gates of destruction. . . . The fiend of the Sussex soli-

tudes shrieked in the wilderness at midnight — he thirsts for thy detestable gore, impious Fergus. — But the day of retribution will arrive. H + D + means Hell Devil. . . . We really expect you to meet us at Clapham in the way described by the *Fiendmonger:* . . . Death + Hell + Destruction if you fail. Mind and come for we shall seriously expect your arrival, I think the trees are on the left hand of the church.

But what special sensitiveness lay back of this sportive exaggeration of death? Not every imaginative boy who reads and writes penny-dreadfuls, even if he has devoured Gothic frightfulness, displays this curious flair for death and ghosts. Critics belonging to the latest physiological school will sagely find the cause in some abnormal proportion of adrenalin, insulin, or thyroxin in the poet's system; in some over-secretion of a ductless gland and a consequent disturbance of the sympathetic nervous system, culminating in pylorospasm and gothospasm. That way to-day lies Africa. But, at any rate, the predisposition is notable, and in the absence of a precise explanation of it we must continue to speak of it somewhat spectrally as a special affinity for the metaphysical. We may not be so very far wrong if in this buoyant, extravagant play in the graveyard we detect the first crude, bizarre symptom of an as yet undeveloped gift for seeing the invisible.

Indeed, there is a striking, even if remote, parallel between these boyish ghost-hunts, and that sustained impressibility toward the mysterious conditions of man's life that characterized Shelley's mature thought and lay at the source of his greatest symbolic creations. It seems a far cry from these spectres to Demogorgon, but pretty clearly the old grey alchemist becomes the " inspired and desperate alchemist " of *Alastor*, and pretty clearly Shelley himself, both in *Alastor* and in the *Hymn to Intellectual Beauty*, regards these earlier imaginings as the rough, childish preluding to his later solemn

songs. Thus, for instance, in *Alastor* he addresses the
" Mother of this unfathomable world ":

> I have made my bed
> In charnels and on coffins, whose black death
> Keeps record of the trophies won from thee,
> Hoping to still these obstinate questionings
> Of thee and thine, by forcing some lone ghost,
> Thy messenger, to render up the tale
> Of what we are.

But in these early compositions death is not always a theme
of Gothic coffins. In two St. Irvyne poems, *Bereavement* and
The Drowned Lover, showing the influence of Scott, and
written, perhaps, in Shelley's sixteenth year, the sorrow of
bereavement is essayed in an utterly incongruous medley of
galloping verse and dancing double rhyme. Again, it is hard,
at first glance, to see in this boy, inexperienced in sadness, riding cock-horse through quiet grief, swelling bosoms, stream-
ing tears, and other soft signs of affection, any promise of the
poet of the *Adonais.* Yet it is not too much to say, perhaps,
that such a set of verses as *Bereavement* is the first scrawling
of an elegiac pattern that Shelley, through the long tutoring
of years of realized grief and deepening poetic power, gradually converted, in many successive amendments, into the
highly wrought art of his greatest elegy. Shelley rarely gave
up an idea or an emotion. The history of his mind and of his
art is the continual repetition, with ever deeper realization
and more entranced utterance, of ideas, moods, and patterns
that are discernible very early in his work. It is especially
interesting to observe, on the one hand, in this most unprom-
ising *Bereavement* what must have been the first, or very
nearly the first, use of the optimistic summer-and-winter
theme of death —

> Ah! when shall day dawn on the night of the grave,
> Or summer succeed to the winter of death —

that, some eleven years later, after several intervening improvements and variations, was to culminate in that memorable closing line of the *Ode to the West Wind,*

O Wind,
If Winter comes, can Spring be far behind?

On the other hand, his skepticism of a crassly personal immortality, bred first at Eton, perhaps, from reading Godwin on God and the future life, or Lucretius on the shackles of religion, finds a rather reluctant expression in *To Mary Who Died in this Opinion.*

Another theme, much fondled by hyperaesthetic youth, appears. Languorous adolescence indulges a sentimental musing upon easeful death, calling it many a soft name, but most of all a sweet deliverer from the pain and weariness of this life. In the plenitude of its vitality youth dotes upon this mood of enervation and defeat, or in the keenness of its first awareness of the suffering called existence finds a promise of escape inscribed above the dark portal.

Of this sentimentalism there are several examples in Shelley's juvenilia. Only one of them, however, is directly related to his own sorrows, and that only retrospectively. In *Cwam Elan,* written in 1812, after his first elopement and after his failure to convert the Irish, he contrasts his present happiness, a result of Harriet's loving sympathy, with the harassed state of his mind at a previous visit to Cwam Elan. The earlier visit occurred just after his Oxford experiences, when the breaking of his engagement to Harriet Grove, the estrangement from his parents because of the Oxford disgrace, and the sentimental importunities of Harriet Westbrook had united to produce an almost unbearable dejection. It was then that his thoughts had wooed death. Recalling, doubtless one of his favourite poems at this time, Scott's *Helvellyn* (how " a young gentleman of talents, and of a most amiable disposition, perished by losing his way on the mountain Helvellyn, and his

remains were not discovered till three months afterwards! ”),
he would repine in the wild wood's gloomiest shade, close his
eyes, and dream he was on some solitary plain, longing to for-
sake existence if with it he might leave pain

> That with a finger cold and lean
> Wrote madness on my withering brain.

Here, or, less certainly, in a few lines in the poem *To Death*
(1810), or in *St. Irvyne's Tower* (1807?), is the first draft
of *Alastor:* excitable adolescence, melodramatic suffering,
Helvellyn, romantic exposure, easeful and pathetic death!

But other praises of release are connected with the political
and religious radicalism he had picked up from his reading,
particularly from Lucretius and Godwin. In oblivion the
good cease to tremble at Tyranny's nod; in the grave the scor-
pions of Perfidy, the phantoms of Prejudice, and Bigotry's
bloodhounds vanish; and where is the horror of death if it
offers escape from the tides of Murder stirred up by Kings?
So in lavish capitals the youth's inexperienced but visioned indignation sets up the trophy of death; or, with swift change,
threatens the tyrant and “ his column of unnatural state ”
with an inevitable departure and extinction. In poem after
poem this double association of death with Godwinian politics and Lucretian philosophy — death as a suffering inflicted
by the oppressor or as a justice meted out to him, death as an
escape for the oppressed — occurs in declamatory violence. In
one poem at least — *To the Republicans of North America*
(1812) — he waves Patrick Henry's and Rouget de l'Isle's
gonfalon of death and liberty — “ Give-me-liberty-or-give-
me-death.” These associations with tyranny and bigotry produce young Shelley's most ardent and frequent theme of
death, succeeding — or, perhaps, transforming — the fierce-
ness of death in *Zastrozzi*, and constituting a noticeable
though crude originality in poetically rendering Godwin's
passive and uncoloured radicalism. Death had been his most

eloquent trope in his Gothic play; by the persistence of habit, and because of its own emotional affinity with revolutionary dogma, it becomes his most emphatic epithet in his serious anarchy. Its use in both cases is dramatic, rather than lyrically personal; but now the romantic note is rendered less sappy, if not less adolescent, by the social indignation with which it is balanced. The change is certainly an intellectual advance, marking a widened interest and a sincere passion; but in these crude anathemas against tyrants there is little promise of the golden transmutation of the theme in *Prometheus Unbound*.

Another romantic theme — the triumph of love over death — which, later, he was also to measure out in gold, makes its first appearance in this early work. The earliest form of the great benediction with which the *Adonais* closes —

> I am borne darkly, fearfully, afar;
> Whilst burning through the inmost veil of Heaven,
> The soul of Adonais, like a star,
> Beacons from the abode where the Eternal are —

is the assertion, repeated in several of these young poems, as in *Bereavement, The Drowned Lover, A Dialogue*, that in eternity " nought waits for the good but a spirit of love." But there is a more interesting example. Judged by the event, by the reversal, that is, of the expectations expressed in it, one of the most pathetic and unconsciously ironic of Shelley's poems is a set of blank pentameters (1812), with a Wordsworthian cadence and atmosphere, addressed to Harriet, beginning

> It is not blasphemy to hope that Heaven
> More perfectly will give those nameless joys
> Which throb within the pulse of the blood
> And sweeten all that bitterness which Earth
> Infuses in the heaven-born soul.

The mystic faith extolled in these verses is common among romantics. Often it is a compensating mood projected from the lover's heart by the grief of real or imagined deprivation.

Rossetti dreamed it, and debated its validity, in *The Blessed Damozel;* and realized it in the passionate hope and questioning of his Willowood sonnets. In young Shelley's naïve poem this mysticism of love and death may be rationalized easily enough. The young, impulsive but book-learned, enthusiast, to whom the ideas of virtue, love, freedom, and unbending fortitude in the face of tyranny, are ecstatic sensations, who like Flecker's Pervaneh is " much entangled in the web of unreality," has had experience, at last, of the physical trance of love. Immediately the keen, fine loveliness of that transport has automatically, with a sense of great discovery and special meaning, united itself with all his dreams of the good, the true, and the beautiful. Platonism and his own original poetic divining of an ideal reality are discovered to be profoundly at one with these exquisite sensations. The beauty of the sensuous transport was thus intellectualized; nay, to him it was so ineffably glorified, in such complete, unique, and magnetic synthesis of all the best he knew, that it seemed spiritualized, rather than intellectualized. At such moments, in despair of any phrase sufficient to the experience, the words spiritual, heavenly, divine, leap to the lips and are uttered with a sudden, surprised confidence in their meaning. Thus, in one of his lush, sentimental, but utterly sincere, phrases, he calls Harriet's kisses " soul-reviving." Her dear love has gleamed upon the gloomy, solitary Alastor-path his lone spirit had travelled; her " spirit beaming eyes " and her glowing cheek had sent a magnetic sweetness through his " corporeal frame," knitting the soul itself to these finely vibrating fibres of the body. Thence comes the mood of faith in the indestructibleness of love; thence comes the mystic, ecstatic victory of love over death. " Let all mortal ties dissolve," he confidently cries, " but ours shall not be mortal." Heaven, he writes in the lines already quoted, will but perfect these nameless joys that throb in the pulses of the blood.

But what does such an assertion really signify? The ecstasy

is obvious enough. Its rationalization is suspiciously facile. Has this impulsive poet but experienced his inevitable fate, to be caught in that web of unreality which is the mistaking of dream and desire for fact? How ironical, indeed, did that faith in an immortal victory prove in the event of mere facts! Harriet was soon to lose the woman-sweetness and enthusiastic heart he here worships, and, her passion burned out, was to suffer that deadly change and deep pollution pictured in *Julian and Maddalo*.

Must our rationalizing stop here, with laying bare youth's passionate self-deception? The answer is a romantic platitude. It has long seemed to the tender minded that such an act of faith implies a philosophy too deeply founded to be overthrown by personal disappointment. For beneath the ecstatic affirmation lies a great premise — a guess, but a rational guess — that all deep harmony, which Carlyle would call " song," and of which love is as perfect a form as we know, is an anticipation, or hieroglyph, of Reality. If it is not so, if all our highest values — of art and ethics and faith — are mere cheats of the life-force to inveigle us into persistence in living, into continuing our blind, mole-like endeavours in a vast theatre of inorganic repetition and organic procreation, terminated by cataclysms, out of which other cycles of repetition and procreation and cataclysm arise, then the waste of universal energy and of human striving and suffering is so inconceivably obscene — not even tragic — that life seems unlivable, and the mind is shattered. The way out of this *reductio ad absurdum* is the act of half-intuitive, half-reasoned faith that every young poet in love performs: that the nameless joys of all deep harmony that we know in our strangely limited consciousness are given more perfectly in Heaven, or Reality. This faith, moreover, is not necessarily, at least, a faith in the everlasting persistence of human personalities — in the infinite Jackyness of Jack and Jillyness of Jill — but in some inconceivable perfecting of the love that does come — and of

13

course sooner or later tumbles down the other side of the hill
— between so many Jacks and Jills. In the poem *To Mary
Who Died in this Opinion*, Shelley had expressed his budding
doubt of the sentimental idyl of an eternity of love in the infinite projection of each Jack-and-Jill affair. But in these lines
to Harriet, caught by the intensity of sensations, he prophesies, too crudely and personally, perhaps, the everlasting con-
tinuation of their mortal ties. From that un-Platonic preoccupation with a particular object, disappointment and suffering
soon forced him away. Life does that. But the disappointment featured eventually as one of those steps upward in the
experiencing of love which Diotima revealed to Socrates.
These verses, then, are only a first sketch and immature essay
in another theme to which Shelley must, by the nature of his
gift, return again and again, as experience further deepens
his realization of the meaning of the book-themes his special
genius has drawn to itself. Of these themes, only advance in
life itself could give him mastery — mastery of knowing and
mastery in utterance.

II

These, then are the chief attitudes toward death that Shelley struck during his first eighteen or nineteen years. In his
teens he was more concerned with the subject than are most
boys, than are most young romantics, even. What, as a matter
of fact, did some of the other young romanticists think, imagine, and feel about death?

It is significant that on the title page of his first volume of
poems, *Victor and Cazire* (1810), Shelley printed these lines
from *The Lay of the Last Minstrel*:

> Call it not vain: — they do not err,
> Who say, that, when the poet dies,
> Mute nature mourns her worshipper —

but that Byron chose for the motto of his first considerable collection Dryden's

>He whistled as he went for want of thought.

One whistled as he went; the other died daily. Both were making-believe.

There is not nearly so much of death, and nothing so extravagant on the subject, in the *Hours of Idleness* (1807) as in Shelley's juvenile work. Shelley was influenced by this earliest of Byron's books, published three years before his own *Victor and Cazire*. But the use that he made of it was characteristic. He was struck, evidently, with Byron's *Lachin y Gair*. He at once hit upon its two most sombrely mysterious lines — quoted lines they are, but they deal, of course, with death — and wrote an entire poem to fit their spirit, viz., the verses, *On the Dark Height of Jura*, included in *St. Irvyne*. Byron's little poem, after Ossianically addressing the dead who ride the night-winds, proceeds with a rather quiet elegiac reflection upon heroic Gordons who died for the Pretender; but Shelley, by changing shades to ghosts, voices to yelling, gales to blasts, and winds to whirlwinds, and by adding dark heights of Jura, a howling tempest, wreathes of dark vapour, and murmurs of death, manages a midnight of ghostly terror. Like Gilbert and Sullivan's famous Koko, he might have confessed,

>If I have a little weakness,
>It's a passion for a flight of thunderbolts.

Byron's *Hours*, a collection of sensational poems on trivial subjects of personal interest, is not filled with death. A commoner theme with this young collegian is " Woman, lovely Woman, my hope, my comforter, my all ": luscious dreaming of kisses and bosoms. And his kisses are physical philandering; not " soul-reviving." Perhaps Shelley was thinking of them when in an early letter, accompanying a poem on love, he wrote: " You well know I am not much of a hand at love songs; you see I mingle metaphysics with even this." Young Byron paraphrases Catullus, Tibullus, and Anacreon; young Shelley follows Godwin, Lucretius, and Plato. In what they say of death there is scarcely anything that is not conventional and ordinary; their ideas belong to open-stock patterns. Both simulate passion; both ape well-known poetic styles. But Shelley is intense and, outside his Gothic fun and adolescent languor, tremendously sincere, quite un-self-conscious; whereas Byron is always conscious of his pretension to easy, aristocratic cleverness and worldly wisdom. With death, as with his Vesuvian passions, disillusionment, and melancholy breast, Byron deals in a spirit now of affected condescension, now of thinly veiled pride, now of maudlin sentimentality; not with that frequency and intensity and social preoccupation which distinguish Shelley's handling of the theme. Both dramatize their death. Shelley loves to think of himself as the poetic youth pursuing — he is never a fugitive — *pursuing* the ideal into a solitary wilderness and dying into the lap of earth. Byron, under the impression that he will soon die, assumes the melancholy air of a theatrical idol, and, gesturing nobly toward the Highlands, ostentatiously declaims a mournful *adieu* full of the various forms of the first-person pronoun. To the importance of this moment, which is such a sad one for his audience, Harrow, Cambridge, the Highlands, his ancestral Halls, his friends, love's deceit, the dear goddess Fame, Heaven, death, and God Almighty, minister. Shelley, labouring under a similar depression, wrote *Queen Mab*, a fervent call to his fellow-creatures to have done with bigotry and tyranny, and to love and serve each other. Over against Shelley's immature idealism should be placed Byron's priggish sophistication:

> Weary of love, of life, devoured with spleen,
> I rest, a perfect Timon, not nineteen.

Like Pooh Bah, he was born sneering!

Playing with Ghosts

Of the poems Tennyson wrote in his first twenty-one years we have approximately one hundred. Less than half of these are concerned with death: twelve mention it only in passing, and only thirty are largely concerned with it. The younger this poet, the greater his dalliance with death; his contributions to the *Poems by Two Brothers* (1827), written in his fifteenth to eighteenth years, show a slight preponderance of poems on death; the 1830 volume contains about twenty poems that are concerned with the subject, as against about forty-five that are not.

The motto from Martial prefixed to the first volume — *Haec nos novimus esse nihil* — may be cited for its contrast to the mottoes chosen by Byron and Shelley for their first collections: Shelley's preponderant theme of death of course got into his motto; Byron's affected dramatization of himself as a peer with a genial gift for poetizing and " whistling " by the way, got into his; a sensitive modesty is expressed in the brothers' motto. And a feminine sensitiveness of mood is the most original part of Tennyson's early utterance on death.

Preceding that soft mood, however, there are less pensive utterances. There is an Ossianic, Byronic romanticizing of an undisturbed boyish faith in Christian teachings concerning the grave and Heaven and dying to live. His sentimentalizing of the sublime, in the verses *On Sublimity*, gives a good perspective of this part of Tennyson's young interest in death: green tender vales and clear, plain things, are not for him; but loud surges bursting o'er purple seas, giant cliffs and melancholy shores, whirlwind and thunder, the secret wood and the blasted heath, the grave, the ghastly charnel-house, the yawning tomb,

> Phantoms and phantasies and grisly shapes;
> And shades and headless spectres of Saint Mark,
> Seen by a lurid light, formless and still and dark!

. . . . .

> Immense, sublime, magnificent, profound!
> If thou hast seen all this, and could'st not feel,
> Then know, thine heart is framed of marble or of steel.

With an almost Shelleyan Gothicism, but with more of serious wonder and less of buoyant play, Tennyson loves to curdle what a lady of Philadelphia once called " the fluid liquids of the circulation." Nor can I resist, in a mood, I admit, of some irreverence, placing beside these lucubrations Charles Tennyson's romantic picturing of the Deity, " fully and palpably displayed," in all heaven's " consummate pomp arrayed." Gazing at His brightness shrivels the flesh, but —

> What tho' this flesh would fade like grass,
>   Before th' intensity of day?
> One glance at Him who always was,
>   The fiercest pangs would well repay.

The English do so love a show! But the horrors of Alfred's *The Coach of Death*, written in his mid-teens, would have thrilled the Shelley of *The Spectral Horseman* and *The Wandering Jew*. The chattering of Death's fleshless jaws, his bones cracking loud as he stepped through the crowd, the infernal glow in his eyeless sockets, and the cockroaches and white flies leaping about his hairless brow, are in the true Spanish or Peninsular style as it used to be practised in England. A Greek name, alas, is bestowed upon Death:

> The skin hung lax on his long thin hands;
>   No jolly host was he;
> For his shanks were shrunken to willow-wands
>   And his name was Atrophy!

And how young Shelley would have enjoyed the infernal pleasantries of *The Devil and the Lady!*

There is, too, the spectacle, in *Memory*, for example, of the adolescent delightfully imagining himself a melancholy, disillusioned old man; or with equal pleasure figuring life as constituted of bleeding Antonies, scalding tears, purpling tides of death, and " thrilling groans re-echoing through the Vale of Bones." Here, too, is Shelley's galloping sorrow — drum-and-fife anapaestics of bereavement and condolence. And, of course, there are owls everywhere, patron birds of the young romantics. And a whole poem on the Ossian-Byron-Shelley theme of the dead riding the whirlwind. And a glimpse, too, of Shelley's fiendish tyrants rushing into destruction, with a vulture behind them, wild for its prey. And tragic historical canvasses, full of the death-to-the-foe sentiment; and Mithridates presenting Berenice with a cup of poison, or Nadir Shah devastating Hindustan, or the fall of Jerusalem, or a lamentation of the Peruvians, or God denouncing the Pharaoh Hophra in little tinkling rhymes!

But the more characteristic, pensive note — not lacking in the earlier collection — dominates the treatment of death in our twenty poems of the 1830 volume. A more mature reflection has started the questions How and Why; there is some play with the paradox, " nothing dies, all things die " — mostly mere pasteboard stuff. Then the sadness of mutability descends upon the young poet, to reinforce his questioning, and give point to it. His sensitive mind is depressed by the chill autumn of an English garden, grows faint, and well-nigh dies with the change:

> Heavily hangs the broad sunflower
> Over its grave i' the earth so chilly;
> Heavily hangs the hollyhock,
> Heavily hangs the tiger-lily.

But his emotion interests the poet, and in poem after poem he becomes more interested in the decadent loveliness of the mood than in any attempt to utter a final criticism of change. In his *Confessions of a Second-Rate Sensitive Mind*, mood predominates. The pain-storm of doubt issues in a longing for a common faith and for a general scorn of death. Evidently he does not understand how auto-suggestion generates first the longing for faith, then the faith itself. He longs for a true religious creed, while he fails to penetrate the psychology of creed — poetry touched by conviction and then enslaved to practical opinion. In this state of mind, in which a mood of doubt temporarily prevails, he might easily be converted, one thinks, through the orgiasm of some old-fashioned religious revival. At any rate, it is only a question of time until the doubt yields to the much desired faith, for there is no sign here of strong intellectual effort, either destructive or constructive. He longs to find somewhere, already formulated, the one true creed, instead of attacking all creeds, with Shelley; instead of realizing the merely approximate character of all creeds, and then escaping their domination in some high argument bred from the great thinkers of the past, or from his own reading of life itself. Rather, he concludes with this weak note:

> O weary life! O weary death!
> O spirit and heart made desolate!
> O damned vacillating state!

Moods and fancies of a sensitive mind, vacillating, not logically consistent, but each interesting in itself, the subject for a poem! Back of Shelley's romances and poems is a mind already teeming with activity, now in wild, fanciful play, now in wild indignation or passionate benevolence, now in adolescent debate and speculation; glorying in attack, too hastily anarchic and destructive, yet instinctively constructive: and all this activity rushes forthright into crude but enthusiastic expression. But Tennyson seems ever on the lookout for subjects he may sweetly fashion into poems. And he writes far better verses than Shelley did at the same age. Romantic emotions, suave pleasures of eye and ear and heart, loveliness — and anguish, and doubt, and tears, and death itself: all these are to be reduced to beauty and a song,

Playing with Ghosts

. . . something which possess'd
The darkness of the world, delight,
Life, anguish, death, immortal love,
Ceasing not, mingled, unrepress'd,
    Apart from place, withholding time,
    But flattering the golden prime
      Of good Haroun Alraschid.

The young Tennyson seems to feel some inadequacy in himself, in face of the world. He instinctively seeks the protection of a forgotten and sequestered life. There is something of the fugitive in his spirit. He seeks the wilderness, less in pursuit of an ever-escaping beauty than in flight from action and conflict and crime and confusion. There is no crusading impulse to turn upon it all and destroy it. A removed, unchanging, peaceful life, culminating in the quiet release of death, is the young Tennyson's heart's desire.

The strangeness and loneliness of death induce a realization of the mystery of life, as does a sudden silence in a city's traffic, or the stillness after a storm. For a heart that feels inadequate to carry on in the tempest, there is an affinity in the peace, cessation, nothingness, of death. Then, perhaps, this peace is dramatized into supreme significance, this cessation into intensest life. This nothingness becomes the All! And he who doesn't run with the pack finds a loveliness, a glamour, a hope, in lonely death.

But Tennyson has not indubitably achieved the full measure of this transfiguration of lonely death. There is that faintness and sadness in the presence of autumnal decay, of which mention has already been made; there is that melodious song of the peace of death, " where Claribel low lieth "; there is the comforting loveliness of the flower-adorned grave, reminding one of a sentence from Anatole France: " the sweetness of life is felt even in the grass growing over the tomb "; there is a dirge of relief at release from the world's woe. There is the idealist's exultation — born whether of desire or intuition or both, and reminding one of that Pervaneh-note in Shelley — the idealist's exultation in a great good in death, and in the poet's power, or love's power, to triumph over death. Tennyson asserts, at any rate, in quite Shelleyan cadence, what he would fain believe of the poet, that

> He saw thro' life and death, thro' good and ill,
>   He saw thro' his own soul,
> The marvel of the everlasting will,
>   An open scroll . . . ;

or what he would fain believe of death, that it is the shadow of life,

> . . . and as the tree
> Stands in the sun and shadows all beneath,
> So in the light of great eternity
> Life eminent creates the shade of death.
> The shadow passeth when the tree shall fall,
> But I [Love] shall reign for ever over all.

In these lines there is more of metaphysical ecstasy than of clear meaning. Likewise, in all the poems the intellectual achievement is small, uncertain, and abortive. Thoughts die out in soft sounds, disappear in ambiguous figures, or are forgotten in beautiful descriptions of silvery marish-flowers and creeping mosses. Promise of the magic artistry of his later verse pervades the great variety of melodious and stanzaic effects; but from criticism of life to sentimental delight of eye and ear the poet is too deliciously persuaded — to airy, fairy Lilians, or to a

> Mystery of mysteries,
>   Faintly smiling Adeline
> Scarce of earth nor all divine.

Surely, too, the account of the wild-swan's death-hymn, how it filled the wilderness with joy hidden in sorrow, is more an experiment in sound than a revelation in poetic truth.

Finally, there is definite debility of spirit. I refer to a positive dread of death, which alternates with his dream of a quiet release. He fears death, as well as life. He shrinks at the thought of the grave and the sharp-headed, fret-working worm. Nor is this faintness resolved by any deep thought or even by any pretty fancy or luscious melody. However it is not the sole, nor even the chief, tone of the treatment of death in these poems, though it has been held to be so. It is, rather, one of the moods in this vacillation in all save artistry that distinguishes the poems of 1830. It alternates with other moods, yet it never fully yields to them. " Sweet and low " is the music, in general; but neither high nor deep nor enthusiastic nor courageous is the treatment of death. If Tennyson avoids, for the most part, the banality of *Zastrozzi,* he fails to attain the courage of *Queen Mab.*

So much for Byron and Tennyson. The comparison with other young romantic owls had better be postponed until the chief of Shelley's juvenile poems has been considered.

III

Professor Walter E. Peck, in an admirable study of the biographical element in Mary Shelley's novels, remarks that Adrian, the hero of *The Last Man,* was much given to wondering about death, the grave, and the Hereafter. Adrian is a full-length portrait of Shelley. But now we perceive that even in the poet's boyhood this interest was already manifest, already dominant, especially in a mood of adventurous and fascinated play. In comparison with the abundance of that healthy mood, there is but little here of melancholy, of adolescent languor. There is nothing of precocious sophistication. There is nothing of faintness and fear. When play deepens to seriousness and the ghost becomes the spirit of the martyr and the villainous murderer becomes a political tyrant, the changes clearly spring from a first inexperienced interest in the affairs and fate of society. When love and disappointment make their entrance, they come not through the well-worn gate of passionate physicality, but through the rarer gate of an impassioned faith in the essential indestructibility of the beautiful and the good. Yet even the new seriousness is only an unconscious burlesque of mature vision; and is a kind of play, after all, with ghosts, with crude images of the ideal, whereas the conventional ghosts of popular story are crude visions of the unknown. To legends of death, of spirits and demons, his very genius was indigenous, as it was also to dreams of the fate of men in this world. Imaginatively to brave the utmost was all his life a prime necessity of his temperament. He was born with a consciousness of the unknown and an inescapable desire to penetrate it, whether it was a concern of politics or philosophy. All his life, in play and love and thought and dream, he ran down the scent of heaven. But at first the pursuit was most of all high-spirited fun.

In that high-spirited attack he made the rude beginnings of most of the themes he was destined to handle with peculiar greatness.

Only a few weeks before he began the *Adonais*, Shelley wrote, in his *Defence of Poetry*, a sentence unconsciously prophetic of what he soon was to achieve in that elegy: " Poetry's secret alchemy turns to potable gold the poisonous waters which flow from death through life." The poisonous waters are the superstitious dread and fear of death, long since infused into many a myth of horror and cruelty. In no other elegy, ancient or modern, is the alchemy of that fear so perfect as in *Adonais*. But the perfection was not suddenly attained. Long poetic practice had to go before, in which death was to lose its ugliness only gradually. It was not an unwitting progress. " While I thought I was learning how to live, I was learning how to die," said Leonardo da Vinci.

But Shelley from the day he began to write was conscious of the dark mystery. He began, its playful rhymester. He progressed, its protestant. He ended, its laureate. Like Notker the Stammerer, he always knew that " in the midst of life we are in death."

Chapter Two

NECESSITY AND DEATH

Neither the Timon not yet nineteen nor the second-rate sensitive mind achieved so great a quantity of composition or so varied a quality of thought within their first two decades as had Shelley when he had finished *Queen Mab* (1813). This poem, representing the growth of his mind from his eighteenth to his twenty-first year, was written between nineteen and twenty. Neither Byron nor Tennyson had felt a compelling urge at nineteen to perpetrate any nine-canto, two-thousand-line poem on political science, atheism, and a rational millennium. Timon-poses and sensuous experimenting do not conduce to such effort. At twelve Tennyson turned out six thousand lines of epic — battles, with sea and mountain scenery, à la Walter Scott; at twenty-one, just after he had taken his seat in the House of Lords, Byron's thousand clever lines of spite and prejudice à la Alexander Pope appeared — *English Bards and Scotch Reviewers*. But out of the romantic ruction of *Zastrozzi*, *St. Irvyne*, and *The Wandering Jew*, Shelley comes forward, à la Godwin, Volney, and Southey, with a serious revolutionary theme of broad human concern, involving the highest interests of humanity, grandiosely conceived and vehemently poetized: perhaps the most often printed, certainly the widest circulated, of his poems. It is the sort of thing that the *Gentleman's Magazine* of 1822 loved to call the " convulsive caperings of Pegasus labouring under cholic pains." But it is also the sort of thing that puts this young poet somewhere in the class of Carlyle, Goethe, and Tolstoi, the poets of social conscience.

In its time *Queen Mab* has been an important document. It exerted a very considerable influence, especially among the working classes, toward ' free thought,' as it used to be called. Though originally but a few copies were printed, for private circulation only, many pirated editions appeared in England and America after Shelley's death, such was the fascination its ardent teachings exerted upon the social idealists of the century. Pocket editions (1826, 1832, etc.) were issued for the use of radical mechanics; Cuthbert Southey spied cheap copies in the cottages of revolutionary farm-labourers. It was exceedingly popular from the 1830's on with the followers of Robert Owen, the philanthropist and social reformer. It was much read by the socialists of the second half of the century, and was praised by their leaders. Karl Marx said that the real difference between Byron and Shelley was this: " Those who understand them and love them rejoice that Byron died at thirty-six, because if he had lived he would have become a reactionary *bourgeois;* they grieve that Shelley died at twenty-nine, because he was essentially a revolutionist, and he would always have been one of the advanced guard of Socialism." In 1886 George Bernard Shaw, at a meeting of the Shelley Society, praised *Queen Mab* for its theme, its grasp of facts, and its anticipation of the modern view that social problems are being worked out by natural laws quite independent of the conscious interference of man. In 1887, by which time more than fifteen editions had appeared, the Avelings lauded Shelley as an inspired forerunner of Socialism — as one of the earliest thinkers to perceive that back of the struggle for political freedom was the deeper problem of economic freedom, and that this problem would develop a class-struggle between the possessing *bourgeoisie* and the producing proletariat. Moreover, as a result of its radical principles, the poem figured in the law-courts: once before Chancery (1817) in the case for the custody of Shelley's children by Harriet; once at the Old Bailey (1821) in the prosecution of Clark, who was the first to pirate it, by the Society for the Suppression of Vice; several times in the years immediately following; and again, before the Queen's Bench (1841), in the case against Moxon for the publication of Shelley's Works. It was in the trial of Moxon that Sergeant Talfourd, speaking for the defence, edifyingly mitigated Shelley's God by likening him to Milton's Satan!

In 1821 Shelley thought it a " droll circumstance " that the poem, " written by him when very young, and in the most furious style, with long notes against Jesus Christ, God the Father, the Bishops, and the devil knows what," should have been pirated by " the low booksellers of the Strand."

To-day the poem is more important as an historical symptom, indicative of the state of mind attending the early stages of an economic and religious revolution that has not yet reached its end. It is also important as marking a definite stage of Shelley's thought. Its varied importance must be our excuse for considering it at some length, although as a poem it is third-rate or worse.

I

A sort of transition from Shelley's Gothic romances to this versified essay in anarchy and atheism is made in several poems of the Esdaile Manuscript, but especially in *Henry and Louisa* and *Zeinab and Kathema*. Both poems culminate in horrible deaths, but each is primarily a bitter indictment of society. In the former, a man seduced by an insane love of political glory and conquest, comes to an evil end, and is followed voluntarily through the gates of death by a lovely and devoted woman, whose innocent life is thus tragically linked with his dark fate. In the latter, the Cashmire maid, Zeinab, having been stolen from her home, is flung by her betrayers upon the streets of a Christian city, there to perish; rising desperately in crime against her persecutors, she is by a blind and pitiless law condemned to death. Dowden unctuously describes the dénouement as follows:

> It is a bitter December evening when Kathema, weary with vain search for his beloved, sinks wearily upon the heath. At the moment of his awaking, the winter moonbeams fall upon a dead and naked female form, swinging in chains from a gibbet, while her dark hair tosses in the wind, and ravenous birds of prey cry in the ear of night. The lover recognizes his Zeinab and is seized with madness; he scales the gibbet, and, twining the chains about his neck, leaps forward ' to meet the life to come '.

Here is the old association of frightfulness and death; but, no longer merely the most gruesome of devices to start shivers, it is now his most indignant and pathetic means of pointing protests against the criminal ambitions of governors and the specious cruelty of organized society. Death has changed from a bogey to a weapon, as the poet's mind has passed from fantastic play to serious protest.

The incessantly reading and speculating boy has conceived the human misery with which history is tragically darkened. Godwin and Lucretius, primarily, and Hume, Volney, Spinoza, Pliny, Voltaire, Condorcet, Rousseau, Helvétius, Holbach, Sir James Lawrence, and others, secondarily, have contributed to this awakening; and the poet's political misadventuring in Ireland has been a practical lesson in human ignorance, prejudice, and affliction. The volcanic lines of Lucretius have persuaded him that popular religion is one cause of the general misery. The cool sententiousness of Godwin's prose has conducted him to a belief, anything but temperate, that kings and governments are the other cause.

To the careful study of Godwin's *Political Justice* he confesses he owes " the inestimable boon of granted power, of arising from the state of intellectual sickliness and lethargy into which I was plunged two years ago, and of which ' St.

Irvyne ' and ' Zastrozzi ' were the distempered, although un-original visions." What Lamb called the " spurious engendering of books " produced in Shelley's case, first, his Gothicism, and, second, his conviction that history is " a record of crimes and miseries." He says, in a letter, Dec. 17, 1812, to Hookham, that the study of history is " hateful and disgusting to my very soul." So, forsaking his Gothic play, he dreams now of becoming a " mender of antiquated abuses." Oppressive despotism, whether of religion or politics, is now the villain in the piece; but a villain conceived with the huge and dreadful seriousness of an inexperienced mind piercingly aware of the sufferings of humanity. With Voltaire, " Écrasez l'infâme," he cries: " Down with this persecuting and privileged orthodoxy! " With Lucretius he thunders oracularly: " I give instruction concerning mighty things, and proceed to free the mind from the closely confining shackles of religion." He conceives himself as handing on the torch lit in *De Rerum Natura*, that most passionate of reflective poems, and as adding new light to its ardent gospel of a mighty truth in irreconcilable conflict with superstition. There is no better, one might almost add, more Shelleyan, introduction to *Queen Mab*, this unorthodox Fairy Queen, than Lucretius's flaming indictment of superstition:

> When the life of men lay foully grovelling before our eyes, crushed beneath the weight of a Religion who displayed her head from the region of the sky, lowering over mortals with terrible aspect, a man of Greece [Epicurus] was the first that dared to raise mortal eyes against her. Him neither tales of gods, nor thunderbolts, nor heaven itself with its threatening roar, repressed, but roused the more the active energy of his soul, so that he should desire to be the first to break the close bars of nature's portals. Accordingly the vivid force of his intellect prevailed, and proceeded far beyond the flaming battlements of the world, and in mind and thought trav-

ersed the whole immensity of space; hence triumphant, he declares unto us what can arise into being, and what cannot; in fine, in what way the powers of all things are limited, and a deeply fixed boundary assigned to each. By which means Religion, brought down under our feet, is bruised in turn; and his victory sets us on a level with heaven.

So, too, burning with this Roman eloquence, the active energy of Shelley's young soul was irrepressibly stirred, not to write an autobiographical analytical tale in the fashion either of *Werther* or *La Nouvelle Héloïse*, but, like Volney, to traverse imaginatively the misery of the past and the present; and to prophesy, perched *extra flammantia moenia mundi* with his imaginative Mab, the fall of selfish governments and superstitious faiths, the extinction of poverty and ignorance, the universal triumph of benevolence, and the advent of peace. Such is the comprehensive and romantic-revolutionary ideology of the poem: after all, a sort of Gothic romance, filled as of old with set bravura pieces of persecuted innocence and utter villainy, but transposed now to a tempestuous seriousness about matters of tremendous human concern.

II

Queen Mab may be as untrue to history as *Zastrozzi* is to human nature, but surely it is easy to discern how the play of the latter was a preparation for the dead-earnest indignation of the former, and how a boy's extreme, excited conception of unmediated struggle between perfect heroes and utter villains is transferred to the two-colour melodramatic problem of tyranny and freedom. And though the political economy of the poem may be quite wrong, the poet's indignation is of the sort that has made new political economies by burning old despotisms. If men's emotions were to be evaluated solely by the truth — so called — of the ideas with which

they are associated, life would be other than it is, and Vai-
hinger's philosophy of the " *Als Ob* " would have to be re-
written.

What, then, in this new and serious but yet romantic ven-
ture, becomes of Shelley's old favourite horror, Death? Death
enters the very first line. Southey among his blank lyric measures in *Thalaba*, one of Shelley's favourite poems, wrote
" How beautiful is night! " In complimentary imitation Shelley opens *Queen Mab* with two similar measures:

> How wonderful is Death,
> Death and his brother Sleep!

Beautiful he cannot call it, yet; for it still remains a horror:
pale, with lips of lurid blue, a gloomy power reigning in
tainted sepulchres. Then he adds, perhaps under the influence
of Shakespeare's allusions to the hideous fretwork of the
coffin-worm, a picture of putrefaction. He feigns for a moment that death — not sleep — possesses and changes the
beauty of his heroine, Ianthe, leaving nothing of her fair form
but loathsome ruin. Such a mutability of bodily beauty, in
spite of any or all philosophy, he could not think of without
horror. One is reminded of a sentence in his essay, *On a
Future State* (1814?): " The body is placed under the earth,
and after a period there remains no vestige even of its form.
This is that contemplation of inexhaustible melancholy, whose
shadow eclipses the brightness of the world." His instinctive
regret at the hideous failure of beauty was at war with any
philosophical view of change that he may have held; especially at this time, when, as we know from a poem addressed
to her, the physical beauty of his young wife, Harriet Westbrook, had made a thrilling impression upon him. The tainted
change of death, then, seems to him, and certainly to the
reader of this passage, rather horrible than wonderful. The
wonder, at any rate, is immediately lost in horror.

But the extreme and grisly theme has a special fascination.

Ianthe, mounting the magic car of the philosophic imagination, passes in a moment through an interminable wilderness of island-universes to the ideal zenith, whence she has vision of the past, the present, and the future. Here, " semicircled with a belt of flashing incessant meteors " and surrounded with shades of infinite colour, is the sublime and fitting temple of the Spirit of Nature:

> Here is thy fitting temple!
>   Yet not the lightest leaf
> That quivers to the passing breeze
>   Is less instinct with thee;
>   Yet not the meanest worm
> That lurks in graves and fattens on the dead,
>   Less shares thy eternal breath!

Thus the enthusiast, in search of a sensational antithesis!

The reader does wonder, after all, but in another sense: Why are the worms and death so loathsome if the same sublime Spirit informs them as well as the island-universes? If the spiritual unity of life pervades the hungry worm as well as the beauty both of Ianthe and of the celestial bodies, there must be less of horror and more of beauty in death. The suggestion, at least, is obvious in these very lines; and it is more than implied in other parts of the poem, as we shall see. But the old mood of horror yet reigns over an idea destined to dislodge it.

Such dislodgment is characteristic of Shelley's artistic and intellectual growth. The principle of that growth, which is by no means operative in Shelley alone, may be stated as follows. With a strong, accustomed emotion a new and essentially incongruous idea is constellated (usually as a result of new reading), but at first the incongruity is not perceived. Later, by a sort of fissiparous birth, this idea breaks away, and, carrying with it some part of its first emotional and imaginative setting, becomes the centre of a new poetic theme or process. Then, accompanying mood and image expanding intuitively, it achieves splendour of utterance. The lack of beautiful image and profound, realized emotion, in these lines, the lack of intimately, sensuously expressive rhythm, are a sign that the idea of the unity of the worm and the star is as yet only an idea — not a vision, not imagination touched with conviction, not an overpowering intimation of some romantic meaning hidden deep in death.

In search, then, for a strong opening of the poem, Shelley turned to his old fascination, his Gothic theme of power, Death; and, handling it in his old way of extravagant terror, but now in conjunction with the idea of an all-pervasive and all-hallowing spirit of nature, fell, rather unawares, into an inconsistency.

It is curious, too, that, in spite of his recent conversion to French materialism, he falls for a moment into the world-wide ascetic, but especially Christian, comfort against mutability — that officious dualism which preaches the glory of the liberated spirit to offset the failure of the too beloved flesh. Like some medieval poem on the yet more ancient theme of contrasted soul and body, the following lines trick out the individualistic melodrama of Heaven and the Grave:

> One [the Soul] aspires to Heaven,
> Pants for its sempiternal heritage,
> And, ever changing, ever rising still,
> Wantons in endless being:
> The other, for a time the unwilling sport
> Of circumstance and passion, struggles on;
> Fleets through its sad duration rapidly;
> Then like an useless and worn-out machine,
> Rots, perishes, and passes.

This is the comfort of Sir Thomas Browne's " resolved Christians," who, " looking on Death not only as the sting, but the period and end of Sin, the Horizon and Isthmus between this Life and a better, and the Death of this World but as the Nativity of another, do contentedly submit to the common Necessity " (*Letter to a Friend*). Elsewhere in Shelley's verse this comfort does not dominate his intense dismay at the mutability of fair forms. Even while he was at Oxford he had written, as we have seen, in the poem *To Mary, Who Died in this Opinion*, that he would barter existence itself for her precious dream of meeting her dear one after death. Only in some of his earliest poems, as *The Wandering Jew*, had the conventional Christian belief in personal immortality received a conventional expression. And it may be worth remarking that in the 1816 partial revision of *Queen Mab*, entitled *The Dæmon of the World*, which gets rid of much of the Mabbishness of the earlier poem, this passage is omitted, and death, represented even more gloomily, is spoken of as a dreamless sleep.

These inconsistencies, then, clearly indicate that Shelley has not yet reconciled his love of beautiful life with his disgust of death; and that his emotions, not yet converted to his philosophy, persist in spite of it. But the inconsistencies are the more striking if the nature of this philosophy is considered.

The supreme generalization of this philosophy in the poem is a personification, the Spirit of Nature. This Spirit is a necessarian. True deity is Necessity. By necessity, Godwin and Shelley, like Hume, meant the universal procession, never interrupted, of so-called cause and effect, apparent no less in the intellectual than in the material world. No action or condition, whether in the outer or the inner world, but is the result of other actions and conditions. If an unusual action occurs, we look for its cause, never suspecting a causeless activity that will forever baffle observation and expectation. Even the superstitious mind, when it is explaining a natural effect by a supernatural cause, is thinking in terms of cause and effect.

In the world of mind every act is determined by a motive, which is a complex of desire and reason. The strongest motive always determines conduct. The advocates of free-will maintain that the individual has the power to refuse to be dominated by the paramount motive; but the strongest motive is precisely that " which, overcoming all others, ultimately prevails," as Shelley is at pains to point out.

Back of every motive, in turn, regarded as an effect, is a long and intricate chain of causation, every act being determined by a complex of conditions. " Trace back the chain as far as you please," says Godwin, " every act at which you arrive is necessary," i.e., is determined by causes. Were it not so, there would be nothing stable about mental life, nothing recognizably repetitive or practically predictable: there could be no 'character,' no 'knowledge of human nature,' no policy in dealing with human affairs; and mind itself could not be realized because it itself is but a general term to name some fairly constant conjunctions in our inner experience.

But just as we can, within limits, modify the material world by acting upon our observation of cause and effect, so, too, in consequence of a similar learning, we are able to modify, within limits, the world of mind and conduct. Persuasion, exhortation, appeals and threats, rewards and punishments, are all addressed to this aim of controlling the conduct of others or of one's own self by rendering certain motives at least temporarily paramount. But in modifying conduct we do not escape or annul the operation of cause and effect, any more than we destroy cause and effect by erecting a lightning-conductor.

There is, then, nothing metaphysical about this philosophical concept of Necessity, even though the poet's capital **N** has been suspect of the taint. The nearest approach to it is Godwin's insistence (which misled Mr. M. T. Solve into asserting that Godwin rejects necessity in the physical world) that cause and effect are only abstractions, or even hypostases, from an observed regularity in the succession of events: " the principle or virtue by which one event is conjoined to another we never see." But this remark pertains more to relativity than to metaphysics. The capital N is, in the first place, at least, and through the greater part of the poem, little more than a conventional personification of what the philosopher himself admits is only an hypostasis of an observed, regular process. Only toward the end of the poem, as we shall see, is this rhetorical personification fused, or confused, with the poet's intuitive animism.

There is, again, nothing fatalistic (in the loose, popular meaning of that term) about necessity. The determinism of cause and effect does not conduce to unthoughtful quietism, or emotional defeatism, or supine acquiescence. Instead, it is the very condition of effort, the very impetus of expectation. Upon observed uniformities in experience we base all our anticipation, all our judgments, all our practical and ethical endeavour.

But we are in the habit of calling some experiences good, others evil. Shelley points out that these terms are relative to our own peculiar mode of being. They indicate phenomena recognized only by the human mind. Yet in our ignorance, he continues, we are apt to annex to the universe, as an essential part of it, what is the particular possession of human beings. Thus we come erroneously to regard things as in themselves either good or evil, whereas good and evil subsist only in our attitudes toward things.

Now from these propositions it would seem to follow that death and decay, considered fundamentally and apart from their relation to our motives, are neither good nor evil. They are involved, like mutability at large, in the very sequential nature of cause and effect. They are necessary. To one enlightened by a profound recognition of their necessity, they should not in themselves appear evil, however regrettable

37

may be their interruption of human activity. Shelley, by his own account, was thus enlightened.

The pictures of the gloomy and hideous accompaniments of death which open the poem are, then, very clearly not in agreement with its fundamental ideas. Survivals of his play with the horrible, they are out of harmony with the worship of all things natural. They are not only antithetical to his new philosophy. By implication, at least, they negative it.

But it should be noted that only the accompaniments of death — the grave, the rotting body, and the greedy worm — raise his horror. Death itself is not pronounced evil. This distinction, to be sure, is not thoroughly logical. It accommodates his emotion while it destroys his rationalism. Before the hideousness of the grave he is still aghast while, in partial fidelity to his philosophy, death itself is regarded as a noble, renovating incident in the progress of life. Therein, perhaps, lies death's title to that wonderfulness proclaimed but not substantiated in the opening lines. And in the body of the poem, as distinct from the introduction in which the vision of Ianthe's fairness yielding to the grave momentarily dismays him, Shelley develops at length this theme of wonder. But in perfect consistency all subjectivity of evil and ugliness, even that attached to putrefaction, should be converted to a glad reconciliation with the processes of aspiring change.

However, another theme alternates with this imperfect philosophy of death: his old political theme, ringing the changes on the sufferings and agonized deaths which tyrants cruelly impose upon weak humanity, and on the mental agony in which the tyrant himself dies. We shall better represent the curious emphasis of the poem, the alternation between argumentative rationalism and rhetorical anarchism, if we interrupt our study of the more philosophical to follow for a moment the more political theme, and determine its relation, likewise, to the underlying philosophy of the poem.

Man's cruelty to man, according to Godwin and Shelley,

may be corrected, ideally speaking, by controlling the paramount motive. The barbaric inhumanity that for selfish ends causes unnecessary sufferings which not seldom culminate in distressful death, if it cannot be eradicated, can at least be amended. Let us endeavour to do full justice to this rational meliorism. It may be objected that a brutal selfishness, rather than a natural benevolence, is so deeply ingrained in most or all of us that in spite of all growth in grace human perfectibility can be nothing but a logical fiction, like the mathematician's upper limit or *nth* degree. Hazlitt long ago pointed out that Godwin, conceiving too nobly of his fellows, absolved them too easily from the gross ties of desire, sensuous illusion, and force of selfish habit, and thereby sacrificed fact to logic in his dream of perfection. It may be that Godwin's argument that political freedom, by removing tyrants and place-seekers, and thus destroying selfishness in general, would annihilate vice, is oblivious to the invincibleness of instinctive selfishness. It may be that the hope of complete political and economic freedom is as much an illusion as the fine-sounding faith that all men are created equal; and that difference in capacity forever makes necessary degree in liberty and wealth. It may be that so far selfishness has been fundamental to the development of life, even if helpful co-operation is equally, or more, common and necessary. It is clear, certainly, that the French *philosophes* were strangely in error when they regarded man as a purely rational animal capable of intelligently pursuing his own best interests, and that the text beloved of Shelley — " Ye shall know the truth, and the truth shall make ye free " — must be taken with a grain or two of salt so far as society at large is concerned. It certainly seems true that, as Mr. I. A. Richards has so well said, " to live reasonably is not to live by reason alone, but to live in a way of which reason, a clear, full sense of the whole situation, would approve." Yet when one remembers the extent to which reason has already developed, from the appearance of the primates, through the courses of pre-history and history, to the present, he becomes cautious in denying the possibility of an even more astonishing improvement during the next several hundred-thousands of years. After all, it must be admitted that in dealing with such questions as these, to think in centuries, or even millennia, is to think in seconds. Moreover, reason already is turning into phantoms most of the assumptions of the last seven millennia, and within one brief century, acting in free experiment, has modified natural events and human behaviour to a highly 'scandalous' degree. When the achievement of psychology becomes at all comparable to that of physics, extraordinary practical results may follow within the realm of behaviour, as yet scarcely even foreseen, save by the wildest of romantic poets and ridiculous philosophers. Highly theoretical, then, as the prognosis of perfectibility may be, is it much more astonishing than the advance from an amoeba to a Thomas Huxley, to say nothing of an Aldous?

The rational meliorism of Godwin and Shelley, then, though their benevolent eagerness deceived them as to the length of time needed for its realization, is not at once to be laughed away for all time, however incongruous with the facts of 1814 or 1914 it may appear. " Reason is never a root, neither of act nor desire," says Robinson Jeffers, following a lead in psychoanalysis. But the *desire* to think and act reasonably, or to be reputed to think and act reasonably, becomes, perhaps, an ever stronger motive as the ages lapse.

The gradual eradication of man's cruelty to man may not be, then, an altogether irrational dream. Here are at least one kind of suffering and one sort of death that may be deliberately modified in a world governed by necessity. By rendering rational motives more and more the *sine qua non* of success and self-assurance (and the very course of evolution may be accomplishing that end whatever may or may not be our little schemes of amelioration), cruelty in conduct may be slowly amortized.

There was enough in that hope, at any rate, to excite Shelley's young imagination to fever-heat, while his own over-generous heart deceived him as to the nearness of the rational Advent. But he had no real hope, as Meredith's Shibli Bagarag *did* have, of shaving Shagpat overnight, at a stroke, in a trice.

One method of humanizing the minds of men is vividly to show them the picture of their cruelty; another, is to show them an idealized, Utopian picture of their benevolence. To the former method Shelley now addresses his energy. As the soul of Ianthe proceeds to its survey of the political history of the past and present, death enters repeatedly as a cruel infliction of man upon man. Nero sits in the Circus, enraptured with the death-agonies of his victims. Widows and orphans curse the conquests, the pyramids, and the palaces that have grown by death. The apotheosis of all this human cruelty in the ideal of an avenging god, true prototype of human misrule, in whose name the innocent are maimed and murdered and whose hell forever gapes for the unhappy slaves he sportively miscreated so that he might " triumph in their torments when they fell " — the apotheosis of all this cruelty and death, which men call god or religion, is assailed with relentless tenacity.

> The name of God
> Has fenced about all crime with holiness,
> Himself the creature of his worshippers,
> Whose names and attributes and passions change,
> Seeva, Buddh, Foh, Jehovah, God, or Lord,
> Even with the human dupes who build his shrines,
> Still serving o'er the war-polluted world
> For desolation's watchword; whether hosts
> Stain his death-blushing chariot-wheels, as on
> Triumphantly they roll, whilst Brahmins raise
> A sacred hymn to mingle with the groans;

41

Or countless partners of his power divide
His tyranny to weakness; or the smoke
Of burning towns, the cries of female helplessness,
Unarmed old age, and youth, and infancy,
Horribly massacred, ascend to heaven
In honour of his name; or, last and worst,
Earth groans beneath religion's iron age,
And priests dare babble of a God of peace,
Even whilst their hands are red with guiltless blood,
Murdering the while, uprooting every germ
Of truth, exterminating, spoiling all,
Making the earth a slaughter-house.

But all the while it is insisted that the passions, prejudices, and interests which sway kings, bishops, and the meanest beings are links in the great chain of nature. The chain of cause and effect lengthens out to the heavenly end, when man, relearning benevolence by hideous experience, shall be perfected morally.

And to that prophecy is added, now, the naturalism of Rousseau. For Shelley eloquently holds up to man as a model of this moral perfection, Nature! " All things speak peace, harmony and love," he cries, " all but the outcast man." This goodness of nature, particularly of the natural man, is, indeed, a fundamental, if not *the* fundamental, romantic illusion, though it was anticipated, as Professor Morley pointed out, in Bernard Mandeville's *The Fable of the Bees* (1714). It is unfair, of course, to attribute the doctrine in its boldest form to Rousseau. It was Chateaubriand who, in 1801 and 1802, with his *Atala* and *Le Génie du Christianisme*, had popularized the romantic thesis of the noble savage, which he inherited from the *encyclopédistes*. But what for Chateaubriand was an actual fact — the essential identity of the Christian virtues and the primitive, or natural, passions — was for Rousseau only an ideal condition, or philosophic myth. Harald Höffding has recently reminded us that the popular conception of Rousseau's naturalism is inaccurate. A careful reading of the opening chapters of *Émile* proves that Rousseau's natural man is ideal man, i.e., Rousseau's idea of the best possible condition of man, just as for him nature itself is a force working in things toward attaining the best possible condition of them. Rousseau's political theory, like Mably's daydream of Communism, was, as somebody has said, a theory of the Kingdom of Heaven. It must be admitted, however, that his enthusiastic and repeatedly vague references to an ideal nature offer excuse for confusing his theory with that of the noble savage. Shelley himself points out, in his *Essay on Christianity* (1817?), that Rousseau did not advocate a return to savagery as a remedy for inequality among civilized men. Nevertheless, following the romantic optimism of the *encyclopédistes*, Shelley did fall into the fallacy of natural goodness. For him, at this time and for years after, the peace of nature is a controlling sentiment if not an unvarnished fact. He honestly believes that the annihilation of selfish privilege in politics and religion will go far toward restoring the innate benevolence of the human heart to its natural preëminence in the affairs of society. He believes, as Carlyle did later, that man's instincts are more humane and wise than his opinions. But against his assumption of the excellence of nature it is sufficient to place John Stuart Mill's indictment:

> The undeniable fact [is] that the order of nature, in so far as unmodified by man, is such as no being, whose attributes are justice and benevolence, would have made with the intention that his rational creatures should follow it as an example. . . . In sober truth, nearly all the things which men are hanged or imprisoned for doing to one another are nature's everyday performances.

And now, to perfectibilism and romantic naturalism is added, finally, vegetarianism! A universal vegetable diet, practicable means to the age of peace, will render man mild and reasonable!

In the future, then, and by these various means, violent death, now inflicted by political and religious tyrants, will disappear; cruelty, crime, and disease will wane; old age will be vigorous and athletic; and natural death will be a mild and slow necessity, an euthanasia, the tranquil spirit failing without a groan, almost without a fear,

> Calm as a voyager to some distant land,
> And full of wonder, full of hope as he.

Very much like a certain death-scene in Godwin's *Caleb Williams!* And not unlike what modern medicine and surgery hope eventually to accomplish in *their* way.

Whether or not decay and the coffin-worm will succumb Shelley does not reveal. But he does, after all, inconsistently, admit the necessity of a sympathetic change in much-admired nature — a sympathetic change, referred to with a sort of pseudo Berkleyism, as though the perfecting of man would produce a corresponding perfection in the so-called objects of sense; and storms, earthquakes, poison, the Sahara Desert, the North Pole, and tigers would become tame and innocuous.

Put the question of fallacies and inconsistencies aside. Admit, too, a degree of possibility in the perfectibilian plan if it is spread over a vast expanse of time. There remains a more devastating question. *Why* must there be this long struggle for the far goal of peace and of quiet death? What weak lack of foresight loaded us with this almost inconceivable penance? What benevolent executive, while he nodded, let progress invent itself at the expense of the individual? What of those whose fate falls in the imperfect days, the shambles of horrid death? In this very poem Shelley has scornfully attacked that Christian scheme of salvation by which millions, never having known their Saviour's name, shall unredeemed go to the grave. But is his own postponed Age of Peace any more humane? This linear-progressive philosophy of the far-off goal is as cruel as it may be pragmatic. Some Unamuno, with the tragic consciousness of existence, always indignantly indicts this childish sentimentalism of the Garden of Eden, whether the Eden be in the Golden Age of the past or the Utopia of the future. The goal, whatever it is, must rather be one that forever is attainable daily. It may be, in reality, only some one emotional attitude, or some quiet balance of attitudes. 'Salvation' may be only some special serenity in our desire-life. Or it may be heroism in the struggle between unenlightened selfishness and that enlightened selfishness we love to call disinterestedness. But one thing it must be if it is to be anything more than a rational make-believe: it must be something each man can attain, at least largely, here and now, within the body of this life. The sacrifice of the individual to the race, as to the state, has its limits. The Kingdom of God lies within the heart, now. Disappointment will eventually force Shelley to acknowledge this proposition, as it has forced other dreamers of a perfected society.

Another method of civilizing the passions consists in displaying to men the reverse of the scene of horror, in eloquently drawing their attention to an idealized account of their moral possibilities. This is the method of Mably and Rousseau. A large part of *Queen Mab* is devoted to such a vision. With this Kingdom of God broadcast upon earth, the present essay cannot properly concern itself. But a little space must be stolen to do another act of justice to Shelley's theories. Shelley's Utopian dreams in *Queen Mab, The Revolt of Islam*, and *Prometheus Unbound* have been held up to ridicule on the assumption that Shelley believed they all could be easily realized and that he put them forward as a programme of immediate, practical reform. There is basis for the charge with reference to *Queen Mab*. That has been admitted, above. But even here, in a measure, and very definitely in the other poems, Shelley's purpose was deeper and different. As to what it was he has not left us in doubt. In the Preface to the *Revolt of Islam* he avers that his aim is not to present arguments in favour of his political philosophy, but only, by drawing an idealized picture of a truly benevolent society, to awaken feelings of admiration, to incite men to think further on this exalted theme, and to arouse emulation in aspiring after moral excellence and in despising " all the oppressions that are done under the sun." He is not, like his critics, confusing argument and poetry. It is his business as a poet, he says, to impart to others the high pleasure he has experienced in dreaming of a perfect world. These Utopias, then, are intended as contagious expressions of the enthusiasm with which he conceived a Kingdom of Heaven. To regard them as programmes for reform is, indeed, both to make them absurd and also absurdly to misunderstand them. Shelley's plans for immediate political reform, always modest and practicable, never those of a maximalist, are to be found in his prose pamphlets and broadsides: not in his poetic imagery of human perfection.

So much, then, for the theme of political death. The other but greater theme, as was said above, is concerned with the nature of death itself, or, at least, with its function in nature.

As the poem advances and the poet's power of composing increases, particularly after he has got himself delivered of his rhetorical anarchism, there occur passages in which his native mysticism — what I have called his genius for the unseen — and his newly acquired materialism approach imaginative fusion, though they do not perfectly attain it. And in this approach to fusion, the inconsistencies, so noticeable toward the beginning of the poem, lose something of their crudity. There are several eloquent expressions of the old *mors janua vitae* idea, quite consonant with the theme of that eternal " storm of change " we imperfectly call cause and effect. At the beginning of the fifth canto, for example, is a fine recognition of mutability as the " imperishable change that renovates the world," and the idea is developed by an expansion of

Homer's great line on the forest's falling leaves — the generations of leaves scattered on the earth, while the forest puts forth again. But where Homer is content to delineate the image, leaving its full meaning a mystery and a challenge to each man's speculation, Shelley labours it to a parable of the loathsome rottenness of the leaves fertilizing the land they long deformed, even as the painful failures of the martyrs prepare a postponed harvest of virtue, delight, and universal love. In the sixth canto, change is called the Spirit of eternal activity, never decaying or ceasing,

> That fades not when the lamp of earthly life,
> Extinguished in the dampness of the grave,
> Awhile there slumbers.

Again, near the opening of the eighth canto, there is another fine passage, the eloquence of which is an anticipation of some of Shelley's most characteristic later work. Here the image is of music catching new life from the ' death ' of sequent and failing sounds; and, again, of winds sinking and rising on an evening sea. Then, alas, he goes on to the benevolent abolition of the North Pole and the Sahara Desert. But the close of the poem holds the best imaged and most musical utterance on " death's dissolving hand," and it is also the poem's most impressive utterance on any subject. Lifted from its context of didactic utopianism, it reads as follows:

> For birth and life and death, and that strange state
> Before the naked soul has found its home,
> All tend to perfect happiness, and urge
> The restless wheels of being on their way,
> Whose flashing spokes, instinct with infinite life,
> Bicker and burn to gain their destined goal;
> For birth but wakes the spirit to the sense
> Of outward shows, whose unexperienced shape
> New modes of passion to its frame may lend;
> Life is its state of action, and the store

Of all events is aggregated there
That variegate the eternal universe;
Death is a gate of dreariness and gloom,
That leads to azure isles and beaming skies
And happy regions of eternal hope.
Therefore, O Spirit! fearlessly bear on.
Though storms may break the primrose on its stalk,
Though frosts may blight the freshness of its bloom,
Yet spring's awakening breath will woo the earth
To feed with kindliest dews its favourite flower,
That blooms in mossy bank and darksome glens,
Lighting the greenwood with its sunny smile.

If these lines are taken by themselves, the precise meaning of the symbols — whether of a far-off semi-divine Utopia or of an end accomplished daily — being tactfully left to each reader to determine, they have the mark and ring of great poetry, or, at least, the promise of it. Their music supports and interprets a notable intuition and a profound, sincere passion. Didacticism, with which the poem sags, passes over into a truly ' possessed ' imagination. Rhetoric, with which the poem clanks and screams, changes suddenly into a mysterious key, distinctly anticipatory of the rapt utterance with which the *Adonais* ends. The young poet speaks better than he knows, perhaps, preluding some of his noblest later performances. The strange state of the naked soul, the restless wheels of being, and the flashing spokes bickering and burning to gain their destined goal, remind one of the final great fragment, *The Triumph of Life*, written during his last days on the fatal Gulf of Spezzia. The middle lines, beginning

Death is a gate of dreariness and gloom
That leads to azure isles,

sound a note that is insistent in *Prometheus Unbound*. The spring-theme, a symbol of a *vita nuova*, is another draft of the memorable closing lines of the *Ode to the West Wind*.

But, mark of the imperfectness of the fusion, death, though a way into a greatening opportunity, still oppresses Shelley with its ugly setting.

The poem ends with yet another intuition of death — the romantic intuition of the lover, of Ianthe herself, that such great beauty as has been revealed in love cannot pass into nothing. This is the message that waxes and wanes in lovers' eyes, already noted in his earlier poems, and to which Shelley will recur more than once, but especially in the fourth stanza of the *Hymn to Intellectual Beauty*. Shelley here speaks solely, I suppose, from direct experience imaginatively projected upon the future. This faith was not borrowed from the cool, dry bookishness of Godwin, or the warmer political prophecies of Turgot and Condorcet, or even the *amours* of the two savages, Chactas and Atala.

With this instinctive faith, less learned but perhaps wiser than most of his ideology, he once again breaks through the thin and temporary veneer of his French rationalism. Again and again his native mysticism has been in deep, half unconscious struggle with the sheer mechanism of his philosophy. *Queen Mab*, indeed, is a story of intellectual apprenticeship. It is the history of an originative mind experimenting with the ideas of its era. Written in the chamber of maiden thought, its very confusions are intensified by the seriousness of the endeavour. But the real fruit of the effort is the fact that contemporary ideas have been studied without sacrificing the poet's special intellectual tendency or temper, even if at the cost of temporary confusion and contradiction. The potential rejection of the philosophy of the poem by the heart of the poet is to be read not only between the lines, but in several mystical passages, which, like this, are out of conformity with the avowed rationalism. It is doubly appropriate, therefore, that the poem should close with this intuition of death: first, because so much of the poem turns on, as it begins with, the idea of death; second, because this last utterance on the subject is by its idealism so thoroughly characteristic of the genius of the poet who, forsaking contemporary French materialism, is to turn to older fields of thought and become the most Platonic of English poets.

In summary what can be said? The whole poem is instinct with death. Beginning with horror at the loathsomeness of the accompaniments of death, not realizing always the implications of his philosophy in reference to this dismay, passing through deserts or mirages of rationalism, naturalism, perfectibility, pronouncing death itself a wonderful engine of Necessity, but all the while never quite reconciled to the mutability of the beautiful, Shelley at the last, thoroughly aroused, in deepening passion, imagery, and music, gives his thus far notablest intuition of birth, life, and death. By poetic magic he endows the already hypostatized Necessity with a burning desire to gain through ever aspiring paths of change a destined goal of some sort of bliss. In this intuition the fear of death itself is purged, but by reason of its unbeautiful accompaniments death yet remains for him a thing of dreariness and gloom. The reconciliation with death is not complete. Only a partly victorious attitude has been struck.

III

Shelley planned a revision of *Queen Mab*, under a new and more dramatic title, *The Dæmon of the World*. There are two fragments of this revision, one published with *Alastor* in 1816, the other, of uncertain date, but probably 1815, scribbled by Shelley in the margins of a printed copy of *Queen Mab*. These two fragments evince a stronger realization of the central theme, throwing as they do less weight on the fairy-creature of old-wives' tales, Mab, who always stands rather incongruously as patron-spirit to a philosophy of necessity; but more emphasis upon a World-Dæmon which, ever struggling against a never-shaken good, is doomed in the end to extinction. Thus the Manichæan dualism of good and evil is preached more clearly and pictured more impressively, at the cost of disregarding the subjectivity of good and evil which he had preached in the notes to *Mab*. This dramatic acceleration is the key to a greater and far more intense poetizing in mood, image, and music. Later, a similar dæmon-of-the-world idea unites with a far profounder realization of the nature of spiritual adventure to produce that splendid fragment in *terza rima* to which reference was made a moment ago, *The Triumph of Life*. To catch a view of how Shelley's mind characteristically re-worked a theme as his artistry and experience deepened, one need only put *Mab*, the *Dæmon* fragments, and the *Triumph* side by side. The history of the development, if not of the making, of a poet's mind is in those three poems. A boy's ardent but rhetorical mouthing of what he has read about life, and a deeper passage or two in which he speaks better than he knows, are in *Mab*; a firmer dramatic grasp and a stronger artistry of image and music, but a yet unconquered bookishness, are in the *Dæmon*; a profound insight and sincerity, fully informed by real and tragic experience, and a new music, the inevitable garment as well as soul of the greater understanding, are in the *Triumph*.

All three are songs in which death makes and sings the burden. In the *Dæmon* the political theme of death is rendered with an increase of dramatic horror; one or two inconsistencies in the handling of the philosophy of death are reduced or removed; the idealism with which he views evil and death he attempts to unite to his necessitarianism; but he yet fails to deduce a consistent function of life and death.

The dramatic improvement is especially notable in the closing lines of the first fragment, which are substituted for, or possibly added to, far weaker lines (109–257) in the second canto of *Mab*. Here is a new picture of the horror of

human murder, which Shelley still attributes to politics and
religion:

> Awhile the Spirit paused in ecstasy.
> Yet soon she saw, as the vast spheres swept by,
> Strange things within their belted orbs appear.
> Like animated frenzies, dimly moved
> Shadows, and skeletons, and fiendly shapes,
> Thronging round human graves, and o'er the dead
> Sculpturing records for each memory
> In verse, such as malignant gods pronounce,
> Blasting the hopes of men, when heaven and hell
> Confounded burst in ruin o'er the world;
> And they did build vast trophies, instruments
> Of murder, human bones, barbaric gold,
> Skins torn from living men, and towers of skulls
> With sightless holes gazing on blinder heaven,
> Mitres, and crowns, and brazen chariots stained
> With blood, and scrolls of mystic wickedness,
> The sanguine codes of venerable crime.
> The likeness of a thronèd king came by,
> When these had passed, bearing upon his brow
> A threefold crown; his countenance was calm,
> His eye severe and cold; but his right hand
> Was charged with bloody coin, and he did gnaw
> By fits, with secret smiles, a human heart
> Concealed beneath his robe; and motley shapes,
> A multitudinous throng, around him knelt,
> With bosoms bare, and bowed heads, and false looks
> Of true submission, as the sphere rolled by,
> Brooking no eye to witness their foul shame,
> Which human hearts must feel, while human tongues
> Tremble to speak; they did rage horribly,
> Breathing in self-contempt fierce blasphemies
> Against the Dæmon of the World, and high
> Hurling their armèd hands where the pure Spirit,
> Serene and inaccessibly secure,
> Stood on an isolated pinnacle,

> The flood of ages combating below,
> The depth of the unbounded universe
>   Above, and all around
> Necessity's unchanging harmony.

The changes in the philosophy of death are less remarkable. The deletion of the passage of Christian comfort has already been noticed. The romantic intuition of the triumph over death, with which *Mab* closes, seems also to have been marked for omission. Thus disappear the nearest approaches in *Mab* to a doctrine of individual immortality. Their place is taken in the second fragment by two cryptic, paradoxical lines (562–563) that may be made to mean almost anything or nothing:

> For what thou art shall perish utterly,
> But what is thine may never cease to be.

Shelley's intention, however, is made fairly clear by two other lines (539–542) that he has inserted in the same passage:

> For birth but wakes the universal mind,
> Whose mighty streams might else in silence flow
> Through the vast world, to individual sense
> Of outward shows.*

Thus is indicated the idealistic theory of a universal mind which is temporarily individualized. The function of this individualistic awaking to outward shows and of the loss of individualism in death is not given, and so a consistent interpretation is neglected. But the intention to dispense with individual immortality is rather obvious. Finally it may be remarked that a difficulty is raised rather than avoided in the beginning of the second fragment. The throne, i.e., the power, of evil is represented as girt with death's omnipotence, but

---

* For birth but wakes the spirit to the sense
  Of outward shows. *Queen Mab,* IX, 155–156.

genius, nevertheless, in its passionate dreams, according to the following lines, has vision of a perfected world in which evil has been overthrown. The implication is that the supporting power, death, will not be overthrown — as Shelley had admitted in *Mab*, in the passage on euthanasia as characteristic of the future; and as he admitted later in *Prometheus Unbound*. But, in strict logic, if evil is to be stamped out, and death is evil, why not regard death as removable? What Shelley really means is that an attitude toward death, the horror and fear of it, will be amended. Therefore it is not with death itself that the power of evil is girt, but with the horror and fear of it — a statement of large practical as well as philosophical import. But the young poet and lover is still so shocked at the mutability of the good and the true and the beautiful *things* of experience that he uses death and the fear of death interchangeably, much to our confusion and to the impoverishment of his own vision and passion.

IV

And now, having considered *Queen Mab* and its related poems, having witnessed therein a growth in serious concern with human affairs, including death, incident to an excursion into Necessitarianism, and having discovered an imperfect reconciliation of necessity and death, we may resume the comparative study of what other young romantics said about death in their first two decades.

For an anti-type to Shelley's juvenile dabbling in death and necessity one need but turn to the early poems of Keats, up to and including the *Endymion*. Here all is honey and hawthorne, moonlight and starlight, the wind along a reedy stream, light-hearted dreams of the loveliness of romance and of women. To be sure, the young Keats rhymes *romantic* and *frantic;* but there is hardly anything frantic about these early poems. His soft, amorous ravishment and " balmy pain "

are scarcely a gesture, even, toward the frantic. To themes
of horror, since they are ugly, he was antipathetic, as may be
divined repeatedly in his work. But he definitely rejects them
more than once, as in a few lines in *Sleep and Poetry*, written
in the third year after the publication of *Queen Mab*, and
describing with curious exactness Shelley's favourite themes,
Gothic and political:

> But strength alone though of the Muses born
> Is like a fallen angel: trees uptorn,
> Darkness, and worms, and shrouds, and sepulchres
> Delight it; for it feeds upon the burrs
> And thorns of life; forgetting the great end
> Of Poesy, that it should be a friend
> To soothe the cares, and lift the thoughts of man.

A few lines later he indicates what then seemed to him the
true function of poets, thus:

> And they shall be accounted poet kings
> Who simply tell the most heart-easing things.

What could be further both from Shelley's earliest play with
ghosts and from his later portentous intransigence, than this
desire to tell simply " the most heart-easing things "?

Death is seldom mentioned in these compositions of the first
five years. One of Keats's earliest exercises, indeed, written
in his eighteenth or nineteenth year, is *On Death*, a comment
on the irrationality of the fear to die. It reminds one of a
slightly similar theme in Shelley's *Dialogue between Death
and a Mortal*, written at the age of seventeen. Both poets, it
is true, turned early to Chatterton, the " son of misery," as
Keats calls him. But, whereas in Shelley's verses the pace of
misery and death is accelerated from year to year, it almost
ceases in Keats's. We find, instead, in his many occasional
pieces as well as in his more considered efforts, a poetizing
true to his heart-easing ideal. He must tell a tale of chivalry,

with huge, cloudy symbols of high romance, filled with gentle knights, dinted shields, and debonair ladies, with Arte-gall and grim Talus, with Archimago, Belphœbe, and lovely Una. Or he turns to write of deep-browed Homer, or to picture Venus looking sideways in alarm; or woos sweet kisses from averted faces, and follows a nymph's enticement,

> Through almond blossoms and rich cinnamon;
> Till in the bosom of a leafy world
> [They] rest in silence, like two gems upcurl'd
> In the recesses of a pearly shell.

Here, too, are " lovely Laura in her light green dress," and the astonished Petrarch. The dew is swept by fairy feet, after a night of quaint jubilee,

> Which every elf and fay had come to see;
> When bright processions took their airy march
> Beneath the curvèd moon's triumphal arch.

A trembling empathy, soft and sensuous, delicate and femi-nine, fills his verses to intoxication: a nightingale singing its undersong in leafy quiet, a bee wrestling with cowslip bells, shining grapes laughing from their green attire, wanton gold-finches pausing in their yellow flights to display their black and golden wings. And many other intense delights, like these:

> Here are sweet peas, on tiptoe for a flight;
> With wings of gentle flush o'er delicate white,
> And taper fingers catching at all things,
> To bind them all about with tiny rings.

>   .   .   .   .

> Where swarms of minnows show their little heads,
> Staying their wavy bodies 'gainst the streams,
> To taste the luxury of sunny beams
> Temper'd with coolness. How they ever wrestle
> With their own sweet delight, and ever nestle

Their silver bellies on the pebbly sand.
If you but scantily hold out the hand,
That very instant not one will remain;
But turn your eye, and they are there again.

Verbal magic such as this reminds one that the old phrase, *ut pictura poesis*, is but a half-truth, or less. At the age of twenty neither Shelley nor Byron had done anything even nearly so beautiful. Among the juvenilia of the poets, those of Keats are amazing, almost unapproachable, for fresh, keen observation and a rich delicacy of phrase. He is, indeed, following the advice he gave Shelley later, which Shelley perhaps liked none too well, though from *Alastor* on he had already anticipated it in his own practice: to load every rift with ore.

When Keats does, so infrequently, refer to death, in the midst of this joyous sensitiveness to all lovely things, he disguises it with enchantment. Taking a view directly opposite to Shelley's prevailing prejudice, he finds loveliness and inspiration in mutability. If he pauses to consider the brevity of life, he tricks out that brevity in beautiful metaphor, calling it " a fragile dewdrop on its perilous way from a tree's summit." He hastens to forget the sadness of decay in a joy in ever-changing beauty, a joy that becomes ecstatic in proportion as the beauty is ephemeral. It is as though he were addressing Shelley:

Why so sad a moan?
Life is the rose's hope while yet unblown;
The reading of an ever-changing tale;
The light up-lifting of a maiden's veil;
A pigeon tumbling in clear summer air.

There, line for line, is Keats's way of reading life, both good and evil, so-called, at the age of twenty: *couleur de rose*, a romantic tale, amorous delight, natural magic — the poetry of heart-easing things. Even the death of a poet he makes proud and happy, by gracing him with the certainty that his verses will please youth and inspire age for generations to come. Even the death of a lover is softened to the picturesque and the mysterious, as when all sweet maids, with sorrow raining from their white eyelids, are summoned to mourn the drowning Leander,

> Sinking away to his young spirit's night,
> Sinking bewilder'd 'mid the dreary sea.

Yet, in the very flush of all this romantic beauty, Keats feels that he lacks a grasp of facts and ideas, that there is sterner stuff in mutability and necessity, which he has ignored, and that therefore his struggle to write will be vain,

> . . . . until I grow high-rife
> With old Philosophy,
> And mad glimpses of futurity!

Shelley made acquaintance with philosophy and politics and had his mad visions before he really commenced poet; perhaps his ideology delayed his poetry. Certain it is that, up to their twenty-first years, Keats wrote better poetry without philosophy, moral and political, than Shelley did with it.

Endymion is Keats's long poem, crowning his juvenilia as *Queen Mab* does Shelley's. Here the contrasts that already have been noted are intensified. There is but little on death: out of some four thousand lines, less than one hundred and fifty. A poem of young, sensuous beauty and ideal love, every line ingeminated with figures of sparkling though luscious delicacy, it has little acquaintance with the gloom of realistic history. Beauty is again the antidote to imperfection, change, and sorrow; the panacea for the cruel, stupid, and cowardly things men do in their rivalries as social beings.

> Spite of despondence, of the inhuman dearth
> Of noble natures, of the gloomy days,
> Of all the unhealthy and o'er-darkened ways

Made for our searching: yes, in spite of all,
Some shape of beauty moves away the pall
From our dark spirits.

So, the poem is a crowded treasure of freshly observed marvels of sun, moon, and stars, old forests, clear rills and cooling coverts, willow trailing its delicate amber, daffodils and the green world they live in, musk-roses on beds of straw, fine herbs whose every name is fragrant, and little rivers in their mid-day gold and glimmer. These brim the measure of contentment. But there are, too, the set scenes of greater loveliness, as the bowers of Adonis and Circe; and the Miltonic splendour of Neptune's palace, with its frontal arch as large, bright, and coloured as the bow of Iris, its titanic gates of carved and shining gold which open swift as fairy thought, with the blue vault above, the lucid depths of the lake-like floor, the great emerald throne, and the gold-green zenith above the Sea-God's head. Frequently some excess of phrase is reminiscent of the Elysian idleness of Spenser's bowers and palaces, or springs from some more vivid sense of beauty than the reader is easily aware of, to which he must penetrate deftly, only in turn to become grateful for the phrase. What a contrast there is between these phrases and those of another long romantic poem that had but recently achieved popular acclaim! Only two years before, Leigh Hunt's *The Story of Rimini* had been published, and in the following year had gone into a second edition. Its unimaged, unmusical lines, flat diction, and vapid sentimentality, its very insipidity, procured it welcome from an undiscriminating public. Sir Walter Scott, himself, carried away a copy of it from Murray's. But the critics, whose business it was to discriminate, saw in *Endymion*, though it is gorgeously written in the great poetic tradition, only an intolerable lusciousness.

The gloom of history is used merely to offset this impassioned loveliness, for Keats can hardly understand that some minds really find more delight and inspiration in woes of

Troy, towers smothered in fire, far-shadowing spears and glistening blades, in struggle, blood, and shrieks, in all the gilded pageants and cheats of history, than in dreaming of beauty and love in whispering groves. Glancing momentarily at the " war, the deeds, the disappointment, the anxiety " of human life, he thinks of them all as a subtle magic to make us feel existence and show us " how quiet death is." Tyrants he contemplates, not to revile their cruelty or picture their own agonies in death, but to wonder whether all regalities are gilded masks, to imagine a supreme Power that keeps a religious and benevolent state high above the " withering of old-lipped Fate," and to envisage all suffering as a lesson in the immortal quietness of death! The death of heroes he makes both noble and lovely,

> . . . . the grandeur of the dooms
> We have imagined for the mighty dead;
> All lovely tales that we have heard or read:
> An endless fountain of immortal drink,
> Pouring unto us from the heaven's brink.

Or, in terms of the sweet idylls of this world, he turns, occasionally, to romanticize the after life. His shepherds, in their holiday leisure, are made to vie in rehearsing each one his own anticipated bliss: loves to be resumed, rosy children to be clasped again; then to sit in almond vales and tell over the stories of their youth; and nightly to summon Vesper, and call the clouds to the west for the sun's couch. Or, again, in a palace under sea he brings to ecstatic life all lovers who have perished at sea; and watches the resurrected joy of this Paphian army pouring down marble steps easily and fast as hour-glass sand, passing into such eternity of lovers' bliss " 'tis dizziness to think of it."

Moreover, the very intensity with which he felt natural beauty and the beauty of love, bred a belief in some unique and sanctifying meaning back of beauty, or rather, *in* it. Intensity of feeling, as so often in the history of the emotions, issued in a half mystical belief in a spirit of loveliness in all things, and in a kind of unity of all things with and in that universal spirit. In love this union is perfected, for with nothing else, says the poet, " can our souls interknit so wingedly."

Endymion's pilgrimage is a pilgrimage through beautiful sensations to the shrine of Diana, or ' Essential Beauty.' Mazes, palaces, bowers, shrines, and temples, the deep glen and the mountain-top, sun and river, under-sea mysteries, and the charm of women and lovers, fulfil his soul in beauty and teach him to read the truth aright — bring him to the worship of Essential Beauty, which is identified with truth. At this time Keats thought of Endymion's experience as a symbol of all search for truth. In a letter of 1819 he refers to the world as the " vale of Soul-making "; and he considered the poem " a regular stepping of the Imagination towards a truth; . . . it set before me the gradations of happiness, even like a kind of pleasure thermometer." But he believed all beautiful things were a permanent possession of the spirit, that

> A thing of beauty is a joy forever:
> Its loveliness increases; it will never
> Pass into nothingness.

That hyperbole he had to recant. The stern facts, the lust and cold cruelty, the desolation and death, " where nought of man's endures before the sun," were yet to be realized, until he should cry, in his *Ode on Melancholy* (1819?),

> She dwells with Beauty — Beauty that must die.

The early florescence of his faith had been too intense and too sudden. While Shelley moaned the passing of all loveliness into nothingness, Keats was so enraptured by the moment's sensuousness that each beauty seemed an eternity. Exultantly accepting beauty, he in a measure disregarded death. " The excellence of every art," he wrote to his brothers, " is its intensity, capable of making all disagreeables *evaporate* from their being in close relationship with Beauty and Truth."

Swinburne's exultant acceptance of the nature-process, wherein " life and sleep and death are one," was a further step in the pilgrimage, never certainly taken by Keats, but tragically and triumphantly accomplished by Shelley toward the end of his life.

Thus, then, Keats, in the years of his apprenticeship, found attitudes of superiority to death, both in his sensuous intoxication with beauty and also in his interpretation of that intensity as a mystical union with loveliness itself. His moods had a more monistic tendency than had young Shelley's. Shelley's very indignation with oppression hurried him into a dramatic dualism.

But there is another aspect of death in the *Endymion*, which, while we read the poem, haunts us. Endymion himself, this pilgrim of beauty, is so closely connected with Keats, soul of his soul, as Shelley would say, that one anticipates in Endymion's adventures the fate of his creator. As Keats, pursuing beauty everywhere, by his expressive sensitiveness to it making the world itself more lovely, passed at length through the change we cannot but foresee and dread in all especially lovely things, and went down through a kind of defeat and gloom to death, so we feel a mortal fate awaiting Endymion. After his *Wanderjahr* in the depths of the earth and sea and the heavens, his exploration of the glories of earth and sky and sea, will not death make an early and necessary close? The brighter the day, the darker the night; the more delicate the beauty, the frailer the life. Those whom the gods love, die young. When the sheer brightness of his dream fails, Endymion cries,

> . . . . I have clung
> To nothing, loved a nothing, nothing seen
> Or felt but a great dream . . . .
> There never lived a mortal man, who bent
> His appetite beyond his natural sphere,
> But starved and died.

Then, as Endymion feels he is about to die, unfitted for life by the very intensity of his idealization of its beauty, our suspense and dread appear about to be realized. This suspense, so far as it derives from our knowledge of Keats and from our identification of the poet with his creation, is, indeed, extrinsic to the poem. Yet, by a sort of sympathetic magic between Keats and Endymion, the suspense seems in some deep way intrinsic, as though Keats himself while creating Endymion were not all unaware of a doom of early change, to go hand in hand with his supreme worship of beauty. Endymion's farewell to life, at any rate, might be pronounced as an elegy for Keats himself.

> Night will strew
> On the damp grass myriads of lingering
> leaves,
> And with them shall I die; nor much it
> grieves
> To die, when summer dies on the cold
> sward.
> Why, I have been a butterfly, a lord
> Of flowers, garlands, love-knots, silly posies,
> Groves, meadows, melodies, and arbour-roses;
> My kingdom's at its death, and just it is
> That I should die with it: so in all this
> We miscall grief, bale, sorrow, heart-break,
> woe,
> What is there to plain of?

But, true to the faith of youth and of all good fairy-tales, though not to commonplace knowledge of the beautiful, Keats gives a sudden turn to the poem, and Cynthia reveals herself, just as her lover had despaired of her and of life. Then, love conquering all, even death, this light lord of ephemerids is translated to the skies, to dwell with his immortal queen of daintiest loveliness. Both Shelley and Keats ended their first long poem with this faith in love's necessary victory over death: youth's attitude of faith, and the dream of old age.

> Unfortunates on earth, we see at last
> All death-shadows, and glooms that
> > overcast
> Our spirits, fann'd away by [Love's] light
> > pinnions.

Thereafter, our reading finished, like Peona we turn home to our dull selves, in wonderment at so much beauty, at so fair an embodiment of the love that ushers us down the sorrow-way to death and then builds a bridge out over the drear abyss. Only love's faith builds the shadowy pylon for the further reach of the bridge to rest upon. In more senses than one we may understand the mysterious call that sent Endymion on his pilgrimage:

> He ne'er is crown'd
> With immortality, who fears to follow
> Where airy voices lead.

The juxtaposition of frail beauty and strong death recalls the work of Dante Gabriel Rossetti. Mr. F. L. Lucas, in one of his brief, intensely readable, but equally penetrative essays, has said that Rossetti had a passion for the loveliness of life more violent than any English poet, even Keats, and that he came to be haunted more and more, as time went by, with the sense of lost days and vanished hours. In spite of much "fundamental brain-work" which he expended upon his poetry, Rossetti was more and more beset by the decay and death of beautiful things.

> There is a change in every hour's recall,
> > And the last cowslip in the field we see
> > On the same day with the first corn-poppy:
> Alas for hourly change! Alas for all
> The Loves that from his hand proud Youth lets fall
> > Even as the beads of a told rosary!

Necessity and Death

What whisperest thou? Nay, why
Name the dead hours? I mind them well.
Their ghosts in many darkened doorways dwell
With desolate eyes to know them by.

.   .   .   .

Ah! who shall dare to search through what sad maze
Thenceforth their incommunicable ways
Follow the desultory feet of Death?

Thus, exquisite sensitiveness to joy in the beauty of frail, momentary things carries its own doom — pain for their quick extinction. " It is a Love that walks hand in hand with Death." So, Keats wrote his *Endymion,* but ended the tale happily. So, Shelley, as we shall see, wrote his *Alastor,* and ended it with death. But in both fictions the quest for beauty is more important than the conclusion, as in real experience the process is more important than the dubious end.

Perhaps, too, this quest carries with it, or leads toward, another doom. In the poppied dream of these sweetly sensuous pictures, social conscience and heroic effort may deliquesce. The creator becomes a thrall to his own sorcery. His witch turns upon him without mercy, *La Belle Dame Sans Merci,* and then forsakes him in the land of reality. Dreams evaporate. The very power of dreaming, unrefreshed by hard forays in the realistic, decays. To replace struggle with dream makes for a kind of death in life. Some such meaning, at any rate, may easily, without fancifulness, be read into Keats's *La Belle Dame:* the knight-at-arms with the armour of his soul all undone, he himself woe-begone and haggard, palely loitering alone by the withered sedge, dreaming of the witch who had lulled him fast asleep:

And there I dreamed — Ah! woe betide!
The latest dream I ever dreamed
On the cold hill's side.

65

I saw pale kings and princes too,
Pale warriors, death-pale were they all;
They cried — " La Belle Dame Sans Merci
Hath thee in thrall."

Heart-easing pictures of death, too, as that of the Beadsman in *The Eve of St. Agnes*, whose breath like his prayers

Seemed taking flight for Heaven, without a death,

leave something of *virtus et labor* to be desired.

But another word on Rossetti. When one remembers that *his* Queen Mab, the exquisite *Blessed Damozel*, was written at the age of eighteen, and that Shelley at eighteen was perpetrating his metrical villainies and prose enormities, one is amazed at the contrast in artistry. But the contrast in the matter of *Mab* and the *Damozel* is almost equally amazing. Even though Rossetti at eighteen was much under the influence of Shelley's poetry, even though there are certain fairly obvious similarities between the heavenly setting of *Mab* and that of the *Damozel* (which students have pointed out more than once), and even though the contrast is not logically, nor even emotionally, perfect, it is nevertheless impressive. If *Queen Mab* makes any one thing clear and indubitable, it is, that of the three major interests Shelley had experienced up to the age of twenty-one — death, love, and humanitarianism — the third was the strongest and the most sincere. Rossetti's poem displays no social conscience at all, but is wholly devoted to an intuition of personal love, so intense, mature, and beautiful that the world has not ceased wondering how a youngster in his teens could have mastered it. It is easier to account for the intense sincerity of Shelley's sociology than for the quintessential truth of Rossetti's romance. And it is precisely where the contrast breaks down that it becomes most notable. Shelley, indeed, concluded his long rationalistic essay with an intuition of that indestructible power of love which is the assured subject of Rossetti's ballad; but how utterly different in intensity and mode of statement are the two presentations of that intuition. Shelley had devoted a large part of his argument to the destruction of the grounds of the very faith which makes the poetic form or truth of Rossetti's poem: the Christian faith, including its assertion of personal survival. Has the benediction of that faith ever been said with more poignant beauty and hope for parted lovers than in the *Blessed Damozel?* Has ever the parting of lovers by death been more sacredly realized and faithfully healed than in the heavenly address of the Damozel as it was overheard by her earth-bound, dream-blessed lover? Even if one remembers how Dante and Petrarch dedicated the theme of ' My Lady in Heaven '? I sometimes think that had never another poem been written in the Christian mood, this one alone would have revealed the essential, poetic truth of the Christian dream: that love somehow conquers death. As one reads the poem, how powerfully he realizes the greatest contribution that Christianity made to poetry — its contribution to romantic love! With what piercing truth the tragedy of parted love is presented, with what tenderness the tragedy is mitigated by the elevation of the sensuous until it is consecrated before the feet of God, and by the calm, yet at the last tearful, faith of the Damozel in an eternal reunion! It is death, and a faith bred of death, that has given this mystic sublimity to passion. Much of it Rossetti learned, of course, from Dante; and he was fortunate to learn it while he was so young. Shelley's debt to Dante was comparatively late, and coincided, as will be seen presently, with the prevailing of his native but tragically tutored mysticism over his acquired learning.

Coleridge's very first poems reveal an interest in sorrow and death, but it is an interest of a kind very different from anything we have hitherto observed. At fourteen he wrote a few lines to the " maid of my Love, sweet Genevieve." The boy's heart is touched less by her physical beauty, so at least he avers, than by her gentle sympathy with woe and suffering. Tenderness — that is Coleridge's characteristic attitude toward woe and death, at once his earliest and his characteristic note. It runs throughout the poems from fourteen to twenty-one, though in his twenty-first year, while he was attending college, there is, naturally, less of death and more of love. But at the age of fifteen he is already waxing solemn, in Christ's Hospital Book, on the tenderness of a wife's love for her " very own " husband " when from death he meets his final doom." At seventeen he pens a hymn to Compassion. At eighteen, and later, he is expressing a deep grief for his sister's illness and imminent death. He performs the regulation homage of a young romantic to Chatterton: not in Shelley's way of imitation or in Keats's way of a memorial sonnet; but in a monody on the death of the poet. It is characteristic that of the romantic poets Coleridge should be the one in his teens to write an elegy. Yes, it is a neo-classical ode, stuffed with personification and other frigid rhetoric; nevertheless, it manages to breathe a heartfelt tenderness toward the lonely, neglected, sorrowing genius of St. Mary Radcliffe's. Of course, these poems have much beside *tendresse*. There is much healthy laughter, in mock heroics, even in mock elegiacs, on noses, bumpy Devonshire roads, and an extinct teakettle. There are friendship and love and happiness, and Christmas tales for younger brothers and sisters, and Ossianic imitations, songs of pixies, and a good deal of nature-poetry. But through it all the note of tenderness continues, in varying connections, but coming to its own again and again in some conjunction with woe or death. The boy, who as he waxed into philosophic manhood, was to know so much of defeat and sadness, seems to foreshadow his own fate as he repeatedly utters consolation to " wounded minds," " sorrow-clouded breasts," " dragon-winged Despair," " Death's dark house," " Tyrant-Pain," and various wistful personifications.

However, there is also a consciousness of danger, terror,

and dreadful death. At times he, too, like Shelley, strove, in
" bloated, puffing " lines, for the intense and vivid; though
this taste was not with Coleridge the all-absorbing habit it was
with the later poet. Moreover, instead of revelling in horror,
he balances dreadful things with gentle moods; or holds them
up as deterrents, as when he pictures the horrid deaths that
may overtake tourists who leave home, and then concludes
on the reassuring theme of home-peace and — tenderness!
Of tyrants, too, he is aware. He exults in their fall, and in the
rise of freedom. At twenty he confesses to " a young lady "
how in his earliest youth he was much given over to gentle
sympathy with sorrow, and how, later, he came to hate tyranny and rejoice in freedom's cause; yet even now his heart
aches for the fallen oppressor, though justice, nay mercy,
struck the blow! So, even these moods of the Horrid Intense
and the Political Intense revolve to tenderness. It is difficult
to avoid capitals when one is writing about the young Samuel
Taylor Coleridge; but the tenderness, at any rate, needs no
capitalization to intensify it: sincerity, and a deep gift for
compassion, are enough to recommend it.

Pater, than whom no one has said anything better about
Coleridge's poetry, remarks upon its being, unlike that of the
" Lake School " in general, " singularly unaffected by any
moral, or professional, or personal effort or ambition, —
' written,' as he [Coleridge] says, ' after the more violent
emotions of sorrow, to give him pleasure, when perhaps
nothing else could '; but coming thus, indeed, very close to
his own most intimately personal characteristics, and having
a certain languidly soothing grace or cadence, for its most
fixed quality, from first to last." Perhaps it is not far wrong
to find in this tenderness, upon which we have been com-
menting, the first instance of this intimate quality of comfort, of soothing grace and cadence, in sympathetic expression. Whether or not it is to be traced, in turn, along with
his " morbid languor of nature, his fitfulness of purpose, and

his rich delicate dreaminess," to what Pater calls " some tendency to disease in the physical temperament," is a question to be left to that branch of criticism which aims to ' explain ' poetry by make-believe clinicopathological diagnosis.

Lamb said that from childhood Coleridge hungered for eternity. There is a touch of this quality, too, in these early poems; and it is associated, not only with languor and a lamenting compassion, but with what was his first attitude of victory over death. Shelley and Keats found a kind of victory in the intensity of idealistic love, because they were unable to believe that such love could perish utterly. Coleridge's theory of victory proceeded from a mood of general imaginative contemplation rising into conviction; from a metaphor graduating to a poetic, if not practical, faith. The experience is imparted in a little poem called *Life*, written in his seventeenth year. As he walked the meadows of the Otter, " musing in torpid woe a sister's pain " — the wistful, sympathetic habit, once more — he woke from his dreamy state to take note, in quick succession, of the details of the landscape: the meadow, the woods, a verdant hill, the " dreary steep." Suddenly, in a moment of intense emotion, he became aware of all the details as one whole. Then, in quick intuition, he realized the experience as a symbol of the nature of life: as his years would advance, new details of knowledge and wisdom would open to view; at length would come Death, with " its undarken'd ray," rapturously to illumine the infinite meaning of life. Death is the great revealer of infinity and eternity: again, *mors janua vitae est*. This expansion of metaphor into faith and victory is a typical phase of much religious, mystical experience, and we shall find both Shelley and Tennyson going through the same phase and drawing deeply from it for their inspiration.

The same faith reappears in these early poems of Coleridge as a power that tranquillizes death. A composition entitled *Happiness* concludes thus:

70

Necessity and Death

Till Death shall close thy tranquil eye
While Faith proclaims " thou shalt
not die! "

Christian teaching pretty obviously here reinforces poetic faith, but the latter has given insight into the former, as it will continue to do throughout the theological disquisitions of later years. Poetic insight always fructified Coleridge's philosophy and theology. Here, therefore, the boy is father to the man.

Up to the age of twenty-one Wordsworth has exceedingly little to say about death. His happy temper is not antipathetic to it, but, rather, oblivious of it. He lives the life peripatetic and contemplative. Already, at seventeen, in his *Evening Walk*, he begins to be a sage of contentment. Already he begins to find that, as he said later, in another of his many walking-poems, *The Excursion*, wisdom is often nearer " when we stoop than when we soar." He writes in a spirit of tranquillity, nurtured by simple, pleased observation of homely scenes into which death enters but quietly, now as a pathetic incident in the suffering of the poor, now as a hushed and healing event at the close of a but little disturbed life. " Solitude," he opines, " prepares the soul for Heaven ", and from a serene participation in the peace of nature one slips almost unawares into death. It is a picture somewhat like Shelley's euthanasia of the good man, only young Wordsworth's good life is rural, private, sequestered, not political or strenuously philanthropic. Indeed, there is not much striving for the intense and vivid, in these early poems. No distressed pondering of the inscrutability of life raises his imagination to an attitude of philosophic victory over death; no ecstatic love of woman presses him to a conviction that love cannot expire in the grave. Instead, there are the jottings of a contented life, which are rounded out by the benediction, *omnes exeunt in tranquillitatem*. At the last, his own

71

large share of happy days well spent, and his small share of hardly-paining sighs all meted out, he will

> Creep hushed into the tranquil breast of death.

Perhaps it was this early disinclination and neglect vividly to envisage death as the possible failure of all human endeavour, that gave to Wordsworth's mature poetry both its special power to impart a healing peace to some troubled but not too critical minds, and its curious insufficiency for other minds more thoroughly critical. For it may be held that the amazing self-confidence of the poet of *Tintern Abbey* and *The Prelude* was attained at the expense of neglecting some of the obvious facts of experience. Retreating in dismay from the tragic sense of life that the French Revolution stirred in him, he too easily found refuge by reassuming the rather uncritical peace of mind he had known in this adolescent intercourse with nature. Hazlitt believed that he was not thoroughly candid in facing the facts of life. It is difficult to defend him against that indictment. One always suspects there was too easy a reassumption of youthful habits of thought and feeling, and that his French experiences had more the effect of intensifying his mysticism as a readily available escape from unpleasant problems than of forcing him to face what his temperament abhorred. The possibility of a malignant, or at least neutral, universe he almost deliberately understated. The desolation of war and death is heard afar, its clamour muted to " the still, sad music of humanity." The " burden of the mystery," " the weary weight of all this unintelligible world," is lightened too readily by the " serene and blessed " mood of the mystic. Shelley's enduring regret for the failure of beauty and his tragic struggle against the triumph of death, for all their exaggeration, were a more candid recognition of the facts with which the ordinary intelligence is attacked; and his own youthful mysticism is refined in repeatedly passing through the fiery crucible of human tragedy. He won his spurs in prolonged conflict. But Wordsworth assumed the mystic mantle almost with a single gesture of thankfulness. The strength and the sureness that he lost by avoiding the battle he endeavoured to make up by a confident, but not perfectly candid, self-assurance. Had his earliest communings with nature in its serene aspects been rudely shocked by its other aspect of internecine murder, his later ministry of peace might have been more thoughtful and powerful. Perhaps, too, in a keener struggle he would have lost the complacency of self-sanctified dullness which spreads through the huge mass of his inferior work. But, in a way, when one is born, one is done for.

Browning at the age of twenty, the reading, dreaming, fortunate boy, spoiled by his parents, writing under the double influence of Shelley and Byron, published *Pauline*, ostensibly a poem of confessions, though not necessarily autobiographical. His other early poetry has not been preserved; but *Pauline*, being his coming-of-age poem, is roughly homologous to *Queen Mab* and *Endymion*. It is remarkable that a poem with so much about Shelley in it should make so little of death, with so much of the Byronic, confessing, gesturing hero should have so little cynicism and so much philanthropy, and with so much youthful storm and stress should be so essentially conventional. From Byron he has taken the dark, theatrically suffering character, without the misanthropy; from Shelley, the philanthropy without the Gothic and political dreadfulness; and, presumably, from some essential bent of his own nature, the persistent faith in God. The confessing hero lays bare, with rather deliberate vagueness as to detail, the story of his soul, of the strange impulses, tendencies, desires, for which he can in nowise account, which he can nowise stifle, but all of which he is bound to trust equally. This is that crowded, romantic life of the feelings which today we do not accept at face-value, but dissect into complexes and basic, selfish, fearful motives. For this hero it is a marvellous personal drama, mysteriously anticipating some unknown state of life, and therefore potent with revelation. The romantic poet who thus carries about with him his own theatre of revelation, believing that at any moment some deep, inexplicable feeling will give him the cue to enter the mystery of mysteries, is the counterpart in subjective adventure of the more objective Arthurian knight, who expected at any moment, at any turn of the dusty road, to chance upon the Grail in its very actuality. For the romantic, *Gefühl ist alles.*

Pauline's hero (Pauline herself may be regarded as a Christian personification of the Platonic Idea of the Good, and even an incarnation of Shelley's spirit) is introduced as one who in his youth never sang but to an audience rising in applause, whose quivering lips were bathed in nature's enchantments, who dreamed wildly of beauty and love and God, but who fell from this high infantine state. Then he became sin's familiar friend, a not too realistic Manfred, knit round with a charm of lust and pride and wandering dreams, thirsting for all experiences, seeing shapes of strange delight, becoming spotted with the world's wrong, losing faith in man and God, draining his own soul's wine, drunkenly, and all the while blasphemously thrilling with a strange delight in causing his own decay. He brokenly, but with a consuming interest in his own sensations, tells Pauline the amazing story, repeatedly assuring her that now it all lies in that dark past before her sweetness brought him once again to the safe harbour where all good Victorians listen to the church-bells on Sundays. For this dramatic introspectionist, after all his titanism, avers, bandying yet more words, that his undying faith in God, truth, and love, having suffered only a temporary stupor, is now revivified. The wild adventurer, companion of Shelley the Sun-Treader, heir to Werther and Faust and Manfred, has all the while been safe because of the deep radical gift of faith, root of his root, heart of his heart. One can almost see Pilgrim comfortably feeling for his through-ticket while he ventures into the City of Destruction. Is there just a touch of Christian's cocksure precocity?

Whither, then, do all these struggles tend? To belief in God and truth and love — the good fight nobly won; and then to death, another fight,

> For I seem, dying, as one going in the dark,
> To fight a giant . . .

So the poem concludes, with but little more on death anywhere in it. The sharp, quick, introspective young man of the many masculine words, ceaselessly revelling in gratified wonder at his own emotions, completes the history of his egotisms in a mood of realized faith in authority, and in one last masculine, courageous enterprise: to go up unafraid against the dark giant of death. One sees a touch of Byron there, and much that one is tempted to call the special note of Browning: a fine attitude, courageously daring to assert what all ' best people ' believe. It is the note that comes out again and again in the later poems, nowhere more magnificently than in the Epilogue to *Asolando*, his valedictory; nowhere more comfortingly than in the *Prospice*, in which, indeed, it is sanctified by the death of his wife and by his faith that he will be re-united to her once he himself has manfully gone up against death,

> Where he stands, the Arch Fear in a visible form.

Browning was always fighting for causes already won. He said it was faith that made him sure of victory. The habit grew on him. From the close of *Pauline* to the Epilogue to *Asolando* one feels that even death has little chance against this very victorious attitude.

V

In various degrees these young romantic poets have found existence good, beautiful, and dangerous. Wordsworth knows that it is good and beautiful to be alive; he is not really aware that it is dangerous. Keats knows it is beautiful, and therefore good; but he ignores or disguises the danger, and then is conscience-stricken for his neglect of the sterner facts. Shelley knows it is dangerous, thinks it ought to be good and some day will be; and as time goes on he will learn more and more to image its sensuous and unmask its intellectual beauty. Byron finds life dangerous, wicked, and beautiful. Coleridge found it strangely beautiful and languorously dangerous; and tenderly believed it to be the precursor of a greater good in eternity. Tennyson finds it a vacillating affair, now good, then evil; now beautiful, again ugly; not seldom too active, often distinctly dangerous, and repeatedly stirring up an impulse to flee; but always, in any mood, however delightful or weary, a possible subject for a melodious poem. Browning, having precociously conquered his doubts, which are more emotional than intellectual, is stoutly sure that life is dangerous and beautiful, a dramatically good place for fighting; and that God is in his heaven.

In varying moods these young romantic poets imagined the issue of living — death. Wordsworth, in his philosophy of homely contentment seldom dwelling upon it, regarded it as the quiet crowning of a tranquil life. There is no need of victory; only the welcoming of a greater tranquillity, the peace of benediction. Coleridge, given to dreamy compassion for those who suffer and die, idealized death as the great revealer of eternity and of the hidden unity of all things. Keats has little to say about death, though more than either Wordsworth or Coleridge. When he does treat it, he keeps close to his rule that poetry should ease the heart. Sensuous beauty is his antidote to imperfection, change, and sorrow; death is disguised with beautiful enchantment of the picturesque and mysterious. The after-life is romanticized — a pastoral idyl projected into the skies. And the very intensity of his love of love, and of all other gracious delicate things, is interpreted as a mystical union with the spirit of loveliness, a triumph over death. Immortality lies where unreal voices lead. Byron, pursuing passion, affecting sophistication, yet languishing in melancholy and sentimentality, theatrically stages his own death — the sad and noble parting of a Timon weary of love, weary of life. Tennyson, after penning boyish essays in groans, bones, and other blood-curdling horrors, and then adolescently, like Byron, imagining himself disillusioned, displays his characteristic moody and fanciful sensitiveness, in a kind of feminine passivity, toward all the dark phases. Fitting his mood to the object, he is faint in the presence of autumnal decay, comforted by the flowers on a grave, pensive before decadent loveliness, sad with the world's woe; reacting from mood to mood, he is afraid of death as well as of life, desirous of fleeing both yet exultant in the release of death, torn between doubt of the old creed and a faith that poets and lovers are clairvoyant of life and death and the everlasting will, eager to believe that death is but the shadow of life. Sad, eager, languorous, afraid, exalted, dubitant, he lives in a vacillation of moods, making no notable critical effort, destructive or constructive; but always intent upon reducing to a sensitive phrase the volatile essence of each changing mood. Browning, already showing promise of the ever victorious champion of established faiths he was to become, calls upon the Sun-Treader ever to be with him in gloom, but most of all when he goes forth into darkness to fight Giant Death.

Shelley, speaking more of the subject than all the others put together, scarcely ever silent upon it, is the young bachelor of death. Approaching all the phases and attitudes discovered by the others, with the exception of Byron's dying Timonism and Browning's Christian heroism, he develops each more frequently and more fully, excepting, again, the fugitive impulse of Tennyson and the sensuous enchantment of Keats. In addition to these themes, which he shares with this company, he has others of which they have nothing or next to nothing; so that in variety as well as quantity of expression he surpasses them, though Keats and Tennyson both outdo him in beauty of expression.

He begins with a raucous delight in harrowing moods of horror on a large but penny-dreadful scale, with a juvenile, playful, and imitative frightfulness of graveyards, ghosts, demons, villains, persecutions, suffering perfection, suicides, and murders — strange preluding to his later themes of the unseen reality. He deals grossly in grief, sorrow, and the soft, pathetic signs of bereavement, before he is acquainted with deprivation — untutored elegiac preluding. He flirts with languor and pain, adolescent weariness with life, and the imagined escape in easeful death — affected preluding of odes in tragic dejection. Becoming aware of society and religion and of their nature and history, he passes to using death as his most vivid colour in painting his political and ethical theories. There is a new essay in shuddering: the persecutions by tyrants and bigots, the sufferings and deaths of their innocent victims, their own agonies in dying, and the victims' heroic choice of liberty or death — earnest but confused preludings of hymns and dramas of freedom. In contrast, death becomes the quietest of colours as he depicts the tranquil, happy death of the good man or prophesies the common comfort of euthanasia in a realized Utopia. There are rhapsodies on the indestructibleness of love and its ecstatic victory over death — rough preludings of mystic lyrics and narratives of passion. He definitely distrusts the sentimental idyl of personal immortality, but wishes his reason might permit him the conventional Christian comfort; he wonders whether death may be a gate to a higher if less individual life; in each recurring spring he ponders a promise of the final triumph of love and beauty — tentative preluding of the great speculative odes. He progresses through Platonic dream, while we hear the accents of Diotima speaking of ideal love and beauty. He versifies the necessity of French naturalism, for which death is an inevitable incident in the drama of universal change; and rises from sounding rhetoric to his first impassioned flight as he beholds the restless wheels of being bickering and burning to gain the destined goal of birth and life and death. Then, indeed, the gate of gloom and dreariness opens momentarily to the awakening of the eternal spring, to " azure isles and beaming skies."

But an instinctive, glowing impatience with all that is ugly and cruel, and a constitutional regret and faintness in the face of the mortality of lovely beings and before the imaged loathsomeness of the grave, are ever-present, always betraying him through his emotions into a dualism of good and evil that is inconsistent with those notes on their subjectivity which he added to *Queen Mab*. As yet he is unable completely to reconcile these instinctive dismays with a mood, attitude, or philosophy of victory over death. His love of the beautiful and his disgust of death have not been definitely harmonized.

But what is the upshot of all this poetizing of life and death by romantic young men? In the first place, and for the most part, it is, naturally, a poetizing of emotional and imaginative attitudes, rather than of highly reflective, persistently rational attempts to conceive the inter-relation of life and death. The vividness of a recurring emotion constitutes it an attitude, raises it to significance, stiffens it with conviction. These attitudes alternate each with each, because there is *some* ground in common experience for each of them. There is just as much justification for Tennyson's attitudes as for Keats's, for Coleridge's as for Shelley's. Some differences of temperament and environment incline one poet to one attitude, another to another; one to nearly all. The reader may occupy each attitude in turn without real inconsistency. There is enough of the ugly in life and death to produce indignation and threnody; enough of the beautiful to motivate joy and dithyramb; enough of the fear of death to make Browning's courage attractive; and so on, for each attitude. In the second place, these emotional attitudes, imaginatively heightened until they become representative and thereby poetically true, are not so splendidly and convincingly representative as to fuse, or confuse, the attitudes with victory. Possible exceptions to this generalization are the trance of beauty in which Keats is able to sacrifice if not forget the ugly, and the intuition of death as a means of life to which Shelley once rises in *Queen Mab*. But even these poetizings have about them something of the vivid insufficiency of youth's imperfectly grounded enthusiasms. A greater utterance, less obviously partial, prejudiced, and temperamental — such an utterance as arises from the disappointing experiences called maturity, the burden of life — must be achieved before these attitudes, common though they be in some degree to most men, can disclose their highest representative power, and so involve that rapt and intuitive intensity which is indeed a kind of victory over death. These young men are as yet living too much in their sensations, too much engaged with their first strange surprises at their own sensations, to speak without surprise and sensationalism — with the exception, possibly, of Wordsworth, who disliked too vivid surprises. In the third place, the most notable attempt to deal intellectually with the subject is that of Shelley, in *Queen Mab*, confused and inconsistent as his thought is. Coleridge, with his sudden vision of a universal identity, emotionally anticipates the goal of his own intellectual struggle. Keats has his intuition that to be lost in loveliness is after all to approximate discovery and victory. Shelley, struggling through materialism, makes the most persistent and conscious effort to come intellectually to grips with death, whatever may be the inferiority of the result when it is compared with the mystical asseverations of

Coleridge and Keats. Byron's attempts are the weakest, both emotionally and intellectually. But of all the moods and images and ideas with which these young poets have surrounded death, it is those of Wordsworth — so simple, so seldom surprising, so easily comprehended, so sentimental, so comforting, often so contrary to fact — that the majority will applaud.

Of the qualities these young men, as poets, have in common, the one most remarkable in relation to death is their habit of living so very largely in their sensations and emotions; though the most inflammable of them, Shelley, was much given, of them all apparently most given, to the pursuit of ideas. Perhaps it was the very ardour of his intellectual excursions that retarded his poetic technique. But these poets not only lived hugely in sensation and emotion: they believed in the meaning of their passionate experiences, believed that from this intensity came or might come spiritual illumination, saw in the emotional life not so much an escape from as a revelation of reality. This welcoming of sensation and emotion and this belief in them as peculiarly significant are the marks of romantic poets. In bringing their sensations and emotions to bear upon death, they had begun to romanticize death, and were not a little persuaded that their attitudes were something else: revelations, or, at least, something by its nature closely connected with, potential of, on the way to, revelation. Some of them really felt, rather light-heartedly after all, as is the way even of romantic youths, that they were coming close to solving the mystery.

From now on they learn otherwise. Shelley, in particular, from now on, from the noble passage in *Queen Mab* to the *Adonais*, advances through romantic idealization, through experience with actual death, through the burden of life, to a vision that is something more than play, philosophy, or dream. His apprenticeship finished, he progresses *Magister Mortis*.

Chapter Three

ROMANTIC DEATH: REAL DEATH

The failure of the quest for an embodied ideal is the great romantic failure. But some romanticists pass through this failure and come out on the further side. Their dreams, modified by the experience, become visions which are contagious to the world. If the romanticist is he who lives hugely in his dream and emotion, with more or less of Rousseau's suspicion of mere reason, and who trusts his imagination and emotion for guidance in affairs and for revelation of reality, his weakness will lie in emotionally running away from facts, his strength in critically correcting dream by fact and purifying fact by dream. The dream may be a supposititious escape from fact, because it has lost contact with fact and is illusory, as is the case with the Gothic romances; or it may be an ideal end, or vision, toward which facts are manipulated, an eternal and wise ideal discoverably and significantly related to the actual, though it always is a receding horizon, as is the case with the humanism of whatever epoch. In Shelley's poetry for the next four years (1814-1817), there is discernible a mutual purgation of romantic dream and real experience, making definitely for greater strength of idea and greater power of utterance. In no other phase of his work is this process more noticeable than in his changing attitude toward death. During these four years he definitely anticipates the three victories over death — the moral, aesthetic, and mystical victories — which he is fully to achieve in the last five years of his life.

Romantic Death: Real Death

I

Two brief poems commence the new artistry: *Oh, there are spirits of the air*, and *Stanzas. April, 1814*. Written early in 1814, while the rift between Harriet and himself was tragically widening, they seem to have sprung from real and poignant suffering; the former, in particular, having an effect of desperate actuality, as against the make-believe tragics of the juvenilia.

With their relation to Shelley's marital experience, the evidence they may give of his conduct in the troubles with Harriet, I am not here concerned. I am not taking sides either for or against Shelley. I am not pretending to know exactly what happened, what Shelley did, what Harriet did. A few unchronicled words spoken impetuously and later respoken in deliberation may have had more effect than all the known events. They do, with sensitive people. And Shelley was preternaturally sensitive; Harriet not so much. I am not preaching what Shelley or Harriet should or should not have done. The story has been told gently by some biographers, ungently by others; but neither apology and sentimentalism, nor innuendo, suspicion, and sarcasm, make impartial biography. So far as I am here concerned, " the book's the man." All that I am noting is that in these few heartbroken lines there is a new strength of passion, simple and unaffected; and, especially, that an important mood of his early affectation — the exuberant insistence upon death — is missing. The younger, inexperienced Shelley, imagining the failure of love, would have had recourse to the melodrama of death. Its macabre rhetoric would have tintinnabulated from the mouths of the two erstwhile lovers, as it did from the lips of the " victim of grief " in the *Dialogue* written five years before, when he was seventeen:

Oh, Death! oh, my friend! snatch this form to thy shrine
And I fear, dear destroyer, I shall not repine.

Now, in the suffocation of reality, the expression is tragically quiet, a line in each poem:

The glory of the moon is dead.

Thou [the poet, himself] in the grave shalt rest. . . .

Two poems curiously mark the transition to this strength in passion. One carries the new tone clearly; but the other sounds only a slight echo of it, the effect being primarily that of some reworking of an earlier poem that had been written originally in his worst style. In *Mutability*, developing his favourite theme that all things change and go down in death while only mutability endures, Shelley achieves verbal harmony and a real fingering of the lines, in place of intolerable jingling. Indeed, most of the poems after *Mab*, from 1813 on, gain suddenly in harmony and melody, the combined result, perhaps, of the opening of his eyes in Wales and Lynmouth to the mysterious beauty of nature, of the access of strength that may come with sorrow, of the music, literal and spiritual, at the Boinvilles, of the reading of Coleridge and Wordsworth, and of the practice-work in *Queen Mab*. The thought itself has nothing of the doctrinaire quality of *Mab*. Mutability is not related grandiosely to any Spirit of Nature, or Necessity. But a sensitive heart, uttering its accustomed instinctive lament for the change of all fair things, is now especially saddened by the failure of its own love. The dream woven around the heart of a child-wife is dead. This is the most extended and imaginative expression, so far, of Shelley's elegiac mood. Less of stock romantic melancholy and more of what appears to be genuine, personal experience make it a poem of some real rank.

The other poem, *On Death*, is a revision of the only verses Shelley cared to preserve from the Esdaile manuscript. It retains some of the jingle and declamation of its first form; yet neither thought nor mood nor music is entirely Gothic.

There is even a reminiscence of the great and mournful oratory of *Ecclesiastes*, growing out of the verse prefixed to the poem: " There is no work, nor device, nor knowledge, nor wisdom in the grave, whither thou goest." At any rate, the political and religious anarchism of his earlier lyrics on death, *A Dialogue* and *To Death*, which gave so radical and raucous a tone to them, is absent.

Yet a third pair of poems, the brief elegy on the Lechlade churchyard, and the long blank-verse *Alastor* written after his return from an excursion up the Thames with Peacock, reveals another phase of his deepening regard of death. Early in 1815, after he had come back from his first trip abroad with Mary, he had been told that he was a victim of tuberculosis. He thought he had but a little while to live. This belief called forth in these two poems a mood of somewhat sombre but decidedly romantic contemplation of the lovely solemnity of euthanasia. Already, in *Mab*, as we have seen, he had eagerly declaimed that although even in a perfected world death is inescapable, yet there it will come upon good men like a mild and gradual sleep. Now, in a graver and more self-conscious, rather Wordsworthian mood, he acclaims the mortal loveliness of such a death in an actual and imperfect world.

In the little elegy, which Matthew Arnold used to pronounce Shelley's " first entire poem of value," the treatment is more gently solemn and less dramatic than in *Alastor*. Here we have his first notable achievement in that *triste* autumnal theme he was so especially to make his own. He pictures the stillness of a September day dying along the river banks, the sere and motionless grasses in the graveyard, the churchspires aflame in the sunset and then slowly effaced in the lessening twilight, and the gathering of darkness among the first stars, while in the little yard the dead sleep on in their sepulchres. The quiet scene stimulates an intuition, " half sense, half thought," of the awful hush and the mild and terrorless serenity of great death, and even a childlike hope that death hides sweet secrets, or that loveliest dreams keep a perpetual watch beside its breathless sleep. Yet the old theme of loathly decay intrudes. It is from the mouldering sleep of the dead on their wormy beds that the mysterious voice of hope arises! The old theme dies hard. The conversion to beauty is incomplete. It is interesting, too, to note an allusion to his boyhood habit of haunting graves in quest of revelation.

The euthanasia in *Alastor* is dramatic, pathetic, self-conscious, and romantic. It is the crest of the poem, for a handsome young idealist, gentle, brave, and generous, wandering abroad to worship beauty, perishes in the solitude of the mountains. The influence of Scott's *Helvellyn* is again obvious.

Hutton, long ago, in what is one of the earliest and best essays upon Shelley's poetry, pointed out that the mere framework of the poem is a romantic absurdity. A lone poet walks from Cashmere across Asia Minor (*not* the steppes of southern Russia, as Hutton has it), traverses Balk (Hutton says the Balkans!), rushing wildly by the desolate tombs of the ancient Parthian kings, arrives at the Black Sea, finds a small, leaky boat, sets up his coat for a sail, voyages two days (while his hair turns grey), sails up a river into the heart of the Caucasus Mountains, and dies in a place of impossible geography — all in search of two eyes he saw in a dream. But, penetrative as most of Hutton's essay is, here it fails to perceive the romantic symbolism of the poem. Indeed, many of Shelley's descriptions of persons and places — a notable instance is the chief character and the scenery of his *Witch of Atlas* — become absurd if applied to mere tangible realities, instead of being regarded as symbolic of mental states. Shelley himself, once for all, in his preface to *Prometheus Unbound*, has called attention to his half-mythopoeic fashion of animating mental experiences in the guise of personages, situations, and even, it should be added, the forms and events of nature. He consciously employed this device, and held it to be a method that, though strange to modern poetry, was used repeatedly by Shakespeare, habitually by the Greek poets, and most of all and with greatest success by Dante. In *The Tempest*, Prospero, Caliban, and most of the other characters, as well as the storm itself, are symbolic, but by no means allegorical, presentations of great-mindedness and brutishness in struggle one with the other. Goethe's *Faust* is replete with such symbolism, the second part even more so than the first. Every stage, though not every detail, of *The Divine Comedy* is a story figuring mental experience. The odes of Pindar and many of the scenes and choral odes of the Greek tragedians, more especially Aeschylus and Sophocles, reach their fullness of meaning in such symbolism, where characters and scenes display not so much different individualities and their operations as different phases of the mental activity of one mind. In *Alastor* the description of the itinerary of the poet is only a way of marking out the mind-history of a poet, of Shelley himself: his glamorous, imaginative youth, his enthusiastic reading, his passionate preoccupation with a higher reality, his deep sensitiveness to all noble ideas and to the incommunicable suggestions of natural beauty, his piercing need of truly beautiful human companionship, his hopeless search for the ideal love, his loneliness, failure, illness, and his solemn anticipation of an early death. The hero of *Alastor* had nurtured his youth with the solemn visions of the ancient philosophers and the choicest responses to natural beauty. He had left a " cold fireside and alienated house " to seek abroad the truths that are all too strange to the conventional minds of father, mother, friends, and wife. He would make in the wilderness a home, " inaccessible to avarice or pride," where

> Nature's most secret steps
> He like her shadow . . . pursued.

87

Thus the tutelage of the poetic mind by literature and nature is imaged. Its fecundation by the lore of the past is represented by the poet's wandering, " obedient to high thoughts," in the ruins of Athens and Tyre, Balbec and Jerusalem and Babylon, and Æthiopia and Egypt, among the stupendous columns of Ozymandias and the remains of ancient temples,

> and wild images
> Of more than man, where marble dæmons watch
> The Zodiac's brazen mystery, and dead men
> Hang their mute thoughts on the mute walls around.

From the past, much as in the second part of *Queen Mab*, a great lesson is learned of man's cruelty to man, of superstitions, and of the ever-enduring search for a supreme reality. His exultant education continues through the strange places of Arabia and Persia,

> And o'er the aërial mountains which pour down
> Indus and Oxus from their icy caves.

Then, resting in the vale of Cashmere, he has the vision of ideal beauty, which gathers into itself and climaxes all the fine, fair learning from nature and man. This spiritual beauty is a woman seen in a dream, that feminine alter-ego of the romantic poet, of whom he ever after dreams, and for some adequate embodiment of whom in an actual woman the rest of his life is a ceaseless quest. This is the " beauty afar," *La Princess Lointaine*, of Jaufre Rudel. This is that romantic worship of beauty, and far, strange search for it, with which Keats endowed Endymion, and of which Rossetti sang so well:

> This is that Lady Beauty, in whose praise
> Thy voice and hand shake still, — long known to thee
> By flying hair and fluttering hem, — the beat
> Following her daily of thy heart and feet,
> How passionately and irretrievably,
> In what fond flight, how many ways and days!

In *Alastor* the search becomes a wild wandering through Asia Minor and a voyage into the Caucasus. The wilderness, the various stream and devious river, and dark, mysterious gorges, are, as the wanderer himself declares, the image of the poet's mental life. The scenes are at once descriptive and interpretive, animistically identifying the experiences of mind with the life of nature. Such dreams of loveliness drive the Actaeon-poet restlessly to his death. Therefore the issue of the quest is in the figure of a romantic euthanasia under a waning moon, with autumnal mountain-winds heaping dead leaves over the corpse of the wanderer.

Death here is no mere Gothic horror. It is the inevitable close of the romantic pursuit of the beautiful, the pathetic mystery that ends the dramatic failure to find the ideal embodied in the actual. Characteristically, for Shelley, this beauty stimulates a ceaseless, febrile pursuit of an ideal which is both a supreme social good and need, and also a personal need and good. His is not a flight from the world to a sequestered beauty, but the pursuit and preaching of a panacea. He cannot lose himself even temporarily, as Endymion did, in the ecstasy of the senses and in the delight of merely imaging the spirit-beauty. He cannot hypnotize himself, as Rossetti did so often, with a haunted contemplation of dead beauty, extinct ecstasies, and desolate eyes. Rather, with native Platonic bent for abstracting eternal invisibles from actual love and concrete beauty, he must at once pass beyond sensuous joy to philosophical meaning. To be sure, the great Wordsworthian invocation of Nature, with which the poem opens, pulses with a passionate love of the things of earth, ocean, and air; and in obvious reminiscence of *Tintern Abbey*, the reading of which must have deepened his sensibility, opened a door of his own spirit, he prays that his verses, breathing the natural magic of air and forest and sea, may become " woven hymns of night and day." This is rich testimony to that poetic baptism in nature which has been the second birth of so many poets. Nevertheless, beside his love of the thing there always exists his love of the idea. He must sanctify the fact by truth. Then, turning back, he searches for the ideal in the concrete, but never finds a perfect incarnation. Thus, almost insensibly, he is forced into that dualistic and dramatic antithesis of spirit and sense that has already been noted in some of his earlier poems.

This failure of the romantic quest for an embodied ideal is the natural catastrophe of a dualism and antithesis of spirit and sense. All such dualism has always resulted in defeated hopes of finding or founding a kingdom of heaven upon this earth. The defeat has been disguised as a mere delay until the kingdom shall be accomplished by the slow evolution of society; or the hopes have been postponed to the realization of a spirit-kingdom hereafter, not made with hands; or, often in unconscious surrender of the dualism, the hopes have been turned individually inward, transmuted into an asseveration that the kingdom of God is within one's self, or that the Kingdom is the community of those hearts in which the ideal has been achieved. Young Keats, too intoxicated with sensuous beauty to face hard facts definitely, removed the ideal pursuit to Endymion's unreal world, where by a boudoir-miracle the dusky, Ganges maid could be transformed to the golden-haired Diana of the quest. Again, the surrender may be conscious and pessimistic, as in Cabell's *Way of Ecben.* It is of the essence of Mr. Cabell's thought that no distinction between the heavenly and the common Aphrodite should be drawn. The Uranian love is but a rarefied and very self-deceiving variety of the common passion; and when old age meets the Uranian ideal it finds only a commonplace girl's body, after all. In spite of faithfulness, all love shrivels with age, and the dream is dead. Thus, in one way or another, failure is the necessary end, intuitively recognized by the poet, of his quest for an objectively realized ideal. Because Shelley had long been preoccupied with death, this failure is at once symbolized as death. However, ' symbolized ' is too weak a word to express his conviction that in the theatre of this life death inevitably puts a *Finis* to the beautiful eagerness of the youthful poet, of himself.

But if the parts of the poem are really symbolical of states of mind, it should be noted that the poet curiously fails to understand that the object of his quest is, properly, too, a state of his own mind. Instead, the end remains an ideal realized in an object external to him, and so forever elusive.

What is *Alastor* without death? What would be the search for perfection, or even for a near-perfect mutual understanding, without disappointment, failure, loneliness, and a new, intimate awareness of the immanence of death? *Alastor* is that romantic dream of youth which time and night must quench forever; or, at any rate, always. Over against the pursuit of a dream of an absolute ideal, youth discovers, there is set a universal drama of perpetual change. All lovely things go down into death, exit into mystery. In the midst of that drama the lonely, eager, puzzled soul itself perishes also, while fallen leaves are spectrally driven by autumn winds. The first part of the great *Ode to the West Wind* will state this theme yet more powerfully, beginning where *Alastor* ends.

More powerfully, yes. For, however sympathetically one may read the romantic symbolism of *Alastor*, the poem leaves him with some sense of a decoration of reality, instead of a mature and resolute grappling with it. Reality is handled picturesquely and immaturely, with the fevered intensity of one expecting to be cut off while life is still a daily miracle, long before it has become customary, and dull with age. The poem, therefore, is really a romantic fantasia of the triumph of death over youthful dreams. Indeed, the smaller and weaker one's individual life may seem, the more incongruous is this sentimentally pathetic euthanasia, so romantically staged, so grandiosely gestured.

The Pursuit of Death

Death, to be sure, has now been poetized more completely than ever before in Shelley's verses. There is an access of vivid doubt, won from his experiences with love, as to love's persistence beyond the grave, quite in contrast to the facile faith expressed in some half-dozen previous poems.

> He eagerly pursues
> Beyond the realms of dream that fleeting shade;
> He overleaps the bounds. Alas! alas!
> Were limbs and breath and being intertwined
> Thus treacherously? Lost, lost, forever lost
> In the wide pathless desert of dim sleep,
> That beautiful shape! Does the dark gate of death
> Conduct to thy mysterious paradise,
> O Sleep? Does the bright arch of rainbow clouds
> And pendent mountains seen in the calm lake
> Lead only to a black and watery depth,
> While death's blue vault with loathliest vapors hung,
> Where every shade which the foul grave exhales
> Hides its dead eye from the detested day,
> Conducts, O Sleep, to thy delightful realms?
> This doubt with sudden tide flowed on his heart;
> The insatiate hope which it awakened stung
> His brain even like despair.

The hope of finding the perfection of love beyond death is gloomy and desperate. Fear of delusion dogs the young romantic, as it is bound to if he really thinks, instead of allowing sensations completely (*Gefühl ist alles!*) to take the place of thought. Moreover, the adolescent, languorous delight in imaginary dying has lost a part of its lenitive charm with the near approach of the reality. All this is true. Yet the poem is a poem of the triumph of death, not of life or hope or faith. And the triumph is rendered with no courageous tragic force, but with a melodramatic, self-conscious pathos, and the nearest approach to Byronic theatricality anywhere to be found in Shelley's treatment of his own fate, whether figured in another's, as here, or rendered directly, as in some of his great odes and in *Adonais*.

The chief advance in artistry remains to be mentioned. At last the poet has turned from the causes he has been advocating to the enforced contemplation of life itself. It is his own life, to be sure; and self-pity plays the usual role, so disconcerting to penetrative self-analysis. But the gain is certain, nevertheless. From rhetorical radicalism to romantic mystery, with a greater sensitiveness to nature, and a new verbal harmony, and some infiltration of the sincerity of Wordsworth and the sorcery of Coleridge, is no slight poetic advance. Nor is there a better measure of the improvement than the incongruity with which one passage on political fear and ruin interrupts the peaceful, moonlit solitude of the poet's death, toward the end of the poem. Yet even it borrows from its context a quieter tone than can be found in the earlier fulminations against tyranny.

The few poems of the eventful and fateful year, 1816, show a remarkable development in Shelley's realization of death. But the mood of romantic peace that he had elaborated to soothe himself in the anticipation of an early death carries over, slightly, into the first poem, *Sunset*, where again death and genius contend in a young poet's " subtle being." Though the poet's death and the grief of the lady of his love, who through the tragic succeeding years patiently tended her aged father, are done with a truer dramatic pathos, yet the enervating spice of romantic self-consciousness is not altogether rejected. The reader is aware of a sad, half-hid delight with which the poet dreams that a fair maid will mourn *him* after he is gone, like the virgins who pined and wasted for the always gentle, brave, and solitary, but never lingering, hero of *Alastor*. Nor does he realize the possibilities of the theme that is actually broached. In one of the best passages it is said of the lady's deep grief that

. . . but to see her were to read the tale
Woven by some subtlest bard to make hard hearts
Dissolve away in wisdom-working grief.

But if this wisdom-working grief were to accomplish anything more than to bring tears to hard eyes, it might be expected to amend her own state of mind with some high faith
in the triumph of spirit over death, after the fashion of the
teaching of *Adonais*. Instead, the only moan she makes is a
despairing cry for the passionless calm and silence of death,
whether the dead live or die " in the deep sea of Love."

The first important event of the year for Shelley, after
the birth of a son in January, and not taking into account the
sordid, long drawn out story of Godwin's debts, was the trip
to Switzerland, May to September, with the sojourn at Geneva with Byron. It stimulated a stronger, serener mood and
freed Shelley from all sickly sentimentalism in the contemplation of death. Again the mountains tutored the poet, as
the impressive poems of these months, the *Hymn to Intellectual Beauty* and the *Mont Blanc*, testify.

What is accomplished in the *Hymn* is in one way not very
notable, in another way highly remarkable. As a reasoned
teaching the poem is as unsatisfactory as Wordsworth's *Inti-
mations;* as a figuration of mood it belongs with the greatest
mystical poems of the language. We must consider it at some
length, for it contains a key to much of Shelley's later
thought.

The thought is Platonic, coming straight from the *Phaedrus* and the *Symposium*. This " intellectual beauty," a phrase
Shelley used two years later in translating the *Symposium*,
though there is no original for it in the Greek, is a happy nam-
ing of that supreme beauty, or love, to the worship of which
Diotima is supposed to have converted Socrates. It is, in fact,
a name for one of the Platonic Forms, or Ideas — the eternal
archetype of beauty from which, somehow, according to

Plato's dream, all beauty in all beautiful things derives. It is the central term in a more or less transcendental explanation of the beautiful.

The method of becoming aware of the archetype is a progressive generalization of our love for beautiful particulars. From a love of one beautiful being men may proceed to that of two, because of the one beauty that is in both; then they may ascend to the love of all forms that are beautiful, because they realize the general beauty in them all; from beautiful forms they pass to beautiful habits and institutions, thence to beautiful doctrines — " until, from the meditation of many doctrines, they arrive at that which is nothing else than the doctrine of the supreme beauty itself." This merely rationalized beauty, as the modern realist would call it, is regarded transcendentally by Diotima as a supreme reality, to which is ascribed the origin of beautiful objects of sense-perception. It is perfect, eternal, and absolute; not subject to change, to increase or decay; not subjective, not varying with different subjectivities; not figurable to the imagination; not subsisting in particular things.

> Nor does it subsist in any other that lives or is, either in earth, or in heaven, or in any other place; but it is eternally uniform and consistent, and monoeidic with itself. All other things are beautiful through a participation of it, with this condition, that although they are subject to production and decay, it never becomes more or less, or endures any change.

This is Shelley's own translation, important to be cited because it gives in his own words his understanding of a Platonic doctrine that repeatedly appears in his poetry from now on, particularly in *Mont Blanc*, *Prometheus Unbound*, and *The Witch of Atlas*.

The run of the thought is, exoterically at least, dualistic. Plato, as Bosanquet observed, was indeed the prophet of a dualism between nature and intelligence, or spirit. Over against all beautiful appearances is set an unapparent beauty, intellectual in its nature, but unlimited, not subjective, of which we become aware by an intellectual discipline that carries us from the contemplation of the many to the one. However, both here and in the *Phaedrus*, there are sentences that supplement this intellectual dualism with that sort of emotional mysticism against which Hegel was wont to protest. From the gradual contemplation of beautiful objects, the disciplined lover comes *suddenly* to his vision of this supreme and sublime beauty. In the knowledge and contemplation of it a rapturous shudder and a great awe pass through him, and at last he reposes in deep, ineffable joy. " He is in contact not with a shadow but with reality," and his human nature puts on ' immortality.'

Here was a union of idea and mood that fitted in perfectly with the unusual personality of the young poet. It appealed to his flair for analyzing the intellectual life, to his love of philosophical synthesis, to his deep emotionalism, his constructive imagination, to his ingrained habit of seeing invisibles, to his native mysticism. Moreover, it ratified his view of mutability as a process somehow set over against perfection, and thus provocative, turn by turn, both of the immediate, tense grief at a loss, and of time's softening of the grief into a perduring sorrow, or general sadness. And it offered a comfort for these elegiac moods by confirming his faith in a real perfection existing outside change yet related to it either as source or as a final cause. Shelley's deep, intuitive assent to Platonism in general, and to the Platonic Idea of the beautiful in particular, is one of those intricate assents of the total individual which modern slang calls a " click."

Shelley had early begun the reading of Plato in French and English translations. Medwin says he studied the *Symposium* at Eton (1804–1810) with Dr. Lind. At Oxford (1810–1811) he read Dacier's translation, and some of the works of

Thomas Taylor the Platonist. Plato's works were sent him at Tanyrallt in 1812. Hogg and Lady Shelley refer to his reading the *Phaedrus* and the *Symposium* at Marlow.

Plato and Godwin were his great books. Back and forth between them repeatedly he passed in his reading, excited both by the transcendental realism of the one and the philosophical radicalism of the other, and deriving mixed nutriment from the confusion. Both Godwin's necessity and subjectivism of good and evil, and Plato's unresolved dualism of natural appearances and their ideal Forms, filled his mind with images of perfectibility and perfection, the one contributing to his political, the other to his religious, or poetic, ideals. In both he found a dualistic *Weltanschauung*. In Godwin, it took the form of a constant struggle to render the higher motives operative in the mind and thus, out of the conflict of lower and higher impulses, to hasten the advent of a perfect political state. In Plato, it took the form of a partly rational, partly intuitive recognition of a metaphysical reality, by which the ugliness of commonplace reality is overcome and a perfect intellectual-mystical state is achieved.

As he sailed about Lake Geneva with Byron, the marvellous blue of the lake, the purple of the mountain-sides, the far snow-capped summits, the flush of sunrise over the white peaks, and the solemn beauty of Alpine sunsets, readily stirred his memories of the *Symposium* and the *Phaedrus*. He must have recalled with awe, and with a thrilling recognition of its spiritual appropriateness, Plato's remark that of all the ideal Forms, that of visible beauty " shines through the clearest aperture of sense ":

> For sight is the most piercing of our bodily senses;
> though not by that is wisdom seen; her loveliness would
> have been transporting if there had been a visible image
> of her, and the other ideas, if they had visible counter-
> parts, would be equally lovely. But this is the privilege
> of beauty, that being the loveliest she is also the most

palpable to sight. . . . He . . . who has been the spectator of many glories in the other world, is amazed when he sees any . . . form which is the expression of divine beauty; and at first a shudder runs through him, and again the old awe steals over him; then looking upon the face of his beloved as of a god he reverences him, and if he were not afraid of being thought a downright madman, he would sacrifice to his beloved as to the image of a god. (*Phaedrus*, 250–251. Jowett's translation.)

Shelley's sacrifice was a Hymn to this divine, or intellectual, beauty.

The *Hymn* preserves and animates the Platonic dualism, for the idea-form becomes the Spirit of Beauty, itself the shadow of an Unknown Power which is the metaphysical absolute, even as all the Ideas emanate somehow from an Absolute. This Spirit comes and goes in the intellectual life of man, as Plato hints in his description of the recurring vision. Its elusiveness and mysterious subtlety, for mortal mind, are symbolized in images of evanescent moonbeams showering behind a pine-clad mountain, of the tenuous hues and harmonies of evening, of the memory of music that has ceased, of

> . . . aught that for its grace may be
> Dear, and yet dearer for its mystery.

While one is aware of it, everything human is consecrated; and " like moonlight on a midnight stream," it " gives grace and truth to life's unquiet dream."

But the *Hymn* is both a pæan and an elegy. It is a song of joyful discovery of a sentiment, or attitude, that resolves for a moment the ugliness of experience. It is a song of regret at the failure, or, rather, evanescence, of that transforming sentiment. The pæan prevails over the elegy in stanzas one, and five to seven, thus enveloping with a kind of mystical rapture the elegiac regret sounding in the three central stanzas.

With this elegiac regret at the passing of the Spirit of Divine Beauty, the unsatisfactory character of the thought, with which both Plato and Shelley must be charged, is apparent. The Spirit is not regarded as being always immanent in nature, but as being, when we are aware of it, only a shadow of some perfection afar. That is, mind conceives a remote, ideal perfection incompletely and inconstantly. To be sure, there is a vague, misleading statement, in the third verse, to the effect that this Shadow " visits the various world." But the opening lines of the second stanza make it clear that this " various world " is the world of " human thought," and in the first stanza it is clearly asserted that the inconstant visitor comes to " each human heart and countenance." If Shelley meant to say that this Spirit resides, but not subsists, in nature, he does not say so clearly, and certainly does not represent it as permanently present there. At any rate, be that as it may, he goes on to deplore that when this inconstant spirit passes away, our commonplace reality, " this dim vast vale of tears, . . . of fear, and hate and despondency, and death," is left doubly vacant and desolate. Now, most characteristically, Shelley's depression recurs, with further reference to death. No other faith — not all the superstitious names of " Dæmon, Ghost, and Heaven " — avail to sever

> From all we hear and all we see,
> Doubt, chance, and mutability.

When the Spirit has passed, the grave, like life and fear, remains a dark reality. Metaphysical Reality, then, is a far God, or Spirit, elusive to mind. And if it is present in things, it is not always present, and is only partially suggested, message-like, by their beauty. Phenomena are declensions from Reality. The implication is that life, or commonplace reality, is a kind of evil, over against the ideal good. Only a vision of the greater reality can hide, and then for but a moment, the gloom and misery of immediate reality.

The Pursuit of Death

The need of some resolution of this sulky Platonic dualism becomes disquietingly apparent. A more monistic, even Aristotelian, generalization is required; some archæsthetism, which recognizes consciousness as a primitive attribute of ' matter,' and as the cause of evolution toward ever more perfect forms, instead of a crude dualism that sees human life as a gloom miserably consummated in death. Death and mutability are not absorbed, as they are in a monistic theory, into the process of evolution; they still stand forth, in this *Hymn* to perfection, as negations of, or at least antitheses to, an elusive perfection.

Analysis of the thought of the poem provokes disappointment. But a poem's meaning is not limited to thought that can be paraphrased in abstract terms. If it were so, there would be less need of poetry than there is. As a unique configuration of profoundly impressive images, intuitive thought, and an ecstatic mood, the poem has an incommensurable meaning. And it is with the fifth stanza, as, the more consciously learned, Platonic address finished, Shelley begins to speak more directly from his own, original experiences, that the greater meaning appears. It is from one's very own imaginative and emotional syntheses of beautiful things, passionate sacraments of love, that the finer meaning always springs, rather than from any reframing, poetic or otherwise, of book-learning. Suddenly Shelley becomes retrospective, linking to his boyhood's extravagant awareness of the unknown, of which we have spoken above, a later insight, or vision, which is the real ground of the poem. In a passage already quoted he recalls his graveyard wanderings and ghost-hunts, and describes his young failure to uncover a true spiritual life either in the grave or in the poisonous conventional religion which youth is taught. These failures left him yet more curious about the invisibles. Then, of a spring day, while he was musing on the mystery, something in the vital, genial warmth of spring's rebirth stirred that glorious intuition of the oneness of all the life-processes which always has been the vision of those greatly endowed with the poetic, animistic imagination. What young Shelley saw on that spring-day was, I am sure, essentially identical with the central visions of Vaughan and Wordsworth, Blake and Tennyson, and all the poets of second sight, or insight. It was what Dante called the universal form of the life-complex,

La forma universal di questo nodo, —

what he endeavoured to symbolize under the figure of the scattered leaves of all the universe bound by love in one volume. Indeed, the *Divina Commedia*, in its three major parts and all the circles and subdivisions of each, is Dante's attempt to unite, through a schematic gradation, all other experience to this central, unique experience. The entire poem leads up to this supreme moment of poetic insight. For Shelley, too, this is the central vision that alone gives meaning to all the rest of experience. He tells us with what ecstasy he welcomed the vision, with what devotion he dedicated his powers to its service, with what faithfulness he has kept the vow in all zeal of study and delight of love, and with what solemn hope he prays that the deep harmony of this vision which descended on his passive youth will supply to his onward life a spiritual serenity, binding him

To fear himself, and love all human kind.

Now this deep faith in a spiritual reality is essentially monistic, escaping that dualism with which Shelley has associated it in the first four, more Platonic, and less personal and original, stanzas of the *Hymn*. Dante speaks for the monistic truth of this by no means uncommon mysticism, which grows nevertheless from a unique experience with a special meaning of its own, when he stresses love as binding the scattered leaves. Love brings all together in one beautiful whole — substance and accidents and their relations fused in one simple flame. In these magnanimous lines he is perilously close to the alleged heresy of Origen, salvation for all through the divine justice and love:

> *Sustanzia ed accidenti, e lor costume,*
> *Quasi conflati insieme per tal modo,*
> *Che ciò ch'io dico è un semplice lume.*

Implicit, therefore, in that generalization is the beauty of mutability and death, and a complete conquest of the fear and the distaste of all kinds of change. But these implications Shelley has not yet definitively conceived. Future pain and sorrow and beauty must teach him. At present, he can associate the crude dualism of the first four stanzas with the poetic monism of the last three, as though the former were but a personification of the latter. Intuition really outran conception. Poetry anticipated reason.

But it is significant that in a previous, blank-verse rendering of the *Hymn* this dualism is not present. The noble address to the "mother of this unfathomable world," at the beginning of *Alastor* (lines 18–49), contains in close composition all the essential ideas of the *Hymn*. The Mother is analogous to the Spirit of the later poem; her shadow and the darkness of her steps, upon which he has ever gazed, become in the *Hymn* the shadow of an Unseen Power; in both cases the story of his youthful search for spiritual manifestation at dead of night in the graveyard is connected with his later divination of nature; in both the fruitless faith of popular superstition is deplored; in both the inability completely to grasp the spiritual reality is lamented; in *Alastor* the intuitions of incommunicable dreams, twilight phantasms, and deep noonday thought correspond to the spring-day vision of the *Hymn*; a mood of dedication pervades both; and, finally, the acme of each is reached in a mystic serenity and an ideal love of humankind. The correspondence of ideas is very striking. But the dualism is absent in the *Alastor* passage. Instead, it

concludes with what is almost an identification of the great
parent-spirit with natural appearances: at any rate, the spirit
is so pervasive that, like the supreme Brahma,* speaking to the
poet in all the voices of living things, it modulates his own
recording of what he hears:

> . . . serenely now
> And moveless, as a long-forgotten lyre
> Suspended in the solitary dome
> Of some mysterious and deserted fane,
> I wait thy breath, Great Parent, that my strain
> May modulate with murmurs of the air,
> And motions of the forests and the sea,
> And voice of living beings, and woven hymns
> Of night and day, and the deep heart of man.

Such a " *woven hymn* " — perhaps in this phrase is the very
anticipation of the later poem — is the *Hymn to Intellectual
Beauty;* but into the weaving was introduced the old Platonic
dualism, not too happily. It is as though in this earlier passage
we had the truer, more immediate expression of his divination of a reality always at one with nature, whereas in the
Hymn the experience is Platonically mediated, bookishly
divided.

Not the least important phase of this self-revealing *Hymn*
is the method of fusing metaphysics with politics. For all of
Shelley is here, as in most of his greater poems from now on:
both his poetic religion and his ideal anarchism. Never, he
avers, since that vision, even in his greatest joys, has he been
without hope

> . . . that thou wouldst free
> This world from its dark slavery,
> That thou — O awful loveliness,
> Wouldst give whate'er these words cannot express.

* The supreme Brahma is thus described: " It hath hands and feet everywhere,
and everywhere It hath eyes, heads, and faces, and ears hath It everywhere in the
world. It abideth encompassing all." (*Bhagavad Gita*, XIII. 13).

Selfish politics, no less than death and all mutability, makes for this "dark slavery." But all ugliness may some day yield to the ideal loveliness. Again the inveterate dualism! Again the postponed Kingdom of Heaven! Dualism must always sacrifice the present to the future.

However, the fusion of death and politics in the concept of ugliness makes clear the essentially aesthetic movement of Shelley's thought. This aesthetic quality, as yet incompletely and even crudely philosophized, is the secret, or originative principle, of his intellectual life. It is what constitutes him a poet. It is that phase of his genius by which he converts into one complex whole physics, politics, religion, love, and poetry. It is the dynamics of his strangely unified interest in all these. His economics is fundamentally aesthetic; so, too, are his politics and religion, his philosophy and love. Therefore, to criticize them from any other point of view, as has often been attempted, is to misunderstand and misrepresent them. The history of his thought in general, as well as of his view of death in particular, is the progressive adjustment of this innate, radical tendency, "soul of his soul," to all his experiences. Therefore his life-long struggle was a struggle to conquer the pain with which he witnessed all ugliness and the fading and death of all fair things. Therefore he loved Plato, and was attracted to Lucretius and Goethe. Therefore, reading Godwin and the French materialists, he transfigured them with a beauty of which their actual thought was scarcely susceptible, and so incurred the superficial inconsistencies of *Queen Mab* and *Prometheus*. Many of the inconsistencies in his work spring from the beauty he imports into thoughts not his own, seeing them thus as somewhat other, and more, than they are. But with time and practice the inconsistencies are burned away by the growing flame of his own thought, his originative aestheticism.

Equally important is the forward-looking, almost practical, faith implicit in this aesthetic fusion of metaphysics and politics. Shelley remains true to his social programme. His vision gives courage to his political faith. The Utopian vision, then, is no mere self-satisfying, sequestered dream. It is not a substitute for action. The poem does not belong to the poetry of escape from a life poets fail to face. It is a poem not of flight but of rescue, giving the very grounds of faith, and of courage to persist in stimulating men to the attainment of the humane ideal. Shelley's visions of loveliness, whether political or metaphysical, are not the reveries of one who has given up the human struggle. They are visions, with the social purpose of freeing men from their banal self-satisfaction in the commonplace. Therein lies the spiritual identity of *Queen Mab* and the *Hymn to Intellectual Beauty*, however great their difference in artistry.

In *Mont Blanc*, properly called by Shelley " an undisciplined overflowing of the soul," for it lacks both clearness and structural unity, the dualism that has been noted, once more obtains. Shelley's own explanation of the poem discloses it. He was concerned to read symbolically " the inaccessible solemnity " of Mont Blanc. The surrounding wilderness becomes a symbol of universal change, of the universe of things that live and die and live again:

> All things that move and breathe with toil and sound
> Are born and die, revolve, subside, and swell.

But the Mountain, gleaming high above all else, still and solemn, is the symbol of the secret, governing strength of things, of both matter and mind. And this hidden strength, like the Mountain, and like the Spirit of the *Hymn*, dwells apart:

> Power dwells apart in its tranquillity,
> Remote, serene, and inaccessible.

The fear and disgust of death, too, reappear, almost like condign punishment for the violence inherent in the dualism. For

in a truly eloquent and no longer merely rhetorical dramatiz-
ing of the vast effort of change, which is likened to a restless
tumult of winds swirling around the serene king of mountains, death is called a " detested trance "; and the destruction
that overtakes the homes of insects, beasts and birds, and
men — " and their place is not known " — is a thing of dread,
the tragic loss of so much life and joy. Yet the poetic animism
is so pervasive of the scene, the sense of a presence everywhere is so deeply felt, the veil is so far lifted from the hidden beauty of the world, and the skill of the music is so en-
chanting, that unless one reads the poem ever so attentively
he feels its general trend and meaning are pantheistic. It is
as though Shelley's reason had here, too, failed to grasp the
full implication of his mood.

In these two mountain-poems, one written among, the
other about mountains, death has been set in melancholy, or
even tragic, antithesis to a great serenity. There is an advance
beyond the sentimental play with death in *Alastor*. Bookishness early developed in Shelley a power of expression out of
proportion to his first-hand knowledge of life. A sporting,
juvenile Gothicism, an earnest, excited, tumid anarchism, and
a personal, sentimental romanticism were effects of that inequality. Then the mountains, and other impressive rhythms
of nature, vastly enriched his experience, developing his sensitiveness, deepening his moods, fecundating his imagination.
He divined vaster meaning. Correspondingly, his verse-music
was modulated by the verbal equivalents of the rhythms of
ocean and earth and air. A serener and more solemn, more
nearly sublime, reading of himself and humankind was an
effect of this advance in experience. But death, and all change,
remained something ugly, apart from serenity and beauty.

II

And now, two actual tragedies, in the closest circle of his human intimacies, were to add their deep, immediate teaching, through suffering, through personal grief and sorrow.

Fanny Imlay, whom Shelley loved almost as a sister, committed suicide the ninth of October, 1816. A month later, one winter day, or night, no human being knows exactly when, Harriet Shelley threw herself into the Serpentine.

Shelley did not write a long poem on either tragedy: only three brief, heartbroken lyrics.

Editors agree that the little *pallida-mors* ballad of twenty-eight lines beginning, *The cold earth slept below*, refers to the death of Harriet. There are several striking contemporary reports of how poignantly Shelley suffered, but this poem is the sole poetic memorial of his grief. Its brevity is significant. The last stanza is heart-rending. No declamation. Stark lyric simplicity. No rhetoric, no tumult, no grandeur. But a new restraint; and a transparent objectivity — the terrible contrast between the fresh, girlish beauty he had once sheltered, and loved so keenly, and the pale, dead face, gleaming in the moonlit water:

> The moon made thy lips pale, belovèd;
> The wind made thy bosom chill;
> The night did shed
> On thy dear head
> Its frozen dew, and thou didst lie
> Where the bitter breath of the naked sky
> Might visit thee at will.

Such a lament! The dear dead under the naked sky; the once beloved body in the sluggish stream: the horrible, unchangeable fact, beyond embroidery of mood and image. It is Shelley's first truly pathetic treatment of death; really, his first actual experience of death. Harriet and Fanny doubly taught the simple, tragic fact.

In 1817 two other very short poems express the same reality of grief. Six little lines on Fanny, recalling his last parting with her, speak his regret that he did not then guess the misery that already had broken her heart. It is a well-known kind of regret — that regret at heedlessness and lack of sympathy, which comes upon us afterwards and leaves us wondering whether, had we been less obtuse, we could have spoken the word that would have meant comfort and have averted catastrophe. Poor Fanny Imlay! Sweet, frail flower! Her mother, Mary Wollstonecraft, had once attempted suicide. Her stepfather, Godwin, preached it. When affairs in the Godwin household grew unbearable to this sensitive spirit, she accomplished it. For her sort of suffering the world, knowing it too well, has a sharp, bitter name — Misery — and too much room for it:

> Misery — O Misery,
> This world is all too wide for thee.

The other poem, entitled *Death*, makes a refrain of the misery of parting. For Shelley, it contains an unusually large number of the common, universal themes of grief: that death is final and the dead return not, that pain remains and goes on and on, that the old familiar scenes remind one poignantly of the dead, that the routine we lived with them is broken forever, that all we have of them is the grave. This access of the all too well-worn, primitive topics of grief, very simply taking the place of the grandiose theorems characteristic of his inexperience, is another sign of the reality of his grief. The would-be sophisticated ideas and moods give way to the primitive when hard experience supervenes. One picture, however, a picture of himself as a youth with hoary hair and haggard eye, sitting beside an open grave, is a romantic intrusion from the *Alastor* phase.

Romantic Death: Real Death

At the same time, his dreams are dying, his dreams of any immediate political revolution, of his power, like an Illuminatus or Eleutherarch, to effect a sudden change in the minds of men. The sanguine hopes give place to despondency and are assimilated somehow to his personal misfortunes, so that one vocabulary serves for his affliction and his dejection:

> That time is dead forever, child,
> Drowned, frozen, dead forever!
> We look on the past,
> And start aghast
> At the spectres wailing, pale and ghast,
> Of hopes which thou and I beguiled
> To death on life's dark river.

There is much meaning in that word " beguiled," as though all his excited mental adventuring had rushed on heedless of its real effect upon human hearts, until the interruptions of death taught regret too late.

Every part of his life seemed infected with failure, loss, and death. Death surrounded him. The very trance of music seemed a trance of death. Constantia's singing moved him to such a trance as sensitives have always known in the presence of beautiful sound, none more than Spenser:

> The whiles a most delitious harmony
> In full straunge notes was sweetly heard to sound,
> That the rare sweetnesse of the melody
> The feeble sences wholy did confound,
> And the frayle soule in deepe delight nigh drownd.

But the stunning familiarity with death at this time must have given special significance to his imaging that swooning trance of delight as the soul's swooning through death into the arms of spiritual reality. In this poem, indeed, *To Constantia Singing*, in which the stanza usually printed first should always be read last, Shelley has united the moods of affliction and dejec-

tion with the promise, the comfort, of the serene Reality of
Mont Blanc and the last part of the *Hymn*. This were death,
indeed, he cries, to be dissolved in such ecstasies and pass
thence, traversing (there is here a reminiscence of the flight
in *Queen Mab*) the " mighty moons that wane upon Nature's
utmost sphere," to the realm of perfected, or intellectual,
beauty. Out of effects of voluptuous, sensuous beauty, he
distils, through yet another euthanasia, the spiritual beauty
the contemplation of which had wrought serenity only the
year before.

It is very characteristic of Shelley, this reunion in a new
and fairer form and lovelier music, of many of his old ideas
and moods: translated echoes of *Queen Mab* and the *Dæmon
of the World*, of *Alastor* (the dying poet), the *Hymn*, and
Mont Blanc, and of the terse tragic lyrics of his personal
affliction. Already, in his juvenile anticipations of his later,
well-known themes and characters, and in imperfect dislodgment in *Queen Mab* of mystic moods by incongruous ideas,
Shelley's characteristic method of intellectual and artistic
growth has been noted: a growth evident not so much in the
appearance of new ideas as in the richer reworking of old
ones — new learning about old ideas. Here, again, in *Constantia*, he is advancing old themes or parts of old themes,
into new beauty, new imaginative and emotional realization.
Really, his thought advances not so much through analysis
and dissection, a scrupulous criticism of the philosophical
propositions he loved so well, as by the natural, primitive,
and poetic method of constantly reanimating old ideas with
new experience, carrying the symbol further in expressiveness as experience itself developed. And the rich increase of
music at each transformation is precisely the sign and measure of the advance in realization, the music being, of course,
at once the soul and life-garment of the vision.

III

But it would be a mistake to consider the year 1817 entirely one of dejection, relieved only by this marvellous lyric to Constantia that almost translates music into imagery. The truth is far otherwise. All Shelley's poems of dejection are short. Nearly all his long poems pulsate with hope and courage. The chief work of the year is the longest of all his poems, *The Revolt of Islam*, and in it he valiantly reasserts his social credo. It is, in a way, a companion piece to his *Ozymandias*, also of this year. The sonnet epitomizes what the epic discourses, the colossal wreck of tyranny.

The Revolt of Islam, an apology for the French Revolution, is a poem of political idealism, of hope, suffering, failure, and death, but eventual triumph: a projection, in all these respects, of Shelley's interests upon an epic canvas. It is a story of violence and revolution. But a mood of peace pervades it; for its comfort for failure and its prophecy of success proceed from a faith in the power of love to survive suffering, lost causes, and death. This faith, in turn, though another example of the repetition of a previous and favourite theme, is here in particular a reflection of the deep, passionate love with which the life of Shelley and Mary was at this time suffused. Moreover, it was written under that new awareness of suffering which had come at the end of the previous year, and the heedful sympathy he learned in that actuality he here began to teach in song. Finally, the precariousness of life, especially of his own life, which influenced him so strongly in *Alastor*, was his constant thought while he sat in Bisham Wood morning after morning, composing this new poem. He tells us this himself. Much of the poem was written, he says, " with the same feeling, as real, though not so prophetic, as the communications of a dying man." How strange it is, this constant genius of death in the work of Shelley! In the *Revolt* that genius is present in added strength, a new lenity, and greater tenderness. Shelley's politics and private life are inextricably interwoven.

These points require substantiation.

But at first, as one reads the poem, and discovers the recrudescence of the old political themes of death, there is disappointment; for there seems to be no advance in treatment, and the serener vision of the *Hymn* and *Mont Blanc* seem nowhere to be found. The four ideas involving death and politics, which we have traced through the juvenilia, enter in unabashed tumidity. Again the tyrant is hurling death upon a bleeding world, again the patriot declaims that death is preferable to loss of liberty, again we behold the grandeur of the past fallen into decay and ruin; and again the poet prophesies the tortured death of the tyrants, but with a difference.

Again, personified Fear, Hatred, Bigotry, and Tyranny spread pestilence, decay, and death. Horrors are described with increased vigour; now in connection with the supernatural, as in his earliest poems; now in a conjunction of nature and death, as in this view of a rotting battle-field, which obviously owes much to Coleridge:

> Day after day the burning Sun rolled on
> Over the death-polluted land. It came
> Out of the east like fire, and fiercely shone
> A lamp of autumn, ripening with its flame
> The few lone ears of corn; the sky became
> Stagnate with heat, so that each cloud and blast
> Languished and died; the thirsting air did claim
> All moisture, and a rotting vapour passed
> From the unburied dead, invisible and fast. (X.13)

The death of a slave condemned to torture is pictured deliberately. The tyrant is a murderer who

> Slaked his thirsting soul as from a well
> Of blood and tears, with ruin. (V.31)

" He murders, for his chiefs delight in ruin." (VIII.14)
The king passes surrounded by the steel

> Of hired assassins, through the public way
> Choked with his country's dead. (X.8)

One recalls two lines in *Queen Mab:*

> War is the statesman's game, the priest's delight,
> The lawyer's jest, the hired assassin's trade. (IV.167–168)

Again, the martyr welcomes death in the cause of liberty. Laon braves one for the other, and invokes his countrymen to do the same. Cythna hopes for either liberty or death. The death of the patriot is a " glorious doom." In the cause of liberty sweet maidens die happily and sentimentally, singing

> . . . a low sweet song, of which alone
> One word was heard, and that was Liberty. (X.48)

The patriot-protagonists, Laon and Cythna, face martyrdom joyfully, though even here Shelley could not but lament that one so young and fair as Cythna should die. Again, the dungeons, palaces, and temples of the past fade like vapour, leaving not a rack behind. But man, with his heritage of perfectibility,

> Remains, whose will has power when all beside is gone.
> (VIII.16)

However, it is when the fourth accustomed theme enters that the new learning becomes apparent. Just what quality in the poem is the effect of the deeper knowledge of life Shelley has been acquiring? I think it is a chastening of the young extremism which first created the romantic villains of *Zastrozzi* and then converted them into the political villains of *Queen Mab.* Hitherto Shelley has exulted in the painful death of bigots and tyrants, and has found therein the cure of all evils. But now he recognizes the fallacy of this hopeful killing

113

off of his personified evils. The tyrants, somehow, must be reconciled with the kingdom of love. Inevitably their evil deeds will draw on punishment, as they sit " aghast amid the ruins [they themselves] have made." Mere self-realization is their inevitable punishment. Yet, they are men — individual, actual men — and as such must have their part in a universe of love, in the theatre of redemption. Merely to avenge the misdeed on the misdoer is only to increase the misery in a world " all too wide for it."

At last, the contradiction of ideas that we have suspected in *Queen Mab* is removed. Necessity, we heard, governs every working of the tyrant's moody mind; the soul of the universe foresees " the events chaining every will " (VI.181–190): yet the tyrant and bigot were in that poem objects of unmitigated scorn. But in the meantime the poet, standing before Mont Blanc, has heard voices that " repeal large codes of fraud and woe," has hymned a wise serenity of the spirit, has been in disgrace with fortune and men's eyes, and has seen despair lead to tragic death. These experiences have softened the indignations of the young idealist, and he learns how to pity, if not to love, the enemies of the public good. The confusion is thereby obliterated.

It is death that teaches tolerance. His young, wild passions and hopes, his disdains and hatreds of unreal, set villains of tyranny, and his hopes of impossible perfections, had indeed beguiled Shelley into the very presence of death. Harriet's death, and Fanny's, too, were tragic commentaries on Godwin's teachings. The logical abstractions and classifications of that strange philosopher, even when they passed into the ardent rhetoric of his chief disciple, were not fitted to the commonplace realities of human nature. Their practice in a perfectly logical world might be undeleterious. But in the actual world of Harriets and Fannies their practice got mixed up with the unpredictable results of passionate weakness and despair. It is in the face of these mixed personal equations that the ideologist learns tolerance through suffering. Classifications of good and evil, and personifications of them as patriots and tyrants, become vanities before the face of individual suffering. Shelley was learning more about individuals, and placing a higher value upon the tragic little theatre that each one is. He no longer could hate even a personification.

The rationale of this moral development, then, perhaps was something like this: Godwin's dream of perfectibility " clicked " with Shelley's ardent, innate benevolence; Godwin's cool logic, satisfying Shelley's conscientious impulse always to appeal to reason when dealing with human affairs, seemed to ratify the dream; his own ardent imagination animated Godwin's theorems into personifications, and insensibly the human quality of the personification was confused with human beings themselves, and he was convinced that his masquerade of personifications was a true picture of persons; then came misfortunes — the loss of his wife's love, the two suicides, the loss of his children by Harriet — at the same time that he was learning more of human sympathy from the Boinvilles and from Mary. He began to learn the difference between the personifications and actual persons. It was what he had to learn in order to proceed poet, for the poet gives us not propositions, even personified, about life, but the very life itself, deepened by a most sensitive, imaginative awareness of actual men and women. After his juvenile practice in themes derived from hearsay, he faces sorrow and derives his major themes from life itself. Then his imagination draws him more and more into concrete, commonplace reality, and passes on intuitively to a knowledge of spiritual, all-unifying reality, so that he feels each individual *sub specie aeternitatis*. So Shelley proceeds, uniting himself in love with persons, listening, though not in Wordsworth's contemplative fashion, to the " deep, sad music of humanity."

In *Islam*, then, Shelley's new learning is evident as a broadening of the power to love, as a more sympathetic understanding of human nature, and as the consequent moderation of his political hatreds. To be sure, the theme of *Islam* is still romantically idealistic, wildly emotional. To be sure, the dream that a perfect and bloodless revolution may result from the contagious genius of beautiful young eleutherarchs, like Laon and Cythna, who preach a gospel of love, is so much sentimentality. These moods leave the political realist cold indeed. But when their tolerance is set over against the fanaticism of *Queen Mab*, a growth in understanding is apparent. It is an advance from hate to love; from ugliness to a measure of beauty; from a crude dualism of evil and good issuing in a fanatical rejection of impossibly wicked villains, toward that deeper and more hopeful humanism which issues in the injunction, "Love thine enemies." It is a step toward that repentant renunciation of hate with which Prometheus opens Shelley's greatest long poem, and which constitutes the spiritual unbinding of the Titan. The beginning of Shelley's own unbinding from extremism is in *The Revolt of Islam*.

Herein, too, lies Shelley's apology for the French Revolution, for in his preface to *Islam* he avers that the failure of the Revolution was not the failure of the ideas upon which it rested, but of the prosecution of its programme by the very means of hatred, murder, and vengeance that were opprobriated in tyranny. His patient, brave words deserve quotation:

> The panic which, like an epidemic transport, seized upon all classes of men during the excesses consequent upon the French Revolution, is gradually giving place to sanity. It has ceased to be believed that whole generations of mankind ought to consign themselves to a hopeless inheritance of ignorance and misery because a nation of men who had been dupes and slaves for centuries were incapable of conducting themselves with the wisdom and tranquillity of freemen so soon as some of their fetters were partially loosened. That their conduct could

not have been marked by any other characters than ferocity and thoughtlessness is the historical fact from which liberty derives all its recommendations, and falsehood the worst features of its deformity. There is a reflux in the tide of human things which bears the shipwrecked hopes of men into a secure haven after the storms are past. Methinks those who now live have survived an age of despair.

Islam is the symbolic presentation of these ideas: the great hopes of Laon and Cythna, their initial successes, the magnificent rejoicing and the *Champ-de-Mars* festival of the benevolent new order, the return of the tyrants, the failure of the Revolution, and the hope of a later and more perfect event, embody these principles. Wordsworth and Coleridge, older contemporaries, who directly witnessed the shipwreck of liberal hopes in the storm of The Terror, made no sufficient distinction between means and end, and with that natural confusion lost faith in revolution; Shelley, escaping the crisis (he was only two years old at the close of The Terror), was free twenty-three years later to make the necessary distinction and realize the eternal nature of the struggle for freedom. Wordsworth's *The Borderers* and Shelley's *Revolt of Islam*, Professor Koszul reminds us, mark the difference in reaction.

But in this poem love defeats a thing less avoidable than hatred. It conquers the ugliness of death, though temporarily, conditionally. The strength for that conquest was the gift of the union with Mary. There we touch upon the other great plastic power of the poem, one that has kneaded its matter into a human beauty that is a companion-picture to the natural beauty of *Alastor*. Its presence is felt at the very beginning, in the seventh and eighth stanzas of the Dedication to Mary. Her loving companionship and the blessing of the " two gentle babes born from her side " are the very parents of this song, he says. It is the love of Shelley and Mary that

makes the love of Laon and Cythna, their children that make
the child of the lovers in the poem. The undaunted, winding
way of the human fellowship of lovers and their children
leads everywhere through the ideal story, from the beginning in love, through the suffering and disgrace at the hands
of men, to the immolation of the lovers and their reunion in
a heavenly paradise. Their revolutionary daring is that of
Mary and Shelley, their rending of the mortal chains of custom, their high hopes for mankind's regeneration, their fortitude in seeming failure, their wisdom of stern contentment
the while they are mocked by poverty and infamy, are the
very things of which Shelley makes his love-song for Mary in
the Dedication.

But it is in the last five stanzas of the ninth canto that the
ecstasy of this love belittles death. The thought is a truism,
like the thought of so many great poems; the mood and its
music are very nearly sublime. The thought is as follows:
the senses and reason discover nought in death but decay and
extinction; but the world is full of delusion, and we know
nought of the Power behind each thing; the mind faints, realizing its impotence to grasp the full nature of things, but this
we know, that extinction is dearer than a life apart from the
beloved; everything is darkly driven toward the abyss of
death, but all change is as nothing *if* only love be not changed.
There is the run of ideas. Now read them in the suggestivity
of mood and image and music. Cythna is speaking to Laon:

> " The while we too, belovèd, must depart,
> And Sense and Reason, those enchanters fair,
> Whose wand of power is hope, would bid the heart
> That gazed beyond the wormy grave despair;
> These eyes, these lips, this blood, seems darkly there
> To fade in hideous ruin; no calm sleep,
> Peopling with golden dreams the stagnant air,
> Seems our obscure and rotting eyes to steep
> In joy; — but senseless death — a ruin dark and deep!

"These are blind fancies. Reason cannot know
What sense can neither feel nor thought conceive;
There is delusion in the world — and woe,
And fear, and pain — we know not whence we live,
Or why, or how, or what mute Power may give
Their being to each plant, and star, and beast,
Or even these thoughts. — Come near me! I do weave
A chain I cannot break — I am possessed
With thoughts too swift and strong for one lone human breast.

"Yes, yes — thy kiss is sweet, thy lips are warm —
Oh, willingly, belovèd, would these eyes
Might they no more drink being from thy form,
Even as to sleep whence we again arise,
Close their faint orbs in death. I fear nor prize
Aught that can now betide, unshared by thee.
Yes, Love when Wisdom fails makes Cythna wise;
Darkness and death, if death be true, must be
Dearer than life and hope if unenjoyed with thee.

"Alas! our thoughts flow on with stream whose waters
Return not to their fountain; Earth and Heaven,
The Ocean and the Sun, the clouds their daughters,
Winter, and Spring, and Morn, and Noon, and Even —
All that we are or know, is darkly driven
Towards one gulf. — Lo! what a change is come
Since I first spake — but time shall be forgiven,
Though it change all but thee!" She ceased — night's
    gloom
Meanwhile had fallen on earth from the sky's sunless dome.

Though she had ceased, her countenance uplifted
To Heaven still spake with solemn glory bright;
Her dark deep eyes, her lips, whose motions gifted
The air they breathed with love, her locks undight;
"Fair star of life and love," I cried, "my soul's delight,

119

The Pursuit of Death

Why lookest thou on the crystalline skies?
Oh, that my spirit were yon Heaven of night,
Which gazes on thee with its thousand eyes! "
She turned to me and smiled — that smile was Paradise!
(IX.32–36)

Thus death, extinction, immortality, love, and mutability are woven into a beautiful and tragic whole, with love dominating fear and hope. Strong, varied, impassioned, undidactic, this is one of Shelley's most direct and powerful utterances on love and death — the most immediately human so far. Here even the old coffin-worm theme is mitigated into something effective, as, too, are all the other vapid anticipations to which we have listened in the poems of the first two decades. One previous theme is only dimly suggested: that great gate-theme, *mors janua vitae*, that stands at the end of *Queen Mab*. Perhaps even it takes second place to this attitude. Here most of us, at any rate, will pause in admiration, even though the Gate glisten afar in the *Hymn*, in *Mont Blanc*, and in *Adonais* itself.

For a victorious attitude, at least its promise, is indubitably present. *Its promise*, because the victory is conditional on the possibility of love's surviving the mutability of all else. This tremendous *if* makes the beauty of the address a tragic beauty, by constraining the dream to a doubt of its fulfilment. The assertion is no mere ecstatic conversion of hope to fact; it is at once both stronger and more contingent than if it were outright delusion emotionally promoted to conviction. Its tragic contingency, indeed, gives it a touch of sublimity; and all moral sublimity conquers the fear and ugliness of death. Sublimity of heroism and sacrifice and courageous self-dependence, of faith and vision, of beauty and love — all these make death small, in very fact negligible.

But, finally, there is even more of comfort than is contained in this moral disregard of death; for in the supreme moment

120

of love, as Shelley says toward the very end of the poem, describing the last great love-moment of the dying lovers,

> . . . the mighty veil
> Which doth divide the living and the dead
> Was almost rent, the world grew dim and pale —
> All light in Heaven or Earth beside our love did fail.
>
> (XII.15)

That assertion rises above contingency by substituting a present value for all fact and possibility —

All light in Heaven or Earth beside our love did fail.

The experience is so supreme that it all but synthesizes within itself the antithesis of life and death — " the veil was almost rent." This intense, mystical annihilation of the dualism of matter and spirit, of life and death, of all such opposites, is the mark of the highest aesthetic moment, as Coleridge long ago pointed out in his doctrine of poetic unity. Moreover, the passage is an anticipation of another such moment, yet more splendidly realized, at the very close of *Adonais*. Shelley's aesthetic mysticism is most fully released, indeed, near the inspired close of certain of his poems: a first release in the great passage in *Queen Mab*, which has been discussed; a second, here; a third at the very end of the *Ode to the West Wind*; the greatest, in the last stanza of *Adonais*. Each of these passages is an impressive example of what James Mark Baldwin meant by his definition of the aesthetic moment: a moment of immediate contemplation in which the dualism of the inner and outer controls is annihilated in a higher reality embracing both. Here the outer control is the fact of life and death; the inner, the dream of survival; and the higher reality is the mystical faith that annihilates the difference between fact and dream. The contrast is annihilated, and a greater reality, including the fact and the dream in its higher synthesis, is ours for a moment. Afterwards we may wonder where we may find the faith to believe in the vision. But the poet, re-making the vision, re-instating the moment, comes ever to our aid.

After the successful portrayal of this great mood and attitude, dwarfing all else, the picture of the lovers' reunion in the heaven-palace of the Spirit is but so much dramatic myth and symbol. Heaven, rather, in reality is in the moment of unfathomable beauty: our moment, here and now. The rest can be taken on trust. Nay, like Dante in beatitude of the vision of God, we are content then to be nothing.

IV

Perhaps it is an anticlimax to consider what of precision there was in Shelley's ideas of immortality up to this time. It is unnecessary to point out again the earliest, flimsy passages on the subject, in *The Wandering Jew*, in which, before he had begun original thought, he merely reflected the conventional Christian belief he had been taught as a child; or to trace the rise of his distrust of that too easy faith in a definitely personal immortality. For a while French materialism, which later he rejected, threatened the promptings of his imagination, and at times he thought death ended all. But his considered opinion at the time he wrote *Islam* was a mixture of impersonal but intense idealism making for impersonal, or at least inconceivable, survival, with an impassioned hope, converted at certain great moments into an impassioned faith, that in eternity lovers will not be lost to each other.

For these beliefs Shelley argued in various ways, and repeatedly he imaged them in poetic figures. Six years earlier, in letters to Elizabeth Hitchener (June 20, June 25, 1811), he had rather speciously contended that the laws of conservation of energy and imperishability of matter assured the soul against perishing; and then had suggested that as the soul's faculties are temporarily suspended during sleep, so they may be in death, and that in its future state the soul will begin life anew, possibly under an inconceivable shape, but forgetful of its previous existence. A few months later in the same year (Oct. 15?, Nov. 24, 1811), he had ingenuously confided to her that though his reason told him death closes all, yet feeling made him believe directly the contrary, and that this deep feeling, or " inward sense," seemed to him a very proof of the soul's immortality. While admitting what so many others, from Cicero to Emerson, have asserted, that the desire for a future state may be a proof of it, Shelley remembers that the wish may prejudice us in favour of the argument. But he thinks that everything lives again, and that the soul of anything, even of a flower, being but the force which makes it what it is (as Aristotle would say, its function or end), cannot be conceived as perishing utterly. Yet where it exists and how we cannot discover. " Have not flowers also some end which Nature destines their being to answer? " he asks. The closeness of this train of thought to Aristotle's teleology of the soul is remarkable. Early in the next year (Jan. 7, 1812), he wrote in a postscript: " I find you begin to doubt the eternity of the soul: I do not "; adding, rather ambiguously, " More of that hereafter " !

In *Queen Mab,* for all its appeal to reason and its *quasi* materialism, the " inward sense " triumphs quite Platonically: soul is the only true reality, animating every atom (IV.139-146). This faith he had put forward tentatively in the letter to Miss Hitchener, dated November 24, 1811. Now he asserts it roundly, and adds that a soul though spoiled by earth may regain its original perfection —

> Soul is not more polluted than the beams
> Of Heaven's pure orb, ere round their rapid lines
> The taint of earth-born atmospheres arise. (IV.151-153)

One recalls a passage in the tenth book of the *Republic:* "Soul does not perish like the body, because its characteristic evil, sin or wickedness, does not kill it as the diseases of the body wear out the bodily life." Moreover, through death's dark gate the soul passes to a greater glory:

> Fear not then, Spirit, death's disrobing hand, . . .
> 'Tis but the voyage of a darksome hour,
> The transient gulf-stream of a startling sleep. (IX. 171–175)

The Universal Spirit, called also Spirit of Nature, Necessity, Soul of the Universe, carefully distinguished from the unreal God of human error and superstition, is represented as ceaselessly active, and as never interrupted by the temporary failure of earthly life in the grave (VI.146–238), though the problem of the exact nature of the relation between the universal mind and the individual, both before birth, during life, and after death, is deliberately avoided. But a positive and fairly definite answer to the question of personal survival was elaborated, we have seen, in connection with his love for Harriet, based again upon feeling. Our best and rarest emotional feelings, especially love, urge us to believe in something beyond death (*Q.M.* IX. 171–184). Birth, on the other hand, is regarded in the *Dæmon of the World* as the means of waking the universal mind to " individual sense of outward shows." *Alastor* develops this transcendentalism in a series of romantic images, and then it is presented with a new awe and serenity in the *Hymn* and *Mont Blanc*.

Intensity of feeling, then, or, rather, of love in particular, as well as a certain deep " inward sense," led Shelley to believe, even against reason, in some kind of persistence beyond the grave. The " inward sense " inclined him to a general and vague conception of that persistence; love in its passionate moments wrung from him a belief in the persistence of the individual, or, at least, of something equal, or finer, in its power to satisfy the desire for the perpetuation of ecstatic states.

But there is a curious relation, partly of contradiction,

partly of agreement, between the ideas in *Queen Mab* and the ideas on survival contained in certain prose essays and fragments written subsequent to the poem. In the first two of these prose pieces, he argues against survival, in the third he becomes doubtful of his ground, in the fourth he disclaims personal survival but argues for some sort of persistence, and in the fifth he rationalizes the Christian teachings of personal survival and Heaven.

Queen Mab was published in 1813. The date of the brief prose tract, *On a Future State*, is uncertain, but in all probability it is not later than the following year, 1814. The tract is written under the influence of the French materialists he had been reading. It contains some ten chief arguments against survival of any sort, and includes reversals of the assumptions he had adopted in the Hitchener letters and in *Queen Mab*. (a) The imperishability of matter is now put forward not as a justification of the belief in immortality, but as an analogy destructive of the grounds of that belief. All matter divides and changes, and therefore gives no warrant for the assumption that spirit (defined as a mere name given to sensibility and thought to distinguish them from their objects) never changes, never divides, never loses a given personal identity. (b) Those philosophers to whom we are most indebted for discoveries in the physical sciences suppose that intelligence, or 'spirit,' is the " mere result of certain combinations among the particles of its objects," and that therefore it must cease with the inevitable dispersal of those particles and consequent annihilation of the combinations. If, then, these natural philosophers wish to believe in survival, it becomes necessary for them to assume the interposition of a supernatural power which overcomes the law of division and change in all matter. (c) The actual decay of the mind during life, seen in madness, idiocy, and old age, does not justify a presumption of changelessness and survival. (d) If mind is a special substance, which permeates, and is the cause of, the animation of living beings, there is no warrant for supposing that this substance is exempt from the general law of substance, viz., decay and change into other forms. (e) The condition of the body at death — the organs of sense destroyed and the intellectual operations dependent on them inoperative — offers no ground for an argument for survival of intelligence. (f) No valid argument for persistence can be drawn from an assumption of preëxistence, for the assumption cannot be supported. The argument that in each living being there is a prior and indestructible generative principle which converts surrounding substances into a substance homogeneous with itself (another of the arguments in the Hitchener letters) is untenable, because this so-called ' principle ' does not really exist, but is only an hypostasis of an observed process, or, rather, of an observed coëxistence of certain phenomena. — These six arguments rest on the naturalistic definitions of spirit as intelligence and of intelligence as entirely dependent on the senses. In the remaining four arguments, an attack is made upon the immaterialistic grounds of belief. — (g) The idea of a survival in a mode of being totally inconceivable to us at present, which had been mentioned in the Hitchener letters and which is developed in some later poems, is called an unreasonable presumption, because it is not supported by a single analogy and because by its very transcendental nature it cannot be brought to the bar of reason. " It is sufficiently easy, indeed, to form any proposition, concerning which we are ignorant, just not so absurd as not to be contradictory in itself, and defy refutation." (h) The argument drawn from the Divine Justice — that a just Deity must compensate the virtuous who suffer during life by providing them with eternal happiness — is lightly dismissed as satisfying no one! (i) Moreover, were it proved that a Divine Power rules the world, survival would not follow as a necessary inference. (j) The secret and real cause of the belief in survival is merely the wish to survive. " This desire to be forever as we are; the reluctance to a violent and unexperienced change, which is common to all the animated and inanimate combinations of the universe, is, indeed, the secret persuasion which has given birth to the opinions of a future state." So he disposes of the argument from the heart, which he has used in his earliest poems, in the Hitchener letters, in *Mab,* and in *Islam,* and which he continues to use in many a later poem. If only that enthusiastic rhetorician, W. R. Alger, had written his *Critical History of the Doctrine of a Future Life* before 1814, what meat he would have been for the Shelley of *On a Future State!* What fun Shelley would have made, for instance, of Alger's picture of mighty man walking the universe, supported by his inalienable instinct for immortality: " Crowned with free will, walking on the crest of the world, enfeoffed with individual faculties, served by vassal nature with tributes of various joy, he cannot bear the thought of losing himself, of sliding into the general abyss of matter "!

In the second pamphlet, the ironical *Refutation of Deism* (1814), the Christian doctrine of the eternal damnation or salvation of souls by an all-foreseeing, all-causing God is ridiculed as inconsistent with any but a savage and obscene conception of deity.

With the fragment *On the Punishment of Death* (1814 or 1815), a change of opinion begins. After asserting that it is quite impossible to know whether death be good, evil, or indifferent, a punishment or a reward, he admits that he thinks the common idea of the survival of " that within us which thinks and feels " is supported by " the accurate philosophy of . . . the modern Academy." This complete reversal in interpreting the French Encyclopedists is made to turn upon a phase of their own teaching, viz., the " prodigious depth and extent of our ignorance respecting the causes and nature of sensation." Shelley has come to realize that the materialists' assumption that sensations are irreducible, or pure, minima of consciousness is highly questionable. In turn, he has recourse to a conception against which he had argued, speciously, to be sure, in the first of these essays: that if we do survive, the manner of our existence must be such as no earthly experience can conceive or understand. But he concludes the matter by observing that if at death the individual soul is merely absorbed in the universal soul, death can be pronounced neither good nor evil, but only indifferent.

The fourth paper is the fragment, *On Life* (1815). Now, definitely renouncing and attacking the materialistic psychology, Shelley tends to take his stand with the idealists. The mind naturally disclaims alliance with transience and decay, and cannot conceive annihilation (this dogma is close to that of the " inward sense " noted above); but idealism leads the mind to such a conception of the unity of all life that the common, intense, and exclusive meaning of individuality is destroyed. Out of this annihilation of the antithesis of the individual and the universal, the poetry of the *Adonais* is to be forged by the heat of tragic experience. But at the close of the fragment Shelley moves away from the idealists, holding that it is " infinitely improbable that the cause of mind, i.e. of existence, is similar to mind," because mind cannot create, but can only perceive.

The last of these prose pieces, the *Essay on Christianity* (1815? 1817?), has definite relations to *The Revolt of Islam*. Christ's traditional teaching concerning the future life is rationalized. The promise that the pure in heart shall see God is understood, not as a reference to a literal beholding of God, after death, but as a poetic way of referring to the blessed and beautiful inner experience of the simple, sincere, and virtuous man: the ideal ' natural ' man of Rousseau. The beatitude is strictly equivalent to the saying that virtue is its own reward. Similarly, Christ's description of the bliss of the soul in Heaven is to be taken as a poetic and enthusiastic hyperbole for the heavenly beauty of the inner life of the good man. Presently we shall have occasion to quote extensively the eloquent exposition of this point, and then its relation to *Islam* will become clear. For the rest of the *Essay*, it need only be remarked that in the course of it are to be found in several places the assumption of an over-ruling Power, by which we are surrounded, from which we experience " benignant visitings." The step from that last phrase to the Spirit of the *Hymn to Intellectual Beauty* and of the *Mont Blanc* is obvious.

These five essays, then, give us some faint and, we may say, in view of their fragmentary, hurried nature, some erratic, suggestions of the change in mind by which Shelley passed from the materialistic psychology of Locke and the Encyclopedists back to the faith expressed in the Hitchener letters and forward to the faith of the *Hymn, Mont Blanc*, and all his later poems. Death and immortality and the nature of God were the crucial problems through which he progressed in making the change from his temporary materialism back to his native gift for the invisible and forward to his more or less reasoned idealism. But it is particularly noticeable that in *Queen Mab*, although it was composed during the materialistic period, the native gift finally triumphed over the acquired materialism, even though the materialistic arguments were resumed in the essay *On a Future State*. His own spirit, when thoroughly aroused, as toward the end of *Mab*, burst through the psychology imported from France or found at home in Locke.

In *Islam*, according to Professor Woodberry, " the expressions with respect to the immortality of the spirit are perceptibly more strong and favorable " than in *Queen Mab* and *Alastor*. I am not sure that this is a true statement. But, at any rate, most of Shelley's previous ideas upon the subject are repeated — the more general ones with greater conviction, perhaps; those dealing more particularly with personal survival, with rather less, it seems to me. For here, again, there is certainty with regard to the existence of a higher power, called both Necessity (IX.27) and Spirit (XII.31.41), which, in a phrase recalling the *Hymn*, is said to "float unseen, but not unfelt, o'er blind mortality" (VI.37). Again, as in *Queen Mab*, and as later in the *Ode to the West Wind*, we are reminded of the social, or influential, immortality of our good deeds and thoughts. The good who die beneath the tyrant's rod are as autumn, dying before winter; but like autumn, they sow in their good works the seeds which spring shall bring to leaf and flower:

> Our many thoughts and deeds, our life and love,
> Our happiness, and all that we have been,
> Immortally must live and burn and move
> When we shall be no more. (IX.30)

Now we live in the winter of the world's discontent, and die therein, even as the winds of autumn expire in the frore and foggy air. But a glorious spring of perfected moral life awaits society, though the good who give promise and prophecy of it must pass. But if the good would behold the glory of that great dawn, they have but to look at the Paradise of their own hearts, which is "the earnest of the hope which made them great" (IX.25–27). Again, mere reason makes him believe in oblivion (IX.32), the extinction of personality (IX.29). But, and, once more, again, reason and the senses cannot give the final answer, and therefore we doubt the blank answer of reason, though we cannot know what mute Power may animate the universe of mind and matter (IX.33, as quoted above). The last recourse, then, is to feeling, especially love,

Yes, Love when Wisdom fails makes Cythna wise. (IX.34)

The love she feels for Laon, typical of all great love, is the only certainty which she knows — the only certainty by which she can interpret death. Because of this greatness and this certainty she is unwilling to believe that Laon's personality and her love for him will be annihilated. Cythna is Love's prophetess of a more perfect life beyond the grave (IX.20). Here is the reversal of the last argument in *On a Future State*.

What persuaded Professor Woodberry that Shelley had reached in this poem a stronger conviction of the personal immortality of the soul was, probably, the definite depiction, in Cantos I and XII, of a paradise for the souls of the good and great. But the very definiteness of these pictures, the wealth of concrete detail lavished on them, their sheer extravagance of imagery, might lead another reader to suspect Shelley never meant them to be taken literally, especially in view of his known objections, both now and later, to confusing such anthropomorphic religious fairy-tales with fact. Rather their very extravagance of bliss is a symbol of the beauty these spirits attained in life, a beauty that cannot die among men, but grows fragrant with time and memory; and a poetic way of suggesting not what does actually lie beyond death, but what is the best possible idea a mortal mind can achieve of a perfect mind. At any rate, they are a part of the fairy-machinery of the poem, floating lightly in the romantic and sentimental atmosphere. Like other marvels in the poem — the child with the silver wings, the boat of hollow pearl, the eagle who refused to bring ropes, and the Tartarean steed — they are properties of the romantic theatre, to be interpreted figuratively, rather than literally.

But Shelley's attitude toward these pictures of heavenly bliss may be gathered pretty definitely from his interpretation of Christ's utterances on a similar theme. I quote, as I promised, from the *Essay on Christianity*:

> We die, says Jesus Christ, and when we awaken from the languor of disease the glories and the happiness of Paradise are around us. All evil and pain have ceased forever. Our happiness also corresponds with, and is adapted to, the nature of what is most excellent in our being.

131

We see God, and we see that he is good. How delightful a picture, even if it be not true! How magnificent and illustrious is the conception which this bold theory suggests to the contemplation, even if it be no more than the imagination of some sublimest and most holy poet, who impressed with the loveliness and majesty of his own nature, is impatient and discontented, with the narrow limits which this imperfect life and the dark grave have assigned forever as his melancholy portion.

So, too, Shelley into his poetry boldly projects the paradise of his own best ideas, making a symbolic external Heaven out of the Kingdom within him, moved thereto by discontent with the imperfections of life and the ugliness of the grave. Of course, such a process again and again must fling out a bolder figurative statement, whether of Utopias or Heavens, than sober sense would allow in reasoned prose. Poetry is a kind, the highest and most natural kind, of intoxication.

Of the classic arguments for the immortality of the soul, which, then, has Shelley, up to this time, put forward? Though Voltaire's epigram, that the problem of immortality has been " discussed for four thousand years in four thousand different ways," well sets out the confusion as well as the indeterminate nature of the discussion — in 1878 Ezra Abbot of Harvard College went Voltaire 977 times better by compiling a list of 4977 books " relating to the nature, origin, and destiny of the soul " — nevertheless some few arguments are outstanding. They are outstanding not because they are convincing, but because they are common or typical, occurring repeatedly in the logomachy, with great variety of specific traits at each occurrence, to be sure. Following Dr. Garvie's admirable *Britannica* article on immortality, I shall pick out five of these common, typical approaches. There is the argument from metaphysics: that the soul, being indivisible and independent of the body cannot perish with the latter — the favourite teaching of Leibnitz and Ernst Platner, to say nothing of many a scholastic, with Albertus Magnus at their head. There is the juridical argument, represented by Kant and Bishop Butler: that the present life is so imperfect there must be another, perfect existence. There is the ethical argument, well developed by Hugo Münsterberg: the more lofty a man's aims, the more incomplete is his life on the earth; therefore there must be another, complete life. There is the religious (Christian) argument: man, being created in God's image, cannot be death's victim. God is the God of the living, not of the dead, as Christ is reported to have said (Matthew 22.32). Finally, there is the argument from the emotions: the heart protests against severance from its love by death, and as man feels love is his most godlike characteristic, love's claim has supreme authority. This is the argument of *In Memoriam.* Now, of these five, the only one that Shelley definitely and directly stresses is the last, the argument from feeling: it is his first argument, in *The Drowned Lover* and the lines *To Harriet;* it survives determinism in *Queen Mab;* it comes back to its own in *The Revolt of Islam,* first with tragic contingency, then with mystic faith; it continues through poems not yet considered in this essay, such as *Prometheus Unbound* and *Adonais;* as late as *Hellas* (1821–22), in a note to that poem, Shelley says that the desire for immortality " must remain the strongest and the only presumption that eternity is the inheritance of every thinking being." This is the only argument for personal survival that he at any time admits, and he stresses it, as is natural, far more in the passion of poetry than in the reflection of prose. Of the four other arguments, the Christian-religious does not at all appear; the ethical and juridical appear only very indeterminately and imperfectly, or figuratively, in scattered suggestions of the hope of final blessedness for the world's political martyrs; and the metaphysical can only with difficulty be read into one or two ambiguous passages.

The other arguments for survival that Shelley has used can

properly be taken only as arguments against personal immortality. His idealistic utterances in *On Life* are connected with a persuasion that personality is a sort of fallacy; and the suggestion that survival must be in an inconceivable mode of being negatives, by implication at least, the definite concept of separate entity. I must conclude, therefore, that Mrs. Shelley's summary of his belief does not fit the state of his published opinions at the time he wrote *Islam*, for in this summary, which follows, she has certainly thrown far more emphasis upon individual survival than appears in these writings, or, for that matter, in his later writings. Perhaps in her eagerness to bridge the gulf between Shelley and the public she unconsciously overestimated the personal element in his opinions or took too literally the Heaven of *Islam;* or, perhaps, she did not fully grasp the impersonality of his idealism. Here, at any rate, is what she wrote:

> Considering his individual mind as a unit divided from a mighty whole, to which it was united by restless sympathies and an eager desire for knowledge, he assuredly believed that hereafter, as now, he would form a portion of that whole — and a portion less imperfect, less suffering, than the shackles inseparable from humanity impose on all who live beneath the moon. (Essays, Letters from Abroad, etc. 1840. I.xiv)

The difficulty lies in the phrase " hereafter, as now," for it seems to designate a survival as personal as is the present life. The rest of the summary is fairly accurate.

But it is high time to hold our tongues concerning these endless speculations. By way of relief, let us remember another of Voltaire's satirical remarks:

> " Hold your tongue," said the dervise. " I promised myself the pleasure," said Pangloss, " of reasoning with you upon effects and causes, the best possible of worlds, the origin of evil, the nature of the soul, and the pre-

established harmony." — The dervise, at these words, shut the door in their faces.

V

Now the story turns back to moods of grief and dejection. *Prince Athanase*, the next document, is a fragment. As it stands it has little about death. Had it been completed, death would have been its pathetic *dénouement*. It is a revised *Alastor*, involving a significant addition. The romantic, hoary-headed young poet of *Alastor*, pursuing his dream of a divine beauty and love, hoping to find it in the actual world, failed in the pursuit, and died in solitude at the touch of winter's changing hand. *Alastor* is a lyric solo of an impossible quest, a failure doomed by the nature of things. But in *Athanase* the poet-prince, also young, hoary-headed, and romantic, was to have won the body-beauty of an earthly love, finding out, too late, that this was not the heavenly love for which he searched. Then, at his death-bed, the spirit-beauty of his quest was to have appeared, to kiss his dying lips. It would have been a lyric drama of pursuit, mistake and repentance, failure, and dying vision.

The theme of the two loves, earthly and heavenly, is taken from Pausanias's speech in Plato's *Symposium*. There are two Aphrodites, said Pausanias, the heavenly, which is pure and noble, called Urania, and the earthly, which is physical and ignoble, called Pandemos. It is natural, and perhaps all too easy, to identify the Aphrodite Pandemos, in the scheme of the proposed poem, with Harriet. The ugly change in her love, at any rate, and the ensuing disappointment and failure, are parallel to the tragic disillusionment of the poem. That Mary was the Uranian love appears from the description of her, as the heavenly love, at the end of the fragment. That she comes too late, while the individual dies, is perhaps a dramatic parallel to actuality — Shelley again, while he wrote this poem, thought he was dying of a consumption — rather than a symbol of some teaching that perfection belongs only to the moment, that all moments in their death give birth to others. That teaching of how to be reconciled with mutability's theft of all beautiful things — that each moment is fulfilled of beauty — was Keats's instinctive teaching; or, at least, an idea his instinct for sensuous beauty demanded of his intellect, so that he need not admit a serpent of ugliness into his young Eden of delight. But it is not yet Shelley's teaching, or realization.

Thus death, dramatic and pathetic, would have been the catastrophe of the poem; but a death true, at least, to Shelley's mournful preoccupation with the failure of loveliness, the brightness of the world ever in eclipse.

But it would have been true, too, to the grief, hardly yet turned through reconciliation into sorrow, which pulses in the poem itself. And, though the actual fragment has so little of death in it, yet for this weight of real grief it becomes an important witness to the growth of Shelley's ideas on death. Athanase is described as bowed with a secret sadness, one that he himself scarcely understands, which his friends emptily conjecture, and which he himself never confesses to them. But the nature of the burden is nevertheless made fairly clear: a deep, almost subconscious intuition of all the evils done under the sun, intensified by a particular, personal tragedy:

> . . . 'Tis the shadow of a dream
> Which the veiled eye of memory never saw,
> But through the soul's abyss, like some dark stream
> Through shattered mines and caverns underground,
> Rolls, shaking its foundations; and no beam
> Of joy may rise but it is quenched and drowned
> In the dim whirlpools of this dream obscure.

This woe for the deep-seated evils of the world was indeed for Shelley embittered to grief by many particulars which had come close to him. We have already rehearsed most of the catalogue. The cruel political persecutions of the time, the causes of some of them deliberately manufactured by the government's nefarious and shameless *agents provocateurs*, inspired him with horror; the loss of his elder children by the court's decision that he was an unfit father to care for them, was the cause of a continual, inexpressible anguish, as both Mrs. Shelley and Leigh Hunt have testified; his fears that little William, his son by Mary, might also be torn from him by the law, embittered him; the loss of friends, the public opprobrium which followed upon the affair with Mary, the deaths of Harriet and Fanny, and his own health failing, as he believed, day by day, filled him with grief, " withering up his prime." Loss of political dreams, loss of family, love, friends, loss of health and hope, the threatened loss of Mary and the new and greater love: — his little immediate world repeated the evils and anguish of the great world. But, most of all, the tragic mistake shared between Harriet and himself shook the foundations of his mental life.

There was this intense mental agony, from which there seemed no escape: " like an eyeless nightmare grief did sit upon his being." That was one half of him, a half that remained untold, except in the disguise of *Athanase*. The other half of him, also pictured in the poem, was the unresting multitude of thoughts driven tumultuously through his mind, a feverish mental activity alternating, in manic-depression fashion, with " lethargy and inanimation." His reason and his feelings, though in some particulars interfused, as in his theory and practice of marriage, led separate but fevered lives, and, like the Prince, he was always disquieted, shaken with " spasms of silent passion."

> . . . there was an adamantine veil
> Between his heart and mind, — both unrelieved
> Wrought in his brain and bosom separate strife.

His mind was indeed in a state of insurrection and terrible confusion. He saw nothing that might help to lighten the load. It must be borne alone and silently. He felt a solemn duty, to keep the worst of it from Mary. "Let it remain — untold," were the words with which he concluded the description of his hero's agony.

The poem, then, is a veiled confession of agony, of tumults of feeling and reason. Shelley, in a note, says he gave up completing it because he feared he "might be betrayed into the assuming a morbid character." There was in Shelley the moral strength that sometimes accompanies sensitiveness. He fought manfully and successfully against his depression in the heroic days before psycho-analysis made paying patients of us all. But the poem is a prelude to the veiled agony of *Julian and Maddalo*.

Nearly all the major themes of death thus far traced reappear in a new unity in the partly autobiographical poem, *Rosalind and Helen*, a poem of love and death, founded on an experience of one of Mary's friends, but amplified to give a picture of Shelley himself under the guise of the dead lover, Lionel. Lionel, like Shelley and the youth in *Alastor*, had looked forward to an early death, a slow wasting away, like a too early blooming flower that droops in an April frost. Something of the romantic self-pity of *Alastor* intrudes again. Like Laon and Shelley, Lionel was a dreamer of Utopias; like Shelley he was for a while crushed by the failure of his political hopes, which were

> Like the life of youth
> Within him, and when dead became
> A spirit of unresting flame
> Which goaded him in his distress.

That is one of the clearest of Shelley's poetic confessions of his political despair, revealing as it does the emotional intensity of his dreams — "like the life of youth within him."

Shelley's political theories, be it said again, were not to him mere abstract ideas; they were sensations of the nervous system, ideas that were tied into all the privacies of his emotional life.

Next comes the story of Lionel's death. His widow, Helen, tells it. The almost unrelieved grief and melancholy of this first part of the poem again reflects the new contact with reality. The pain of utter despair which the death of a loved one unseals, until agony obliterates even the hope of rest in death, is presented simply and poignantly, as of one

> Walking beneath the night of life,
> Where hours extinguished, like slow rain
> Falling forever, pain by pain,
> The very hope of death's dear rest.

Yet he cannot resist using his old theme of the ugliness of death, the coffin-worm, though he no longer employs it to create a mood of horror. It becomes expressive of the bitter despair with which the living contemplate the physical failure called death; even of the hideousness of life itself that must experience grief and go down to obscenity. Then, after the pessimistic gloom has settled over poet and reader, almost unbearably, there comes that optimistic turn, toward the end of the poem, which one finds so often in Christian elegy, and in so many of Shelley's poems — in *Queen Mab, The Revolt of Islam*, and, finest of all, *Adonais*. It is, once again, the conviction that love dies not with the dead. The very passion of Helen's love for Lionel leads her to feel, like Cythna, that the thing which she loves and finds so beautiful must be eternal:

> And in my soul I dared to say
> Nothing so bright can pass away;
> Death is dark and foul and dull,
> But he is — Oh, how beautiful!

The Pursuit of Death

Once more death is defeated through desire, by the emotion of personal love, by the intensity of the sacrament of the union of two individuals. That sacrament is too exquisite to mean nothing; it is the incandescence in which what all life burns toward, is realized. But from this passionate conviction the thought rises to the serener perception of a universal beauty which includes and answers death. This is the mood of the *Hymn* and *Mont Blanc*. But this serenity is here united with that special intensity which impassions the lyric to Constantia. Lionel, speaking comfort, had said in a kind of revelation:

> Heard'st thou not that those who die
> Awake in a world of ecstasy?
> That love, when limbs are interwoven,
> And sleep, when the night of life is cloven,
> And thought, to the world's dim boundaries clinging,
> And music, when one beloved is singing,
> Is death? Let us drain right joyously
> The cup which the sweet bird fills for me.

All these figures — the intense union of love, the intense vision in dream, the intense abstraction of thought, the intense ecstasy of music — are figures of those uttermost moods of which we are capable, which seem to have a unique and mystical meaning of their own, and which persuade us, at least momentarily, that all beauty is but an anticipation, in comparison dull enough, of the perfect beauty of a reality that encompasses death serenely. " Perchance this were death indeed."

This aesthetic ecstasy in which Lionel dies is a kind of death, i.e., it transcends the common and false antithesis of life and death in a more than ordinary, or mystical, state of awareness, wherein thought clings " to the world's dim boundaries " as it all but escapes those boundaries. This ecstasy is the ' death ' of the misleading antithesis. Hence it is

that, as Shelley himself enters this ecstasy while he is composing *Adonais*, he cries " Die, if thou wouldst be with that
which thou dost seek." Lionel's death, in its mystical con-
summation, is an anticipation of the central theme of *Adonais*.

In *Rosalind and Helen*, moreover, a remarkable link
between the pathetic death of the poet in *Alastor* and the
comfort of death in *Adonais*, is discoverable. Rosalind's description of the place where she wishes to be buried is distinctly reminiscent of the burial of the poet in the former
poem. She wishes her grave may be on some Alp, whose
snowy head is islanded in the azure air (the *Mont Blanc*
theme), for, as her lover had said,

> 'T were sweet
> 'Mid stars and lightnings to abide,
> And winds, and lulling snows that beat
> With their soft flakes the mountain wide . . .

Similarly the leaves of the mountain wilderness had covered
the body of the *Alastor* poet. But the quiet union with nature
thus accomplished in a romantic solitude had carried with it,
even in *Alastor*, some undersong of natural, or even spiritual,
deathlessness. Here the undersong sounds forth more clearly:

> Who knows, if one were buried there,
> But these things might our spirits make,
> Amid the all-surrounding air,
> Their own eternity partake?

Surely the next link in this chain of thought, which with
each link becomes more masterfully conceived and beautifully fashioned, is the famous metamorphosis of the poet in
Adonais:

> He is made one with nature; there is heard
> His voice in all her music, from the moan
> Of thunder to the song of night's sweet bird.

Thus Shelley's poems are continually, not merely echoing
each other, but striking each into each with such an ever

deepening harmony as makes all seem one increasing composition of ever repeated themes.

Rosalind and Helen is one of Shelley's many minor, second or third rate, poems. It largely though not entirely lacks his distinctive race — his special excitement that springs from the union of mystical abstraction and sensuous vividness, as though Brahma should become an impassioned lover, dancing like Siva, or even Kali. It is probably the most pedestrian of any of Shelley's poems of equal or greater length. It seems an exercise faithfully fulfilled for the less intuitive mind of Mary, who asked him to tell the story. But it is a peculiarly interesting poem for the student of Shelley's thought. For in it, for the first time after his contact with tragic reality in his own life, and after the maturing process of composing the long *Islam*, he has united his old book-bred ideas about life in general with his new realization of it through particular personal happenings, in an extended scale of finished composition. And something new has descended upon him: the fructification of ideas by pain, the humanizing of his youthful, inexperienced tragic gloom, the poignancy of realized grief, the quite genuine submersion in sorrow, and then a sincere revulsion to hope and faith.

Such is the result of the alternation of moods and ideas during these four years, 1814–1817; such is the mutual purgation of romantic dream and real experience. Shocked out of the romantic self-pity of *Alastor* by real tragedies, converted in *Islam* from vituperation to sympathy and pity, plunged into despair by the wreck of his hopes, reaching uncertainly toward serenity in the *Hymn* and *Mont Blanc*, stifling his agony in *Athanase*, making a new love into a spiritual dream of personal immortality, manfully re-creating hope and faith out of their own wrecks, Shelley is becoming acquainted with the burden of life — its many kinds of death.

Chapter Four

THE BURDEN OF LIFE AND THE MORAL VICTORY

But, ah, no fairyland is with us now!
But life, how grey and cruel — ah, and death!
(Stephen Phillips, *Pietro of Sienna*)

How a poet conquered a living death is the story now to be unfolded. The story stretches from the *Julian and Maddalo*, through the *Prometheus Unbound* and *The Cenci*, to the *Ode to the West Wind*, taking in lesser poems on the way. Back of the conquest lies one of the most heroic struggles ever maintained, beside which such romantic efforts as those of Amiel, Byron, and the young Goethe appear sentimental journeys. Beside this difficult endeavour, Browning's daily victories are suspiciously eupeptic, Wordsworth's complacent, sequestered faith seems a religious " retreat," and Tennyson's faithful eloquence of a sensitive heart grows all too effeminate. Spenser's sweet dreamery of good and evil is gently distilled into an antique style. Keats moves toward death through a bewitchment of the senses. Rossetti builds a tragically beautiful house out of love's death only. William Morris finds life full of absorbing occupations and has no time to die. George Meredith, by far at his best in his poetry, not too happily exchanges personal immortality for the corporate immortality of the race. James Thomson sang the " restful rapture of the inviolate grave." The young Swinburne, before *Hertha* and *Thalassius*, accepting the tragic significance of defeated ideals, praised death and romanti-

143

cized oblivion; but the maturer Swinburne, by annihilating hope, and fear of death, became free, and found a breathless rapture in contemplating the everlasting drama of change, and at intervals even hymned Brahmanically, or debated hopefully, the " soul within sense." Milton sought to justify an inherited theology, and made death a terror and a punishment. Shakespeare, with the gift of multiple personality, explored in many a tragedy the mind's slavery to passion, evinced, possibly, at times, a despair at the evil in the world and at the power of evil to drag down with it in its fall so much of good; and toward the end of his life went into a retirement where, perhaps, like Prospero, every third thought was of his grave. But Shelley, who never knew a living first-class mind — neither Godwin nor Southey nor Peacock nor Byron nor Leigh Hunt nor Trelawny was such — who drew all his knowledge from books and his own fatal mistakes, who had no person of real wisdom to stand beside him in his dejection and misery, who spent all his practical life in helping men and women who little deserved his philanthropy, who was an outcast from society for certain ideas which he held in advance of his time, most of which have since his death been adopted by society, — this Shelley, frail of body and preternaturally sensitive of spirit, by his own integrity and by the help of the great dead, notably Plato, Sophocles, Dante, and Spinoza, endured a burden of life at least the equal of any the other of these poets and heavier by far than what fell to most of them, passed through its living death, and in the result produced two of the greatest English literary dramas and one of the greatest English odes. All these poems were compounded of his struggle and his victory. Death is a protagonist in each poem.

The Burden of Life and the Moral Victory

I

Julian and Maddalo, with its veiled confession of some deep mental injury, may be regarded as a sort of prelude to *Prometheus Unbound*, though its last revision was subsequent to the completion of the first two acts of the latter poem. Out of the depths of hysterical agony that are revealed dramatically in the ravings of a maniac, arose the great theme of conquered agony in *Prometheus*. Here is the personal, human original of the Titan's godlike misery. That Shelley's own dejection, the abyss of despair into which he was plunged by the failure of his adventure with Harriet, is the reality back of the maniac's mysterious story, is almost certain. The stark suffering with which the poem is convulsed is something more than the grief of a fictitious maniac. Shelley himself, in a letter to Leigh Hunt, said that the madman was " in some degree a painting from nature, but, with respect to time and place, ideal "; and he once referred to the poem as among " his saddest verses." But in prying into the matter-of-fact causes of the suffering that has been idealized here, we are not interested. The state of mind that is unfolded is sufficiently typical to make the particularizing of its causes otiose. The more important question is not how some one person got into this state, but how anyone may get out of it. We are concerned, then, to realize that this poem is a study of an intensely personal yet representative agony and of the means of mitigating that agony, to point out the relation of this personal agony to the vicarious suffering of Prometheus, and to remark the conjunction of this personal agony with madness and death.

A conversation on the general subject of human suffering and death leads up to the specific case of the madman. Maddalo, who is Byron, points out the dreary, windowless madhouse, and an open belfry on the top of it. With desperate cynicism he compares the tolling of the bell, which calls the maniacs to prayer, to the soul, " hung in a heaven-illumined tower," summoning our thoughts and desires to worship amid our rent and baffled hearts, until, in the end, death destroys all, memory and everything. Our misery is expended for nothingness. Man is a weakling, doomed to long torture, and then to black extinction. Shelley, appropriately called Julian, after the great apostate emperor, replies that man need not be a passive sufferer. Let him educate his will (in *Mab* he would have said his ' motives ') and be free of evil:

> It is our will
> That thus enchains us to permitted ill.
> We might be otherwise; we might be all
> We dream of happy, high, majestical.
> Where is the love, beauty and truth we seek,
> But in our mind? And if we were not weak,
> Should we be less in deed than in desire?

This is the way to relieve us from the tragic sense of life: by strong self-control to realize in the one proper place, viz., one's own mind, that love and truth and beauty which we all seek. Only so can man be free — free of grief, but not (be it added) of death.

Now this little passage, which repeats an idea we have already found in *The Revolt of Islam* and in the *Essay on Christianity*, is in turn the first draft of the great passage at the close of the *Prometheus*, soon to be quoted, which sums up the methods by which everyman, like the Titan himself, may disentangle the doom of suffering and unbind himself from evil and agony. " These are the spells," as Shelley puts it in the greater poem, " by which to reassume an empire o'er the disentangled doom." This conversation, then, which stresses first the evil of life and its culmination in annihilation of the sufferer, and then the splendid mitigation through self-culture, is a *précis* of *Prometheus Unbound*. Moreover, Maddalo's retort brings us yet nearer to that Utopian poem, for he cries out, " You talk Utopia." And Julian, using the very metaphor of the Utopian title, answers hopefully:

> It remains to know,
> . . . and those who try may find
> *How strong the chains are which our spirit bind.*

The rest of Julian's speech is a direct transition to the theme of personal agony. Whatever the individual's suffering may be, he continues, " much may be conquered, much endured "; and the striving to achieve this self-control is " something nobler than to live and die ":

> So taught those kings of old philosophy,
> Who reigned before religion made men blind;
> And those who suffer with their suffering kind
> Yet feel this faith religion.

" Fine words," replies Maddalo; " Lucretian words," he might have added. " As words go they may be made refutation-tight. But only a short while ago I had this same argument with another like you. He has now gone mad. That is the answer. Such aspiring theories are all in vain." Julian holds his point. It was only some want in that unhappy man of the true theory of a " soul of goodness in all things ill," that broke him. Or, Julian again surmises, he may be one of those who, patient in everything else, yet demand " to love and be loved in gentleness " —

> And being scorned, *what wonder if they die*
> *Some living death?*

The living death of one hurt to the soul by one beloved! Yet even that agony is not destiny, " but man's own wilful ill." Such is Shelley's sthenic faith, his own medicament of his own despair and living death.

So they visit this madman whose woes point the argument. The ravings begin like a minor *Prometheus:*

" Month after month," he cried, " to bear this load,
And, as a jade urged by the whip and goad,
To drag life on — which like a heavy chain
Lengthens behind with many a length of pain! "

And, as in the first act of the greater *Prometheus*, there is a
continual refrain of " Pain, Pain." But the ravings are not un-
meaning. All is clear enough. One who is preternaturally
sensitive, having hoped too much of love, has been scorned
by a beloved who had made mere pretence of love, then had
taken lightly the loveless embrace, had referred to it coarsely,
and so had come to loathe their love. It were cruel, indeed,
cries the sufferer, to punish even *cruelty* by making its love
the instrument of the torture —

But *me*, whose heart a stranger's tear might wear
As water-drops the sandy fountain-stone,
Who loved and pitied all things, and could moan
For woes which others hear not, and could see
The absent with the glance of fantasy,
And with the poor and trampled sit and weep,
Following the captive to his dungeon deep;
Me — who am as a nerve o'er which do creep
The else unfelt oppressions of this earth,
And was to thee the flame upon thy hearth,
When all beside was cold: — that thou on me
Shouldst rain these plagues of blistering agony!
Such curses are from lips once eloquent
With love's too partial praises! Let none relent
Who intend deeds too dreadful for a name
Henceforth, if an example for the same
They seek: — for thou on me look'dst so, and so —
And didst speak thus — and thus. I live to show
How much men bear and die not!

He endures a life of envenomed agony. His madness, indeed,
is no more than a metaphor for the intensity of his suffering.
In truth he is not mad, but great-minded. He is too mag-

nanimous to sink his intelligence in hatred. That the woman may "have less bitter cause to grieve," he even disappoints his craving for death, the peace-giver. For he has forgiven darkest wrongs, and would intend not even the slightest harm to the one who has humbled him.

But we must pass over the shocking eloquence of this deep despair, not pausing even to note a most extraordinary fantasy (ll. 383–397) of his meeting his dead bride, at the grave's call, in a ghastly wedding dance — clearly a remaking of those few sad lines on Harriet's death that have been noted above. Instead, the emphasis must be placed upon the victim's faithfulness to his highest dreams of good; for, out of the misery and the longing for death, rises an unbent will, like Prometheus's own; an untamed determination to pursue the good and the beautiful forever, at whatever cost:

> Believe that I am ever still the same
> In creed as in resolve; and what may tame
> My heart must leave the understanding free,
> Or all would sink in this keen agony;
> Nor dream that I will join the vulgar cry;
> Or with my silence sanction tyranny;
> Or seek a moment's shelter from my pain
> In any madness which the world calls gain,
> Ambition or revenge or thoughts as stern
> As those which make me what I am; or turn
> To avarice or misanthropy or lust.

This ethical self-dedication is an example of the very fortitude in which Julian finds a mitigation of evil. And the so-called madman avers that it is the only way out from his agony, for if the disaster that broke his heart had also shattered his reasoned faith in a spiritual universe, everything for him would have been lost. His metaphysics, therefore, converges on this ethical ideal. Maddalo's pessimism and cynicism for him would be a surrender of mental integrity — a failure to "think through" his emotional crisis.

149

The Pursuit of Death

One is reminded of J. R. Green's analysis of Virgil's piety:

> An inscrutable mystery hangs around the order of the world. Men of harder, colder temper shrug their shoulders and like Augustus repeat their " *vanitas vanitatum* " with a smile of contempt at the fools who take life in earnest. Nobler and more sensitive souls like that of Virgil carry about with them " the pity of it." . . . Even with death and ruin around him, and the mystery of the world darkening his soul, man remains man and master of his fate.

But both the madman and Julian, while rejecting contempt, accomplish more than pity. They outface fate and death with determination. Death and heroism are great antagonists.

However, the death which Byron hated is the reward of the madman's fortitude. At some time subsequent to the visit of Julian and Maddalo, the shallow-minded, indelible woman saw her victim again. There was no erasure of her enmity or of his grief. Then the sufferer — determination and all — was snuffed out by death, his only peace. And this mortal release makes the contrast between his agony and the vicarious suffering of Prometheus, the contrast of death and the grave's peace with life and victory. Perhaps, therefore, we had better call *Julian and Maddalo*, not a personal prelude to *Prometheus*, but an interlude of agony and failure and courage and death. Nevertheless, out of this fatal agony was born that living victory.

The madman's story, then, shot through with the longing for death, ends in the peace of death. Two lyrics, written at Naples toward the close of 1818, in the interval of composing the first and second acts of *Prometheus*, further reveal Shelley's longing for death at this dark period. They, like the ravings, are the speech of a soul in despair, however matter-of-fact may have been modified as it was changed into poetry. The *dolores vitae* were overwhelming him. In the *Stanzas Written in Dejection* the tale is tallied:

The Burden of Life and the Moral Victory

Alas! I have nor hope nor health,
  Nor peace within nor calm around,
Nor that content surpassing wealth
  The sage in meditation found,
  And walked with inward glory crowned —
Nor fame, nor power, nor love, nor leisure.
  Others I see whom these surround —
Smiling they live, and call life pleasure; —
To me the cup has been dealt in another measure.

Let us itemize the salient phrases of this tale, at the cost of repeating the schedule of his sorrows. *Nor hope:* at times it seemed to him that he was hunted by calamity. The suicides of Harriet and Fanny, the loss of his children by Harriet, the turning of family and friends against him, his public reputation as a moral pariah, the death of his little daughter, Clara, in September of this year, a host of minor difficulties, financial and other, the constant worry about Claire and Allegra, some mysterious affair at Naples, concluding seemingly in the death of an English woman who was infatuated with him — all these events tortured his memory. It is little wonder that, as he wrote sometime later, it seemed to him as if the destruction that was consuming him was as an " atmosphere which wrapt and infected " everything connected with him. *Nor health:* he had come to Italy for his health, he was continually subjected to intense physical pain and overwhelming lassitude, and at Naples he had suffered particularly through the egregious blundering of a physician. *Nor peace:* in the midst of all these wearing memories and ever-recurring problems, he had been cautioned to avoid even the comfort of composition, and not even the translating of the *Symposium* had restored the tranquillity of mind he had praised in the *Hymn. Nor fame:* his published works were neglected — for example, the public indifference to *Alastor;* or bigotedly rejected — for example, the *Quarterly Review* criticism of *The Revolt of Islam,* by John Taylor Coleridge, who vili-

151

fied the author and pronounced the work a " laboriously obscene " farrago of lawlessness, atheism, and immorality. *Nor power:* his hopes of bettering society had ended in failure, both his practical attempts, and his endeavours in his poetry to awaken men from " the trance of ordinary life " and stimulate them to a noble rivalry in working for moral progress. On every side he saw the vast accumulation of stupid, selfish opinions and institutions, against which virtue itself seemed powerless. Typical, for example, was that scene he witnessed the following spring in the great square before St. Peter's, which he described thus in a letter (April 6, 1819) to Peacock:

> In the Square of St. Peter's there are about 300 fettered criminals at work. . . . Their legs are heavily ironed, and some are chained two by two. They sit in long rows, hoeing out the weeds, dressed in party coloured clothes. Near them sit or saunter, groups of soldiers, armed with loaded muskets. The iron discord of those innumerable chains clanks up into the sonorous air, and produces, contrasted with the musical dashing of the fountains, and the deep azure beauty of the sky, and the magnificence of the architecture around, a conflict of sensations allied to madness. It is the emblem of Italy: moral degradation contrasted with the glory of nature and the arts.

If this be an example of Shelley's excess of " unbalanced sensibility," one nevertheless is at no loss to sympathize with the despair with which a mind nurtured on the great humanitarian teachings of the past beheld this human degradation in the very courtyard of Christ's capital temple. *Nor love:* it was a time of loneliness for Mary and Shelley, for friends were few, especially at Naples. Then, too, there was his feeling that he ought to keep Mary in ignorance of his despondency, so far as possible. She curiously united, as Dowden has observed, to something of her father's desire for temperance of emotion a habit of looking " over-intensely at the dark side of human things " (Leigh Hunt's words, in a letter addressed to her); so there was good reason for guarding her peace of mind. Much as she had always aided him to overcome his gloom, at this time, apparently, he suffered alone, preserving for her sake an appearance of cheerfulness. Later she came to realize a part, at least, of what he had kept from her:

> Many hours were passed when his thoughts, shadowed by illness, were gloomy; and then he escaped to solitude, and in verses, which he hid from fear of wounding me, poured forth morbid, but too natural bursts of discontent and sadness. One looks back with unspeakable regret and gnawing remorse to such periods; fancying that, had we been more alive to the nature of his feelings, and more attentive to soothe them, such would not have existed.

Thus, dying daily, as it were, he suffered an accumulation of tortures that must have been like that " cloud of winged snakes " with which the mind of Prometheus was tormented. " It would be difficult," wrote Professor Hotson, after discovering Shelley's lost letters to Harriet, " to find in all history a mind so sensitive, loving, and generous, which had its best efforts more cruelly beaten by disappointment and disillusion."

In the *Invocation to Misery*, the second of the two lyrics mentioned above, his grief is poetized into a marriage with misery underneath the grave — a figure that recalls the bridal-night in *Julian and Maddalo*; while, once again, too, we remember those sad lines to Fanny in which the world was accounted all too wide for misery. Truly Shelley, as he himself intimated, has become too adept in depicting sadness. The poem, which has some slight, superficial resemblance to " Come away, come away, death," is in an intense, rather than reflective, mood, vibrant with a kind of desperate welcome of desolation, as though he were bound once for all to cast away all hope by identifying himself irretrievably with pain and death, until annihilation should blot out all the sorry scene. Does it not read like a lyric epilogue to the maniac's monologue in *Julian and Maddalo?*

Misery! we have known each other,
Like a sister and a brother
Living in the same lone home,
Many years — we must live some
Hours or ages yet to come . . .

Hasten to the bridal —
Underneath the grave 'tis spread:
In darkness may our love be hid,
Oblivion be our coverlid —
We may rest, and none forbid.

Clasp me, till our hearts be grown
Like two shadows into one;
Till this dreadful transport may
Like a vapour fade away
In the sleep that lasts alway.

This longing to bury misery in oblivion was a frequent theme in the juvenilia: one recalls the ranting cries of misery in *The Wandering Jew*, the fierce and deadly agony in *To a Scene of Former Times*, the fiends of despair in *A Dialogue;* and in one of the early *Fragments* there is a maniac who seeks slumber in the grave of the loved one. Out of such ranting, real suffering has at last made true poetry.

But in the former lyric, *Stanzas Written in Dejection*, there is a more reflective spirit, or perhaps a deep lassitude — a dull, relaxing, hopeless dejection, and a quiet dreaming away into death:

Yet now despair itself is mild,
    Even as the winds and waters are;
I could lie down like a tired child,
    And weep away the life of care

The Burden of Life and the Moral Victory

Which I have borne and yet must bear,
Till death like sleep might steal on me,
And I might feel in the warm air
My cheek grow cold, and hear the sea
Breathe o'er my dying brain its last monotony.

These lines are in the later vein of Keats, for they are the tired utterance of one who would escape pain in oblivion. Courage is at its nadir. Much of the effectiveness of the poem results from the contrast of the beauty of nature and the woe of a human heart, and from that association of death and sleep beloved of all human hearts and so often recurring in Shelley's earlier as well as later poems, including *Queen Mab* and *Alastor*. Here, too, is the desire, strangely casting forward to his own fate, to meet lone death on the ocean's waste, to "hear the sea breathe o'er my dying brain its last monotony." In *Alastor*, also, the poet longs to die at sea; and in *The Wandering Jew* Victorio seeks friendly death in a watery grave.

What remains to be done? There is nothing, he answers, in the second and last sonnet of this year. All has been vanity. Why lift again the "painted veil called Life" (cf. the poem *Death*, written in 1816), with all its unreal shapes which only mimic the ineptitudes we endeavour to believe? Behind it, he moans, are only Fear and Hope, weaving their vain but cruel shadows. Then, turning to a sad self-portraiture that recalls lines in *Alastor* and *Prince Athanase*, but very definitely anticipates the memorable portrait in *Adonais*, he cries:

I knew one who had lifted it [the veil] — he sought,
For his lost heart was tender, things to love,
But found them not, alas! nor was there aught
The world contains the which he could approve.
Through the unheeding many he did move,
A splendour among shadows, a bright blot
Upon this gloomy scene, a Spirit that strove
For truth, and like the Preacher found it not.

Here is intellectual surrender — far worse than death. He had written in much the same mood his impressions of the English burial ground at Rome, where later his own ashes were to find forgetfulness. The place seemed very beautiful to him, with the sun shining on bright grass fresh with autumnal dew, the wind whispering in the trees above the pyramid of Cestius and the quiet tombs of those, mostly women and young people, who were buried there. " One might, if one were to die, desire the sleep they seem to sleep. Such is the human mind, *and so it peoples with its wishes vacancy and oblivion.*" But these surrenders were only " passing spasms " of the Titan who was Shelley. The *Prometheus* ends otherwise.

So also does that miniature of the *Prometheus*, the *Lines Written Among the Euganean Hills*, another poem that belongs to the interval between the first two acts of the drama. Written in deep despondency, with yet other veiled references to personal misfortune, and ringing once again the changes on tyranny and death, it is concluded by a brief picture of a perfected life, which reaches back to the last part of *Queen Mab* and forward to the last act of *Prometheus*.

To the nobler moods of *Prometheus Unbound* we may now turn, which towers splendidly above the lower but related poems of its period — the *Rosalind and Helen*, *Prince Athanase*, the *Julian and Maddalo*, the *Euganean Lines*, the *Invocation to Misery*, the *Stanzas Written in Dejection*, and some others to be noted. These poems of depression, clustering about the *Prometheus*, give, then, some idea of the deep spiritual gloom out of which Shelley courageously reared his greatest single poem and greatest single ethical appeal. It is his own splendid and unaided answer as well to his own misery, as to the misery of mankind. The answer is an exhortation undauntedly to conduct the inner life of the spirit nobly. Its text we have already found in *Julian and Maddalo*:

The Burden of Life and the Moral Victory

It is our will
That thus enchains us to permitted ill.
We might be otherwise; we might be all
We dream of happy, high, majestical.
Where is the love, beauty and truth we seek,
But in our mind?

II

In very fact, *Prometheus Unbound* is a great poem of self-culture; but this self-culture is dramatically conceived, and — unintentionally — disguised, as a regeneration of society.

The poem comes straight from Shelley's own experiences. Prometheus dreamed of a better world, attempted to aid men to realize it, encountered vested selfishness, bigotry, tyranny, suffered in persecution and failure, and became acquainted with pain that seemed well-nigh infinite — as Shelley had; was a rebel, and cursed tyranny — as Shelley had in *Queen Mab;* persisted in his faith in man and in ultimate social regeneration — as Shelley had in *The Revolt of Islam;* knew love and its idealism — as Shelley had; and longed for his feminine other-self, Asia — as the poet in *Alastor* had. High hopes, vivid objurgation; piercing sensitiveness to the sufferings of men; worship of justice, hatred of injustice; disappointment and dejection, but persistence in faith: all this, the story of the binding of Shelley, as of Prometheus, is told in the poem. But there is an even more important connection. The poem opens with Prometheus suffering his doom, to the repeated refrain,

Ah me! Alas, pain, pain ever, forever!

But it proceeds to the unbinding of the Titan, his loosening from dejection and pain, when he learns, at long last,

. . . the spells by which to reassume
An empire o'er the disentangled doom.

157

These spells were the projection, into dramatic and symbolic form, of the next great moment in Shelley's self-culture: his own moral victory over failure, pain, and despair.

That the personal story took the form of a social evangel was no accident, for, we have remarked, Shelley's inmost spiritual history was a history of ideas about society, and of premature attempts to realize these ideas in action, until his whole theatre was " beguiled to death." The gospel for society and the tragedy of the evangelist were inseparably linked, for Shelley saw the social implications of all his personal experiences. He saw himself as a specimen of human nature. Thus it is with the poet, with one who lives the intellectual life ardently. It was inevitable that Shelley should eventually make a synthesis of his own experience in a great world-theme. In Prometheus, at last he found an adequate theme, in which he could unite social breadth of meaning with personal intensity of feeling.

It was a dramatic theme that could carry all his extreme idealism, and suit, nay, demand, his extremest power in sublimity of phrase and image. Hitherto his characters, especially in the long poems, had not been conceived with a grandeur adequate to his style, so that repeatedly there was an effect of tumidity. But in Prometheus he found a figure so elevated by popular tradition and former poetic treatment, that no splendour of phrase could seem inappropriate; and so peculiarly suited to his own experiences and temperament, that it inevitably called forth his greatest poetic genius. Moreover, Shelley's impulse to identify himself with society, hitherto too romantic and self-conscious to escape an effect of sentimentality, had now been wrought, as the result of intensity of real suffering, to a truly dramatic, re-presentative power. The dramatic manner, therefore, was no more an accident than the significant social form which his personal experiences assumed.

But a first reading of the poem does not always set the

reader in the right way for discovering this intricate implication of the personal and the social. Lamb, believing no one
was ever the wiser or better for reading Shelley, and that
his poetry was "thin sown with profit and delight," found
Prometheus Unbound just a capital story — which surely it is
not — and nothing else. A story that does not keep one's un-
flagging interest until the end is hardly "capital." How many
readers finish the fourth act of *Prometheus?* Arnold, less
mischief-loving than Lamb, nevertheless agrees that Shelley's
poetry "avails nothing, effects nothing" — and proceeds,
therefore, to angelicize him; though in all fairness to the
apostle of culture one must quote the limiting adjectives: "a
beautiful and ineffectual angel beating in the void his luminous wings in vain." A conclusion almost in the old *Quarterly
Review* style! Arnold surely read at least some of Shelley
more than once. But I prefer to suspect he dared the length of
Prometheus only once.

If the poem is really a dramatic projection of Shelley's
experience, it must bring to a focus his old utterances concerning death, since death has ever been a major-theme in his
thought. Often and variously as he has wrestled with this
theme, his responses have not yet vitally cohered. Thus far
he has reached only a momentary or conditional, not a final,
triumph over its ugliness. How near to that durable triumph,
or, at least, to a reconciliation with death, does he come in
this, his greatest single poem?

Three of his familiar death-motifs open the first Act: the
murderous tyrant, the all-enduring martyr, the extinction of
the tyrant. Toward the beginning, death is lightly associated
with them. But as the Act unfolds, and the story of evil and
hate progresses, while the emotions grow intense and complicated, death darkens the scene more and more, and dominates the climax; then plays a tragic part in the great unbinding of the spirit through repentance, renewed temptation,
and resistance; then a saddened under part to the winning

of wisdom from misery; and finally is almost lost sight of, though not completely, in the compensatory closing moods of love and hope.

This is the thought of the first Act, in the abstract. Let us turn to concrete details. The Caucasus mountains are represented as rising to a great height, shouldering their way into the heavens. From their crawling glaciers, the vast, dun plains below and the ever-changing sea are visible. The environment is Aeschylean, elemental: the eternal snow and ice, the night, starry and slow, the leaden-coloured east, the hoar-frost of daybreak, the burning cold; again, whirlwinds, storm-filled abysses, earthquake, and endless hail. In such scenes the mind, often to its own amazement, expands marvellously to meet its surroundings. Prometheus himself is such an expansion of the mind — an expansion, on the grand scale, of the mental travail of the idealist and martyr. Nailed in misery to these eagle-baffling mountains, the martyr-Titan utters his soliloquy, itself elemental and vast and stormy, like his outlook: a splendid summation of rebellion against evil, of courageous failure, endless suffering, and infinite defiance. Two alone, Jupiter, the murderous tyrant, the archdoer of evil, and Prometheus, the divine sufferer, the dreamer of good, behold sleeplessly the rolling worlds, where slaves for their hecatombs of broken hearts are requited by the tyrant " with fear and self-contempt and barren hope." But over misery Prometheus perforce has triumphed. Torture and solitude, scorn and despair, have become his empire. Each word — torture and solitude, scorn and despair — like nearly every word in the soliloquy — refers straight to Shelley's bitter days, from the alienation of Harriet to the exile; and Prometheus's victory over defeat is his own success in building up, out of the failure of his own life and service, a will further to live and further to serve.

Through this dithyramb of tyranny and martyrdom run dominating chords of defiance, hatred, and disdain. Then, even as the lagging ruin and death of the tyrant are exultantly prophesied, another note comes forth suddenly, *de profundis:*

> Disdain! Ah no! I pity thee [the tyrant] . . .
> . . . for I hate no more,
> As then ere misery made me wise.

This pity, born in the depths of misery, marks the beginning of the end of Prometheus's pain, for when love or pity takes the place of hatred the worst of pain is over. So long as against the oppressor the oppressed wish to use the destructive instruments of hatred, they themselves are caught painfully in the wide-spread net of destruction. This truth had been Shelley's explanation of the failure of the French Revolution. But when the higher principle, "Love thine enemies," is actively realized, the way out from the net has been found. Incidentally, one may remark the appropriateness of the fact that again and again the teaching of the poem can be epitomized in some well-known phrase from the Gospels; for even as the Gospels represent the triumph of a spirit of love over the fierce jealousies of the Old Testament, so Shelley's *Prometheus* is his own new testament of the power of love to vanquish tyranny and misery. But before he himself could see this phase of what men sometimes call God, he had to be cast down and become " poor in spirit." A similar experience may lie back of the epitaph Epictetus is famed to have composed for himself: " I was Epictetus, a slave, and maimed in body, and a beggar for poverty, and dear to the immortals." Only in suffering is freedom to be found, for it destroys egotism. That is the sudden note of glory *de profundis,* known to many sufferers, to Oscar Wilde not least nor first nor last. To Prometheus it sounds, indeed, the beginning of the end of his travail of spirit.

The next step toward that end is repentance of violence.

Prometheus recalls the curse he had levelled against tyranny in the young days of his bitterness. That dread curse had riven the world with fear, and darkness had then stood over the living day like blood, while the tongueless caverns of the mountains, the emptiness of heaven, the ocean waves and pale nations, had endlessly repeated a refrain of " Misery, Misery." Violence breeds misery; hate, death! Now death, indeed, begins to darken the mood of the poem. The misery of violence is known to all things that die, and their whispers are awful with the terrible curse. But Prometheus, as a deathless spirit, cannot understand their language. Yet he would hear the curse. The melancholy Earth-Spirit remembers the flood of evil over the world when Prometheus was chained, and recalls the joy of the inarticulate dead at the mighty curse, which they have hopefully treasured through the ages, even as men have always looked for vengeance on their oppressors. In the world of dreariness vengeance is darkly treasured. Then a way is found to rehearse the curse. Beneath the grave lie the shadows of all things that be. There they inhabit until death unites their living forms with them, no more to be parted. It is the unfathomable world of Demogorgon, the tremendous gloom beyond and underneath the utmost reach of the mind. From this reverse, or hidden source, of consciousness a shade may be summoned to utter the curse. By this device the revenge of Jupiter upon him who voices the curse can sweep through the land of shadows only, " like a rainy wind through the abandoned gate of a fallen palace." Prometheus summons the phantasm of Jupiter himself, so that the evil words may not pass again the lips of anything good. The spirit of tyranny appears, to the accompaniment of destructive forces of nature: Shelley's utmost picture of political evil.

> The sound is of whirlwind underground,
>   Earthquake, and fire, and mountains cloven;
> The shape is awful, like the sound,
>   Clothed in dark purple, star-inwoven.

The Burden of Life and the Moral Victory

A sceptre of pale gold,
    To stay steps proud, o'er the slow cloud,
His veinèd hand doth hold.
Cruel he looks, but calm and strong,
Like one who does, not suffers wrong.

We have come a long, but discernible, way from the villains of *Zastrozzi!* And certainly the God anathematized in *Mab* and in the original draft of *Islam* has become this Jupiter. He is the god of ignorant superstition, whom Voltaire had in mind when he ejaculated " God created man in his own image and man returns the compliment "; of whom Stendhal said " God's only excuse is that he does not exist "; whom Nietzsche objurgated — " What has been the greatest objection to life hitherto? God! " Or one may reverse the criticism thus, with Ingersoll: " An honest God is the noblest work of man." He is the God whom Asia (Act II., Sc. iv.) denounces as the creator of hell and of " the sharp fear of hell ": repeatedly in the poems and prose works the cruelty of hell is taken as the symbol of this god's all too human ferocity. He is the god Victor Hugo and Mazzini and, it might be added, Christ himself, attacked. In this indictment the pure in heart of all ages unite; and Shelley, who of course took a somewhat perverse and thoroughly ironic delight in being called an atheist for such religious idealism, has given us in this picture of Jupiter his simplest, fiercest, most controlled and most impressive rendering of the indictment. Swinburne has said much the same thing in prose, in his *Dedicatory Epistle*, viz.,

. . . that the spirit and the letter of all other than savage and barbarous religions are irreconcilably at variance, and that prayer or homage addressed to an image of our own or of other men's making, be that image avowedly material or conventionally spiritual, is the affirmation of idolatry in all its attendant atrocities, and the negation of all belief, all reverence, and all love, due to the noblest object of human worship that humanity can realize or conceive.

And now this god speaks. While all dead and mortal things eagerly listen, the tremendous shade repeats the defiant curse of envenomed agony, filled with bitter reference to ghastly suffering, frenzied fear, and furious death. The curse was a curse of death, a climax of hatred, a symbol of the mind's tragic error in lending itself to brutish violence.

But Prometheus, listening in horror to his own words, cries out, at the end,

> It doth *repent* me; words are quick and vain;
> Grief for a while is blind, and so was mine.
> I wish no living thing to suffer pain.

Thus repentance — the next stage of his unbinding — is accomplished: another piece of transmuted autobiography.

But the Earth-Spirit, misunderstanding this repentance as surrender, in despair calls upon the living and the dead to bemoan the failure of their champion, who lies fallen and vanquished. " Fallen and vanquished! " cry the echoes the world around. Very true to life is this littleness of knowledge, faith, and vision in the followers of a leader. The populace, bound to attribute infallibility to the hero, cannot permit him to grow in grace and wisdom. How effective, too, after the clear utterance of self-conquest, is this querulous cry of the earth and the echoes. With such misunderstandings the helper of men must always reckon.

Two temptations of the idealist, and his rejection of them, complete the unbinding. The temptations are drawn from tragic suffering. Mercury, the messenger golden-sandalled, purple-plumed, approaches through the azure chasm of a snowy hill, attended by crowds of tempest-walking Furies glutted with the groans and blood of the thin dead. The hope of torturing the Titan excites these obscenities, as the reek of corpses stirs death-birds after a battle. They rush upon him avidly. But the beautiful god restrains them until he has delivered Jupiter's message, which involves the first temptation. It is the characteristic temptation that both mightily and insidiously, with promise of beauty, comes to the idealist when, having lost his urgent hatred of the enemy, he sees himself face to face with the furious vengeance of malice: viz., to compromise, and thus achieve peace. It is the temptation of the noble. Mercury, prophesying the vanity of struggle, announcing the unimagined pains yet to be incurred, bids him sue for peace:

> . . . bend thy soul in prayer,
> And like a suppliant in some gorgeous fane,
> Let the will kneel within thy haughty heart,
> For benefits and meek submission tame
> The fiercest and the mightiest.

The answer of Prometheus is that strong, stoical acceptance of suffering with which each Utopian ekes out his aeons of waiting for the ever-postponed City of his dreams. His suffering, Prometheus knows, must last while Jove reigns: " no more, nor less do I desire or fear."

But what may be called a class-conception of good and evil — the governed being naturally good, all governors inevitably becoming evil — lies back of this stoicism. The issue, the defeat of the evil doers and the triumph of perfection, lies far off in time. Preferable, perhaps, is the individualistic conception of the war, that good and evil contend in each being for the mastery, in a constant, ever-renewed struggle for individual self-control. The warfare is within one. The kingdom is within one. Salvation is individual, both momentary and continual, rather than social and remote. Such salvation was what Shelley was in reality experiencing, after the madness of *Julian and Maddalo;* but still he must unwittingly disguise it in large social terms, making out of what is a personal reality a social mirage.

Thus repulsed, the beautiful messenger of compromise " with wingèd feet runs down the slanted sunlight of the dawn," leaving the sufferer to the foul Furies, ministers of pain and fear and hate and clinging crime, who " track all things that weep, and bleed, and live." The first temptation sprang from the extreme suffering of the Titan himself; that now brought by the Furies springs from the tragic suffering and death of others. The Furies come upon him fresh from their feasting in the red gulfs of war, in famine-wasted cities, in ships wrecked in mid-ocean; from their delight in the maniac dreamer's wretched threats of Hell, in the furious tyrant's conclave " where blood with gold is bought and sold "; from their delight in nurturing

> . . . the self-contempt implanted
> In young spirits, sense-enchanted,
> Misery's yet unkindled fuel.

Before the tortured eyes of the great martyr they unfold, in ever darker climax, visions of supreme suffering. First, the Christ. Had Prometheus flattered himself with joy for the clear knowledge he had given man? With that gift went a fierce thirst — hope, love, doubt, desire, which consume men forever — quite outrunning the perishing waters of knowledge. Then,

> One [the Christ] came forth of gentle worth,
> Smiling on the sanguine earth;
> His words outlived him, like swift poison
> Withering up truth, peace, and pity.
> Look! where round the wide horizon
> Many a million-peopled city
> Vomits smoke in the bright air!

The Burden of Life and the Moral Victory

> Mark that outcry of despair!
> 'T is his mild and gentle ghost
>   Wailing for the faith he kindled.*

Second, the French Revolution:

> See! a disenchanted nation
> Springs like day from desolation;
> To Truth its state is dedicate,
> And Freedom leads it forth, her mate;
> A legioned bank of linkèd brothers,
> Whom Love calls children —
>   'T is another's.
> See how kindred murder kin!
> 'T is the vintage-time for Death and Sin;
> Blood, like new wine, bubbles within;
>   Till Despair smothers
> The struggling world, which slaves and tyrants win.

These failures and tragic deaths, endlessly accumulating, promote the great doubt-temptation of the altruist: the doubt

---

* It is interesting to read beside this poetic account of the 'wailing Christ' (so different from the attack on Christology in *Queen Mab*, VII) the previous prose-study of the theme in Shelley's *Essay on Christianity* (1817?): "Jesus Christ opposed with earnest eloquence the panic fears and hateful superstitions which have enslaved mankind for ages. Nations had risen against nations, employing the subtlest devices of mechanism and mind to waste, and excruciate, and overthrow. The great community of mankind had been subdivided into ten thousand communities each organized for the ruin of the other. Wheel within wheel, the vast machine was instinct with the restless spirit of desolation. Pain has been inflicted; therefore, pain should be inflicted in return. Retaliation is the only remedy which can be applied to violence, because it teaches the injurer the true nature of his own conduct, and operates as a warning against its repetition. Nor must the same measure of calamity be returned as was received. If a man borrows a certain sum from me, he is bound to repay that sum. Shall no more be required of the enemy who destroys my reputation, or ravages my fields? It is just that he should suffer ten times the loss which he has inflicted, that the legitimate consequences of his deed may never be obliterated from his remembrance, and that others may clearly discern and feel the danger of invading the peace of human society. Such reasonings, and the impetuous feelings arising from them, have armed nation against nation, family against family, man against man." There is a remarkable parallel in Swinburne's *On the Persecution of the Jews*.

of the pre-eminence of righteousness and the efficacy of evangelism; for devotion to the Truth seems merely to provoke misery, not only for one's self, but for mankind. Great hopes " beguiled to death," indeed! More transmuted autobiography!

> Behold an emblem: those who do endure
> Deep wrongs for man, and scorn, and chains, but heap
> Thousand-fold torment on themselves and him.

So cries the Fury; and Prometheus, visioning the tortured deaths of the Christ's followers, groans aloud. But the catalogue of agonies mounts yet higher, to a picture of the inextricable confusion of good in evil the world over, the dead weight of that fact, mountainous, seemingly immovable, unchangeable — fear ever surmounting it all.

> Worse! In each human heart terror survives
> The ruin it has gorged: the loftiest fear
> All that they would disdain to think were true.
> Hypocrisy and custom make their minds
> The fanes of many a worship, now outworn.
> They dare not devise good for man's estate,
> And yet they know not that they do not dare.
> The good want power, but to weep barren tears.
> The powerful goodness want; worse need for them.
> The wise want love; and those who love want wisdom;
> And all best things are thus confused to ill.
> Many are strong and rich, and would be just,
> But live among their suffering fellow-men
> As if none felt; they know not what they do.

Here are the ultimate causes of dejection, the temptations to despair, for the idealist who labours in the class-conception of good and evil: Shelley's experience generalized — each sentence reminiscent of his hopes and failures. Yet the whole passage is instinct with a latent, almost audible, individualistic conception; for this intricate confusion of good and evil unto death is the very crucible of each and every human being, and the very dayspring of ethics, of the struggle to lead a good life. But the Utopian dream again disguises this liberating and stimulating truth. However, Prometheus's reply to the Furies puts into two brief but entirely adequate lines the agony of Shelley's own dejection and the courageous patience by which he overcame despair:

> *Thy words are like a cloud of wingèd snakes;*
> *And yet I pity those they torture not.*

Those lines are in epitome the inner life of Shelley at this time: the first plunges us into vivid realization of what he suffered; the second reveals his present way out, the way of pity and love. To pity for those whom he had hated has been added repentance of the hatred itself, and now, finally, pity for human insensibility. This is the last spell by which both he and Prometheus reassume " an empire o'er the disentangled doom." " Thou pitiest them? " cries the Fury, and vanishes.

The unbinding is spiritually, though not yet materially, complete. But the refrain remains one of pain and death, though grief is muted to sadness and endurance:

> Ah woe!
> Ah woe! Alas! pain, pain ever, forever!
> . . . Peace is in the grave.
> The grave hides all things beautiful and good.
> I am a God and cannot find it there,
> Nor would I seek it; for, though dread revenge,
> This is defeat, fierce king, not victory.
> The sights with which thou torturest gird my soul
> With new endurance, till the hour arrives
> When they shall be no types of things which are.

This is the philosophy of defeat, the wisdom of misery. Its noble assertion of will reminds one of Epictetus's saying, that the will alone is ours to do with as we choose. But Epictetus added that we must learn to wish to have things as they are

— instead of waiting for a far-off divine event, when the Furies no longer will be " types of things which are." Perhaps Shelley's outlook is more like that of Marcus Aurelius: that the good man must live on a mountain, as men were intended to live, and if men cannot endure him, let them kill him, for that is better than to live as men do. The good and the beautiful go down into the grave! The ugliness of the doom Shelley has not yet thought away; but he has reduced the ugliness of suffering and of the grave by substituting pity for hatred.

Teufelsdröckh, when he began to think, was blasted by the Furies, types of things that are, and in the first horrid vision of them plunged to his Everlasting No. But, as he became accustomed to his pessimistic, destructive *Weltschmerz*, the constructive power of his mind, outgrowing a temporary paralysis, began to take note of the other side of the picture, of the loveliness in life. Forthwith he moved from his Inferno, through an intervening Purgatory, to the Paradise of his Everlasting Yes. Such is the typical history of the individual who thinks. And now upon Prometheus, having escaped the negation of evil and hate and scorn, there come visions of the good, " like flocks of clouds in spring's delightful weather, thronging in the blue air." They are personifications of that benevolence which begins and ends in man, and is destined, by the perfectibilian creed, to triumph over evil, completely, at last. They come: spirits of bloodless revolution and of freedom, of self-sacrifice, of wisdom, and of poetry that so " adds spirit to sense " as to make the whole world beautiful; and, last of all, the spirit of love itself, prophesying that though as yet ruin is love's shadow,

> Following him, destroyingly,
> On Death's white and wingèd steed,

nevertheless the grim horseman shall be quelled, and as spring succeeds winter so justice and love and peace shall succeed tyranny and grief. Most vain is all hope but love, replies

Prometheus; and he dreams of the Uranian Aphrodite, here called Asia:

> Asia! who, when my being overflowed,
> Wert like a golden chalice to bright wine
> Which else had sunk into the thirsty dust, —

one of Shelley's most daring figures, in which, with characteristic intuition, sense and thought are fused into one.

The second Act iterates love's Everlasting Yes. Fierce hatred and proud disdain overcome, persecutors forgiven, the gospel of suffering learned, all most subtle temptations to fall into compromise or dejection resisted, pity and love triumphant — the constructive powers of the mind awaken from their coma and take note once again, as in ardent youth but with what added power dearly won from misery, of the loveliness of the world. Then one achieves his best guess, or deepest intuition, of the nature of being: his profoundest oracle.

This loveliness of the world, which is the path to the oracle, has a double glory — feminine beauty, which is really a quality of the soul in both man and woman, and the beauty of natural forms. These two phases of beauty are expressive of each other, or are but two faces of one reality. Here the feminine quality is Asia, and she dwells in a " far Indian vale," once rugged, desolate, frozen. But now, with the release of the Titan's constructive vision, which might be called the release of Asia herself, the release of the divining, feminine quality of the soul, this rugged place has changed to a bower

> . . . invested with fair flowers and herbs,
> And haunted by sweet airs and sounds, which flow
> Among the woods and waters, from the ether
> Of her transforming presence, which would fade
> If it were mingled not with thine [i.e., with
> > Prometheus's spirit].

Shelley's bower of natural loveliness, which he uses repeatedly and which he seems to have borrowed from Spenser, is
indeed a figure symbolic of the one ideal beauty, for the bower
is but natural beauty in sympathy with moral perfection.
Other examples of this bower-theme occur in Act III, Scene
iii of *Prometheus*, in *Epipsychidion*, in *The Sensitive Plant*,
in *The Revolt of Islam*, and in *Lines Written among the
Euganean Hills*. In each case, the outward form of the bower,
or garden, is expressive of an inner experience, viz., moral
loveliness. Moreover, the two are so fused, intuitively, that
the objective form can hardly be said to be a mere symbol.
In some deep sense, perhaps, no thing is a symbol: each thing,
deeply realized, is the very truth itself.

Swinburne, in his quick, hyperbolic way, in his essay on
Wordsworth and Byron, has most suggestively praised this
power of Shelley to visualize emotions and to give corporeal
existence to abstractions by an intuitive fusion of inner experience with natural forms:

> There is much study, there is much knowledge, there
> is much sober and sedate enjoyment of nature, much
> deep and thoughtful thankfulness for such enjoyment,
> made manifest in the poetry of Wordsworth: there is
> a singular intensity, a matchless refinement, of relish for
> the pure delight of communion with natural beauty, per-
> ceptible in the poetry of Keats: but to neither was it
> given, as it was given to Shelley, to rise beyond those
> regions of contemplation and sensation into that other
> where the emotion of Keats and the emotion of Words-
> worth become one, and are superseded by a greater; to
> breathe, in Shakespeare's audaciously subtle and success-
> ful phrase, the very " spirit of sense " itself, to transcend
> at once the sensuous and the meditative elements of
> poetry, and to fuse their highest, their keenest, their
> most inward and intimate effects, in such verse as utters
> what none before could utter, *and renders into likeness
> of form and sound such truths* of inspired perception,

such raptures of divine surprise, as no poet of nature may think to render again.

The italicized words very clearly indicate this reciprocity of mind and nature, or " natural magic," in Shelley's pictorial way of thinking. Pater, much more successful in defining Arnold's critical phrases than was Arnold himself, was really clarifying the Arnoldian " natural magic " when he spoke of " that strange, mystical sense of life in natural things, and of man's life as a part of nature, drawing strength and colour and character from local influences, from the hills and streams, and from natural sights and sounds." But it is to the poet whom Arnold called a pseudo-Shelley, to Swinburne, that we are indebted for the deepest criticism of this natural magic. The poet of the intense activity of wind and wave and sun, the poet of *By the North Sea*, who thought in tones of verbal music as intuitively as Shelley thought in images of nature, easily divined the secret of Shelley's supremacy in revealing

> Soul within sense, immeasurable, obscure,
> Insepulchred and deathless.

Asia, who is called " the light of life, shadow of beauty unbeheld," even as in the *Hymn to Intellectual Beauty* Shelley had spoken, Platonically, of the shadow of that beauty visiting this world inconstantly, now divines from natural beauty the supreme vision, or oracle. Not only do her own " footsteps pave the world with loveliness," but she herself goes down the path of that loveliness to meet her vision. These, again, are but two ways of speaking of the reciprocal loveliness of beauty in soul and in nature. On every petal and leaf, each herb, each shadow of morning clouds athwart the purple mountains, were stamped the words, " Follow, oh, follow " — signifying the summons of natural beauty to spiritual vision. Winds shook the clinging music from the pine-boughs, and

Low, sweet, faint sounds, like the farewell of ghosts,
Were heard: Oh, Follow, Follow, Follow Me.

Fine, clear sounds came from the crags, spirit-tongued —
the intense violin-music one hears on balmy days along rocky
shores or in mountain solitudes. Delicate music, in variously
beautiful symmetry and convolution, issued from the many-
folded hills, and nightingales sang ceaselessly in the windless
ivy-boughs. Led, or, better, impelled, by these reciprocal
harmonies of nature and the poetic mind, each striking into
each in true concord, Asia and Panthea arrive at the place of
vision, the deep gorge leading to the realm of Demogorgon,

> Like a volcano's meteor-breathing chasm,
> Whence the oracular vapour is hurled up
> Which lonely men drink wandering in their youth,
> And call truth, virtue, love, genius, or joy,
> That maddening wine of life, whose dregs they drain
> To deep intoxication; and uplift,
> Like Mænads who cry loud, Evoe! Evoe!
> The voice which is contagion to the world.

And now, at the acme of the climax, death again enters mightily. For, to come face to face with Demogorgon,
who is but the symbol of " the ultimate of being conceivable
by man's imagination," Asia must pass down through all
glooms, through sorrow and despair, through " the cloudy
strife of Death and Life,"

> Through the veil and the bar
> Of things which seem and are,
> Even to the steps of the remotest throne,
>   Down, down!

Milton's description of Death and the dark pavilion of Chaos,
" and the dreaded name of Demogorgon " (*Paradise Lost,*
2:666-965), were obviously in Shelley's mind as he pictured

the cave of his own Demogorgon and the " veilèd form on an
ebon throne " within:

> . . . a mighty darkness
> Filling the seat of power, and rays of gloom
> Dart round, as light from the meridian sun,
> Ungazed upon and shapeless; neither limb,
> Nor form, nor outline; yet we feel it is
> A living Spirit.

Here is Milton's picture of Death:

> The other shape —
> If shape it might be called that shape had none
> Distinguishable in member, joint, or limb;
> Or substance might be called that shadow seemed,
> For each seemed either — black it stood as Night.

The meaning of death is the culmination of the questions
Asia addresses to Demogorgon. Who made life and thought
and passion and imagination, and the " sense " of intellectual
beauty, which

> Fills the faint eyes with falling tears which dim
> The radiant looks of unbewailing flowers,
> And leaves this peopled world a solitude
> When it returns no more?

Who made terror and madness, crime and remorse, and self-
contempt, " bitterer to drink than blood "? Who made pain
and the sharp fear of Hell? Who made ghastly death?

The answer of Demogorgon is fittingly ambiguous: " the
deep truth is imageless," says the awesome voice, and of it
each one to himself must be the oracle. Unsatisfactory as this
conclusion must be for those mystics who, to use Mr. Tom-
linson's phrase, " find it easy to explain intuitively what no-
body can know," it is a singularly impressive testimony to
Shelley's intellectual honesty. He never listened sanctimoni-

ously to his own phrases as though they were definite oracles of God. Much given to argument and disquisition on many matters, and always determined to exercise reason to its utmost limits, he nevertheless resolutely preserved an agnostic attitude toward what he considered to be beyond the limits of reason. Fables in the Platonic manner he often constructed. Asia is the mouthpiece of one, a little further on in the very scene under consideration — a myth of the origin of man, the intrusion of death, and the Promethean gifts that alleviated man's lot and disguised or medicined death. But always they are palpable fables — an indirect way of stating the problem of what is by poetizing what might be, for the sake of elevating our minds above the commonplace; never an asseverated revelation of what really is. This wise indefiniteness, therefore, centered in the midst of much beautiful and symbolic fabling about the approaches of the mind to its greatest moments, preserves his intellectual honesty in the face of a temptation to put definite words into the mouth of God. That pious fraud, that religious ventriloquism, so characteristic of uncritical religious writers, he avoided. He preferred the truth — that in answering first questions each mind must be its own oracle. If Shelley was a mystic, he was a singularly honest one.

His Demogorgon, indeed, must not be given too specific a meaning. A French critic writing recently in the *Révue Anglo-Américaine* (Dec. 1929) has spoken of Demogorgon as the missing link between mind and matter. Rather, he stands for that mystical persuasion, vague but intense, that mind and matter are an untrue antithesis, and that what we call mind and matter are somehow one, without any erasure of the disparateness of individual things. For in the true mystical state multiety is not carelessly sacrificed to unity. The mystic says that unity both is and is not; variety both is and is not. In other words, mystical experience is beyond reason, indefinable by the being-categories of Occidental logic; and therefore to the non-mystic contradicts reason. It is an experience in which the paradox of unity and variety is solved without sacrificing either term of the antithesis, but by uniting them in what the mystic believes is a higher, super-sensory, super-definable awareness. Demogorgon is but a name for this mystical state of mind, I believe; and positively to define the state is to misconceive its nature, or, at any rate, its own claims. Therefore, " each man must be his own oracle " where Demogorgon is concerned. But, though Shelley is consistent in avoiding definition of the indefinable, he is repeatedly at pains to point out that it is love and beauty which draw us on to our deepest possible awareness of life, making us " seek to awaken in all things that are, a community with what we experience within ourselves." The poetic animism, then, of the aesthetic experience leads us toward this mystical state of mind, this ecstatic state of mind in which Lionel died and in which Shelley penned the closing lines of *Adonais*. But this point we shall elaborate in the last chapter.

Shelley is not to be blamed, then, for not pretending a definite answer to the problem of death and the hereafter of the individual. He is, rather, to be praised for not confusing the various attitudes he assumed toward death with literal revelations of its meaning.

But his real problem, clearly, is the conquest of his disgust of the ugliness of death. The commoner problem of the fear of death he seems not to have entertained. Nowhere in all his utterances upon death is there any fear of the hereafter, any pondering of Hamlet's indecision.

What, then, are the oracular vapours that lonely men drink in their youth? Not practical revelations of an actual heaven or hereafter, but youth's visions of best possible conditions and ideas — of ideals — which are, indeed, " the maddening wine of life " and a " contagion to the world." Such ideals were the life-blood of Shelley's intellect. And it was the very intensity of his love for his ideal of beauty that made it so hard for him to adjust himself to the loss of loveliness in the grave.

Did he make any advance toward a satisfactory, strong adjustment in the *Prometheus?* Here, as is his custom, he has used death to intensify the tragic picture of life. Our review of the first Act has shown that. But the heart of Prometheus is itself purified of the contempt and hatred that the world over contribute mightily to the hideousness and darkness of this tragic picture. Then pity for the doers of evil has further mitigated the tragic sense of life. Finally, the renewed summons from womanly and other natural loveliness to dare again the vision of an ideal beauty measurably liberates the purified mind from the ugliness that culminates in death. Our review of the second Act has shown that. But is death quite swallowed up in loveliness?

For the answer to this question the third Act must be explored. After the fall of Jupiter, the way is open to the reinstatement of earth and all its creatures in their primal innocence and good. Prometheus anticipates this renewal of the Golden Age — a poetic hyperbole symbolizing the ideal of Intellectual Beauty — by describing a bower of exquisite, unchanging beauty, where Asia and he will dwell in love. The joys of all loveliness will be theirs forever — of music and deep thoughts, of romantic, strange beauty made by new combinations of common things, of ideal beauty and its immortal shadows that are painting, sculpture, rapt poesy, and unimagined arts yet to be. Then, themselves unchanged, they will pensively debate the mutability of the world's life, but smile again for its loveliness, losing the pain of death in the sensations of beautiful things — almost in the early manner of Keats:

> . . . we will sit and talk of time and change,
> As the world ebbs and flows, ourselves unchanged.
> What can hide man from mutability?
> And if ye sigh, then I will smile; and thou,

Ione, shalt chant fragments of sea-music,
Until I weep, when ye [Asia] shall smile away
The tears she brought, which yet were sweet to shed.

Thus death, which for Shelley has always been the central
symbol of the cruelty and darkness of life, is softened; it is
shrouded in beauty. But the beauty is transparent. Death is
romanticized, perhaps sentimentalized. But it remains, nevertheless, the one dark and ugly event in this renascence of the
Golden Age. Other ugliness, much of what death symbolizes,
disappears; but not death itself. Tyrants and bigots fail, but
biological death goes on.

The Spirit of Earth develops the same theme of a perfected world, but she, too, concludes with a reference to
death. Her comfort consists of the promise of an euthanasia
— that death will be the last dear embrace of " her who takes
the life she gave " —

    . . . even as a mother,
Folding her child, says, " Leave me not again."

But Asia is not easily appeased by such sentiments. " Oh,
mother! " she cries,

    . . . wherefore speak the name of death?
Cease they to love, and move, and breathe, and speak,
Who die?

At one bound we are back to the old tragic questioning, death
having suddenly sloughed the thin veil of beauty. Has Shelley felt the inadequacy of the romantic evasion? Temporary
forgetfulness, while the attention is distracted by beauty; artistic admiration of a painless death: such weak aestheticism
will not stand the wear of experience. At any rate, the Earth
Spirit's reply to Asia is a well-known speculative paradox to
which philosophers the world over, as well as poets, have had
recourse repeatedly; and which Shelley has vaguely adum-
brated in *Mab, The Dæmon of the World, Mont Blanc, Islam,*

and *Prometheus* itself, but which now takes definite form for the first time. And it continues to grow in his thought, until it receives its most impressive statement in the *Adonais*. The spirit answers thus:

> It would avail nothing to reply;
> Thou art immortal and this tongue is known
> But to the uncommunicating dead.
> *Death is the veil which those who live call life;*
> *They sleep, and it is lifted.*

Life, really, is death; and only with the cessation of that death is the greater reality, or the true life, released! With some, the paradox may be no more than an epigram of immortality — a heightened way of praising the after-life; with others it may be only a way of expressing the hourly jeopardy or even horribleness of this life, like the old Senecan and " Pauline " reminder, beloved of the Fathers of the Church, that we die daily (1 Cor. 15:31). It is with a glance at the second meaning that Plato in the *Gorgias* quotes the famous line from Euripides,

> Who knows if life be not death and death life.

But Euripides, himself, uttering the idea more than once, seems rather to have meant that the conscious life of men may be all an illusion; and that meaning of the phrase brings out its relation to Plato's own surmise that all appearances are shadows of Ideas. Obviously, it is in this more philosophical mood that Shelley uses the paradox, moving therein, as someone has noted, toward a sort of Mahayana teaching of the apparitional character of all consciousness, and of salvation as consisting in the progressive comprehension of this fact and a consequently gradual union with the reality behind the shadow. Every art of knowing thus becomes a step toward " salvation "; and each act of knowing is in itself a faint revelation of what existence is.

The Burden of Life and the Moral Victory

It is worth remarking that when Asia revivifies the tragic question, the answer is made in a phrase reminiscent both of this Euripidean passage in the *Gorgias* and of Plato's own basic doctrine. A Platonic answer takes the place of the near-Cyrenaiscisn of the aesthetic evasion. The paradoxical answer, therefore, is something more than an arresting epigram, or ingenious trope; something more, too, than an arbitrary act of faith. It is based upon a reasoned guess that the limitations of consciousness, reason, and appearances, in analogy to all practical limitations, suggest a something beyond themselves. Then, since every this and that of our experience is related to a beyondness, not to say the Absolute, their significance lies in that relation. But, since in our limited condition, a kind of death, we cannot conceive this significant relation, it follows that for each individual the significance can be completed only in a beyondness, or real life, of the thinking individual himself — which is a sort of argument for some kind of persistence beyond our limitations. This is a line of thought pretty close to Professor Royce's argument for personal immortality. It has an affiliation, also, with two arguments which were noted in the last chapter as not definitely appearing in Shelley's poetry up to the end of 1817. First, it recalls the juridical argument of Kant and Bishop Butler: that life is so imperfect there must be another, perfect, life. Second, it recalls the ethical argument, that from the fact that the loftier a man's aims the more incomplete is his life here, it must follow that there is another life. Subject as both these arguments are to the suspicion of a hidden motive of self-interest, they nevertheless are more respectable, more reasoned, attitudes toward death than is what I have called the aesthetic evasion. It follows, therefore, that this new attitude of Shelley's, with its several affiliations to some of the standard arguments for immortality, marks a significant advance in his speculation about death.

It becomes necessary at this point to remove a possible confusion of this idea with one that bears to it a superficial and quite misleading similarity. Death, or death-in-life, is here called a veil. In two other passages *life* is called a veil in quite another sense; indeed, with a Godwinian, rather than Platonic, reference. In a sonnet, written in 1818, which already has been noticed, life is called a painted veil whose unreal shapes mimic all our crude beliefs. We are adjured not to lift the veil because, though its ugly shapes are unreal, they are the weaving of those blind human fears and hopes which, in government and religion, make up the sorry tragedy of life; and because one (i.e., Shelley) who had tried to pierce the veil and find a true loveliness, had come to grief:

> Lift not the painted veil which those who live
> Call Life; though unreal shapes be pictured there,
> And it but mimic all we would believe
> With colours idly spread, — behind, lurk Fear
> And Hope, twin Destinies, who ever weave
> Their shadows o'er the chasm, sightless and drear.
> I knew one who had lifted it — he sought,
> For his heart was tender, things to love,
> But found them not, alas! nor was there aught
> The world contains the which he could approve.
> Through the unheeding many he did move,
> A splendour among shadows, a bright blot
> Upon this gloomy scene, a Spirit that strove
> For truth, and like the Preacher found it not.

The sonnet, in effect, is a momentary confession of Shelley's failure to win peace and love for himself and his fellows by practical application of Godwin's theoretical anarchy. The veil, in this case, is the loathsome and unnecessary (in that sense " unreal ") phantoms of state and religion, ruling by blind fear and hope. The lifting of this veil would disclose not Plato's Ideas, or life eternal, but Godwin's perfected society. The second passage, from the closing lines of Act III of *Prometheus,* corroborates this interpretation. A splendid vision of mankind freed of political and religious illusion is introduced by three verses almost verbally identical with the opening lines of the sonnet. A fourth line definitely calls the veil a loathsome mask; and the rest of the selection pictures society as it will be when this loathsome veil has been destroyed:

> The painted veil, by those who were, called life,
> Which mimicked, as with colours idly spread,
> All men believed and hoped, is torn aside;
> The loathsome mask has fallen, the man remains
> Sceptreless, free, uncircumscribed, but man
> Equal, unclassed, tribeless, and nationless,
> Exempt from awe, worship, degree, the King
> Over himself; just, gentle, wise; but man
> Passionless — no, yet free from guilt or pain,
> Which were, for his will suffered them.

Very different is the Platonic " veil " which is death, though mortals call it life, the removal or lifting of which discloses the immortality of spirit. But the figuring of the two ideas under the one device of a lifted veil is very Shelleyan, for it marks the double significance death always had for Shelley: death as a symbol of cruelty and all ugliness, and death as a biological fact. Both deaths release perfection, one of society, the other of spirit.

The spiritual, Platonic idea appears again toward the end of the third Act of *Prometheus,* though Shelley seems to veer from it suddenly and completely. For after associating it rather cryptically with a suggestion previously used in the poem — that the immortal gods cannot understand the language of those who are doomed to die — and thus keeping up the mysterious and solemn effect of the whole Demogorgon episode, he goes on to describe at length the perfect peace and beauty of the new life of nature, which is to parallel the perfection of humankind. As in the Scenes already described, the theme is one of joyful contemplation of a world that has put off evil. In fact, the four or five lines that contain the Euripidean paradox are followed by over two hundred verses devoted to the new order.

Yet, at the very close of the Act, unconquerable death is remembered. Death has the last word. Society may be perfected, but man will not be exempt from death:

> Nor yet exempt, though ruling them like slaves,
> From chance, and death, and mutability,
> The clogs of that which else might oversoar
> The loftiest star of unascended heaven,
> Pinnacled dim in the intense inane.

And there, at last, I think, he has struck out a truly sublime conception of death: that were not the spirit rendered human by the circumstance of death it would in its own proper freedom transcend time and space, and become incommensurable by matter, even by the loftiest star " pinnacled dim in the intense inane." Understood in its obvious reference to Platonism (a reference quite missed by Arnold in his famous conversion of the last line to characterize Shelley's genius), this passage is no mere aesthetic subterfuge, no pretty flourish to close an act; but a sudden, magnificent poetizing of one of the world's most famous attitudes toward death. It brings to an inspired conclusion his treatment of the dark enigma which, by its symbolism of all imperfection as well as by its own native right, has been the burden of the drama, as of life itself, throughout the first three Acts.

Here the poem originally ended. The fourth Act was an afterthought. It repeats, on a wider scale, the glory of the sympathetic change in nature — the old Empedoclean fable converted into a poetic hyperbole — which we have but just now contemplated. It is a thing of scintillating joy, a marvellous effulgence of brightest verse. " Lyrics of the Golden Age," it might be called. In sustained beauty it is easier to write of sorrow than of joy. Where else can one find so rich an example of the rarer beauty? Yet even here there is material for our dark study.

Some matters may be passed with a glance. The Act opens with a procession of dark forms and with shadows passing confusedly. These are the spectres of dead hours, and they sing a dirge as they bear Time to his tomb in eternity. Yet it is only the old time of the tyrannies dissolving away before a diviner day. There is another reference to Platonic illusionism as the chorus of hours hymn the withdrawing of " the figured curtain of sleep," i.e., again, the death men call life, which so long had shrouded their being. There is a lyric of spiritual freedom that sums up all Shelley has yet said on death, for it names love, thought, and breath as the powers that quell death: love's ecstasy defying death, thought's power assimilating it to a higher reality, and breath symbolizing the everlasting renewal of life in successive forms. There are verses that put most clearly the reason for Shelley's continual association of tyranny and death: lines that picture the ruins of old horrors — shipwrecks, weapons, armour, scythèd chariots, royal emblazonry, and armorial beasts — " *round which death laughed.*" And other allusions of one sort or another. But two circumstances claim special attention.

In all this triumph of perfection — in the drama as a whole, in the third Act in particular, and in the paeans of the fourth Act — Platonism has been superimposed upon Godwinism. What was begun in the *Hymn* and *Mont Blanc*, the assimilation of Shelley's reforming zeal to the calm serenities of Plato's thought, has here been carried to a conclusion. This it is that makes the great difference between the more strident declamation of *Queen Mab* and *Islam*, and the lovely wisdom of *Prometheus Unbound*. The Godwinian thesis of the overthrow of selfish power by the innate benevolence and reason of men — for a while, in the ardour of his inexperience, blazoned by the young poet in his own impatient conflict with

society, or in the less impatient suffering of Laon and Cythna
— has been revised as a Platonic thesis of the tearing aside
of the illusions of death-in-life and the consequent unveiling
of ideal reality. Plato's Ideas have absorbed Godwin's benevolence, as a question of practical politics has merged into transcendental philosophy. A theory of political justice has been
married to an epistemological theory, and a theory of the
nature of knowledge and of reality has been converted into
a poem of perfectibility. Mr. Yeats, in his very sympathetic
and penetrative study of Shelley's poetry, has seized upon
this fundamental fact and brought it forward to refute the
popular misconception that *Prometheus Unbound* is only a
versifying of Godwin's *Political Justice*. The liberty of the
poem he says, " was so much more than the liberty of *Political Justice* that it was one with Intellectual Beauty. . . . He
calls the spirit of beauty liberty, because despotism, and perhaps . . . all authority, pluck virtue from her path towards
beauty, and because it [beauty] leads us by that love whose
service is perfect freedom."

Yet Plato himself, in his *Republic*, endeavoured to show
how a clear knowledge of what life is — i.e., of the Ideas in
relation to appearances — might ameliorate the conditions of
social existence. What, then, is the relation of the *Prometheus*
to the *Republic?* Since in the course of his appropriation of
Platonic doctrines Shelley acquired a new attitude toward
death, this question can appropriately be asked in the present
essay.

Plato planned a philadelphian state, and Shelley sang a
philadelphian mood. Plato laid down a system, and Shelley
uttered its song. The system provided for a standing army
to wage defensive and aggressive wars, for philosopher-kings
whose minds should be filled with heavenly light, for skilled
artisans whose workmanship should be finely tempered of the
spirit, and for the holding in common of goods, wives, and

children. Shelley's song was the spontaneous overflow of powerful feelings arising from the contemplation of the ideal beauty, peace, and love, the ideal temperance, knowledge, and justice, of such a system. With all the practical details of the system, Shelley could not sympathize. Standing armies and offensive wars he could not approve. He must have been as suspicious of kings, even philosopher-kings, as Plato was of poets. He may be said, then, to have written a poem in praise of Plato's Ideas rather than of any city-state definitely planned with reference to them; of those highest realities functioning freely in the emotions of men. He pays little attention to practical affairs. Even his anarchy is more a symbol of ideal peace than a programme of revolt. He trusts to a beauty innate in the human spirit. Benevolence is the true character of man. To this Godwinian teaching, he adds, in the first Act, the lesson of his own adventuring: that benevolence is unchained by suffering, by repentance of scorn and hatred, by pity for the wicked, by unfailing fidelity to the higher vision, and by love. In the second Act, he adds the Platonic dream that this innate beauty is redeemed from decay by visitations of the Idea, or Reality, of Beauty; and imagines an outer world brought into conformity with this innate beauty by the destruction of the horrors of injustice, intemperance, and hatred. Then, in the third Act, he avers that Life, which is a veil of this spirit, had better be called Death, for death has long since become his symbol of all imperfection, ugliness; but what he and other men have called death, is the true life, the greatest visitation of the divine. Platonism, superimposed upon Godwinism, has inverted the meaning of death. Thus, at last, in the triumph of benevolence and beauty over the ugliness that is falsely called life, a perfected moral character is achieved. The emotional harmony of that character, and a sympathetic harmony, or peace, in all natural things, overflow into the lyrics of the fourth Act. Such hymns of moral beauty Plato required for the delight and edification of the youth of his ideal republic. While he sang thus, Shelley would not have been excluded from the City.

But just as soon as one discovers that in these attractive pictures and lyrics the moral renascence is again disguised as a general, or communal, perfection, the emotional appeal suffers before skepticism. Perfecting society by unchaining the benevolence of men is one thing. Asserting its possibility stirs more doubt than hope. And doubtless will continue so to do until biology finds a way of breeding moral individuals who will not slough their virtue as soon as safe opportunity offers. " Ah, dear Marwood, what's integrity to an opportunity? " But the everlasting struggle of each individual to move toward perfection through the maze of his failures, is another thing. It is the ethical tragi-comedy known to us all, and we have developed an affectionate humour toward the incongruity between what men are and what men think they are or would like to be. The inevitability of the incongruity is the sanction of the humour. Also, experience shows typical stages of ascent in this struggle; and for each stage we have set up those expressive signs noted above: Forgive thine enemies, Love thine enemies, The pure in heart shall see God, The Kingdom of God is within you. Now, just because the hero of the *Prometheus* is an individual, howsoever representative, who passes through these stages (the alleviation of humour was not a part of the plan), the effect of the play is so individualistic, and thereby profoundly appealing, that one remembers almost with a shock that, after all, the play is intended as a story of the regeneration of mankind at large. The unbinding of Prometheus is in fact a story of what has actually happened, in some degree short of the ideal perfection, to each of countless millions of men. But the perfecting of society is a story of what has never happened, of what perhaps never can happen until there is biological change in the fundamental nature of man.

The Burden of Life and the Moral Victory

May not one be warranted, then, in detecting in this poem a movement, unrealized by the poet himself, away from the preoccupation with the perfection of society toward the perfecting of the individual? from the dream of Utopia to the drama of the aspiring individual? To any ground for this surmise that may have been cleared in our examination may be added one more piece of evidence, from the very close of the poem. Shelley seems, as he penned the last lines, to have become skeptical of a permanent moral paradise upon earth, for, in a significant afterthought — I think it may be called that — he admits the possibility of a cataclysm of all the perfection he has imaged, and the need, then, of beginning over again the anabasis of society. For that long and renewed ascent Shelley gives as a programme a magnificent inventory of the means by which the *individual* gains control over himself. These, he says, " are spells by which to reassume an empire o'er the disentangled doom " —

> To suffer woes which Hope thinks infinite;
> To forgive wrongs darker than death or night;
> To defy Power, which seems omnipotent;
> To love, and bear; to hope till Hope creates
> From its own wreck the thing it contemplates;
> Neither to change, nor falter, nor repent;
> This, like thy glory, Titan, is to be
> Good, great, and joyous, beautiful and free;
> *This is alone Life, Joy, Empire, and Victory!*

" This is alone Life, Joy, Empire, and Victory! " This self-conquest is alone Utopia! Sufferings are trials of fortitude. Could there be a clearer paraphrase of the old victory-cry, " The Kingdom of God is within you "? That cry, too, came after the hope of a new Jerusalem built by hands had gone the way of all Utopian expectations. Here the cry becomes a paean of the moral victory over the ugliness of social cruelty and of physical change and death. Here is no aesthetic evasion of social phenomena and biological fact, no idealistic and paradoxical inversion of them, but an identification of their function with the individual's moral struggle that culminates in a realized higher beauty of heroic conduct. *Prometheus Unbound* is, indeed, a great poem of a self-culture that was in the making.

How soon will this tendency toward the drama of the individual be fully realized by Shelley? How will it colour his poems from now on? And what will be the effect of its realization upon his conception of Death? We shall find the answer to these questions in *Adonais*.

III

From this poem of political tyranny we turn to a drama of domestic tyranny, *The Cenci*. Shelley said of it, in a letter to Peacock (July, 1819), that it was written " without any of the peculiar feelings and opinions which characterize my other compositions." It is free of Godwinism and Platonism, to be sure; and, unlike most of his poems, it is written in a severely unfigured style. But a tragic union of loveliness and death, like that of the Medusa, is the heart of the poem. It is a tragedy of worse than death, but with death in every line. Count Cenci is mad with lust of cruelty and murder. His victims fall into despair, and desire death. Beatrice suffers a doom worse than death — the incestuous passion of her father. She plots his murder. She spends her eloquence defending the deed, and anticipating her own death. One of her tools, Marzio, dies on the rack. The state executes her and her brother and her stepmother, Lucretia. And there is not a passage in the poem that can be read without suspense from the threat of death. It is not a melodrama of blood, like *The Spanish Tragedy;* but a veritable tragedy of blood, like *Macbeth* or *Medea*.

Through this dark theatre Cenci strides to death. He belongs to the monsters of fiction. He is, with a difference, of the race of the Barabbases, Volpones, Sir Giles Overreaches, and other Elizabethan monsters of evil. He is a development of one of Shelley's earliest fascinations, for he is a Zastrozzi matured; another study in that absolute villainy which already had gone through one translation — from shuddering fiction to indignant political theory. Yet he is neither mere fustian nor mere abstraction. He is too eloquent for the one and too ingenious for the other. Henry Sweet has said that in creating a character Shelley " had only two alternatives: either to reproduce himself or create an abstraction," and that in the Count, Shelley has merely combined " every imaginable depravity into one abstraction." But Professor Herford, with keener observation, remarks that Cenci is Shelley's first success in creating an adequate antagonist. Jupiter is the abstract antagonist of Prometheus. But Cenci is no Jupiter. He is too varied and inventive, and yet always consistent, in his cruelty; he is not uncomplicated, for he has qualms of conscience, and is one of those strange passionate individuals who in self-deception unite evil with piety. He has one absorbing motive for his wickedness, a realistic philosophy of conduct, like that of Callicles in the *Gorgias*, to the effect that the strong man lives in excessive intemperance, pleasing all his desires to the uttermost, whereas only the cowardly and weak, being unable to satisfy their desires, praise temperance and justice. Moreover, his eloquence in expounding his theory is so convincing, so removed from bombast, that one feels he is driven relentlessly forward to his fate by some demoniacal influence. He has the dignity and awesome grandeur of one fated to perform what he does perform. His overmastering desires seem even to himself to rush forward under some more than natural impetus, and Beatrice voices a similar feeling about him. He belongs in part to Greek tragedy, not wholly to Elizabethan melodrama. He is a monster, under fate; not a mere ranting, impossible villain. He does not change. But he does hesitate. Then the fury of his perversion carries him headlong to incest and destruction. Murder is his *milieu* and his compulsion, his weapon and his destiny. He is a study in demonic ugliness, a Gorgon without the veil of loveliness. He is all that Sir Giles Overreach fails to be.

In this connection it is appropriate to cite Professor A. C. Bradley's judgment of the character:

> It is customary to say that Count Cenci is only Shelley's usual tyrant, magnified into an absolute monster. But this is to be more obsessed by Shelley's ideas than Shelley himself was. In his Cenci there is surely as much insight into the dark places of the soul as in many of the villains of Elizabethan tragedy; and, if Shelley had been Shakespeare's contemporary, we should be wondering at powers which now we wholly deny to him.

But that Beatrice Cenci is flesh and blood there can be no doubt. She, in the selfsame drama, is the refutation of Sweet's charge. She is neither Shelley nor an abstraction; but one of the great studies in tragic womanhood, of the race of Antigone and Medea, of Vittoria and the Duchess of Malfi. And Shelley's magnanimity has given her a quality of her own, in virtue of which she stands with these other heroines, but above them.

Keats, in a seldom quoted part of his oft quoted advice that Shelley should be more jealous to load every rift with ore, cautioned him to lay aside for a while his magnanimity, to be less concerned with the sufferings of men and the ideals of philosophy, and to permit his mind to be more completely immersed in sensuous beauty. Now, Keats himself never succeeded in creating a great character. In particular, his women characters are, as Bridges has noted, conventional or insipid. He failed to delineate human passion. But to Shelley's very magnanimity, speculatively exercised, but purified in suffering, we owe the distinctive excellence of Beatrice. She contrives the death of her father in no Medean spirit of mad

vengeance for her own sufferings; but, as Herford has so well
pointed out, as herself being the instrument of divine justice.
I cannot agree with Herford that she acted primarily to preserve her father's honour —

> Because my father's honour did demand
> My father's life.

Other reasons for her conduct are very plainly indicated.
Her magnanimity in murder — for that is the paradox with
which we are faced, and the casuistry of which, in the better
sense of the term, would have powerfully appealed to any
one of the three Greek tragic writers — her magnanimity in
murder is deliberately and repeatedly anatomized in the play.
Her first great tragic moment is one of suffering rather than
action. At the beginning of the third Act she staggers upon
the stage, speaking wildly and disjointedly, but in veiled
words, of the unutterable attack upon her. In the first frenzy
of her torture she is intuitively certain that the punishment
must be stupendous,

> something which shall make
> The thing that I have suffered but a shadow
> In the dread lightning which avenges it;
> Brief, rapid, irreversible, destroying
> The consequence of what it cannot cure.

But presently she debates her problem. " I pray thee, God,"
she cries, " let me not be bewildered while I judge." Merely
to endure her fate, and let her body, unworthy temple of the
divine spirit, become a foul den from which what the divine
abhors may mock it unavenged, is to her unthinkable. That
way lies only repetition of the crime — " day after day load-
ing with crime an overburdened soul " — until she herself
will be reduced to the hideousness she permits. Her body and
soul could but become that " monstrous lump of ruin " that
Cenci himself intends they shall be. Suicide she rejects out of

religious awe: " Thy decree yawns like a Hell between our will and it." Neither life nor death can give her rest. There remains recourse to law. But she is convinced that the strange, overpowering horror of the accusation would baffle belief, and that that handicap would be mightily exploited by her father's great influence and wealth. Lucretia states the danger vividly:

> But if one, like this wretch,
> Should mock with gold opinion, law and power?
> If there be no appeal to that which makes
> The guiltiest tremble? If, because our wrongs,
> For that they are unnatural, strange and monstrous,
> Exceed all measure of belief? Oh, God!
> If, for the very reasons which should make
> Redress most swift and sure, our injurer triumphs?
> And we, the victims, bear worse punishment
> Than that appointed for their torturer?

Only a miscarriage of justice could result; and Beatrice's unpolluted innocence would be turned into a " stale mouthèd story " by vilest gossips. Man's law cannot be trusted.

> Oh! in this mortal world
> There is no vindication and no law,
> Which can adjudge and execute the doom
> Of that through which I suffer.

Death itself, she realizes, is an equivocal thing. Law calls it a punishment; religion, a reward. " Mighty death! Thou double-visaged shadow! " Yet, there is no other way out. Absorbed in thought, it comes to her at last that death is the " only judge, the rightfullest arbiter." Thus she unravels her entangled will, and makes her decision as deliberately as is possible to one in such agony of mind.

The choice once made, Beatrice, despite her gentleness, becomes an Antigone for resolution. " We must be brief, bold, and prompt." Henceforth she never hesitates. The plan for murdering Cenci is perfected. Assassins are hired. But the plot fails. A new plan is at once invented. But before it can be executed, there is a hideous scene in which Cenci gloats over his scheme for bringing his daughter to complete ruin — soul and body to that " monstrous lump of ruin." Because of this fiendish intention, the murder appears all the more necessary. The new assassins are fearful. A sudden noise disconcerts them. Then the ecstatic courage of Beatrice speaks:

> Ye conscience-stricken cravens, rock to rest
> Your baby hearts. It is the iron gate,
> Which ye left open, swinging to the wind,
> That enters whistling as in scorn. Come, follow!
> And be your footsteps like mine, light, quick and bold.

The murderers go in to the sleeping man. Overcome again by fear, they return on the pretext of hearing her call. Her reproaches are sudden and fierce. She has a measure of her father's headlong spirit. Whence conscientious fears in such a cause? she storms. Mercy would insult heaven.

> We do but that which 't were a deadly crime
> To leave undone.

Snatching a dagger, she threatens to do the deed herself. Whereupon they enter again, strangle Cenci, and throw the body into the garden. Beatrice feels a vast relief. Her blood, that had seemed congealed, runs freely again in her veins. The darkness of hell that had suffocated her is dissipated. Dismissing the assassins with gifts, she bids them repent their crimes. "This deed is none." They have, indeed, been the instruments of Heaven.

Thus we have one and the same high-souled Beatrice in suffering, in deliberation, in decision, in deed. Now, with the discovery of the murder, we hear her restate her case in defence. She has no feeling of guilt. To the Pope's legate, Savella, she says:

> Guilty! who dares talk of guilt? My Lord,
> I am more innocent of parricide
> Than is a child born fatherless.

The unnatural crime had unfathered her. A mighty idea! She attacks worldly justice, which seems keen-judging, but is not. In the case of such a power as Cenci, human laws, or rather their ministers, would have barred retribution. And now,

> When Heaven doth interpose to do
> What ye neglect, arming familiar things
> To the redress of an unwonted crime,
> Make ye the victims who demanded it
> Culprits? 'T is ye are culprits! That poor wretch
> Who stands so pale, and trembling, and amazed,
> If it be true he murdered Cenci, was
> A sword in the right hand of justest God.

It would have been a crime no less than Cenci's, had her fierce desire for his death faded for one moment in her heart. This was her only rest on earth, and only hope in Heaven. In contrast to her stout spirit, her brother, Giacomo, is subject to a thin remorse, which sets off her heroism much as Ismene's weakness is a foil to Antigone's strength. Yet it is Giacomo, nevertheless, who gives the perfect picture of his sister in this tragic event:

> She who alone, in this unnatural work
> Stands like God's angel ministered upon
> By fiends; avenging such a nameless wrong
> As turns black parricide to piety.

But the height of her ecstasy is reached when, under torture by the rack, Giacomo and Lucretia confess the plot. What had they to confess? she cries. Some wicked lie to flatter their tormentors! Ignoble hearts, " false to their deserted selves." They have lost their vision of the higher justice, and, falling back into the shortsighted ways of human justice, have acknowledged what only blindness can call guilt.

> Have they said
> That they were guilty? O white innocence,
> That thou shouldst wear the mask of guilt to hide
> Thine awful and serenest countenance
> From those who know thee not!

There needs but one more mood to complete the story of her exaltation. When, after their doom has been pronounced, mother and brother, broken-hearted for their momentary weakness, turn to her in repentance, Beatrice comforts them with these high words:

> Take cheer! The God who knew my wrong, and made
> Our speedy act the angel of his wrath,
> Seems, and but seems, to have abandoned us.

Such is the magnanimity of Beatrice. Like Antigone, she perceives a higher justice, and boldly asserts her duty to become its instrument. It is not so much that her father's honour demands his death, as that the unnatural crime demands an unnatural punishment, to the vision of which conventional law cannot rise. And she, in turn, is punished by law lawfully, but not justly. The reader to whom this contention is convincing, holding her guiltless, cannot have pity for her, if pity implies sympathy with one who suffers not without culpability but beyond the measure of his guilt. He must feel, instead, an intense, almost unbearable compassion for sufferings attributable, not to any demerit in the victim, but to a stupendous misfortune. In this interpretation, *The Cenci* is a tragedy of fear and compassion for the misfortunes of a guiltless and magnanimous heroine.

But many a reader, even if he admits Shelley's intention to produce this effect, will feel that Beatrice with all her deliberation and defence makes but a weak argument to support her right to interpret and administer the divine justice. He will find a flaw in her judgment, the result of a passion akin to her father's. He will then discover less magnanimity, and more culpability; and compassion will yield to pity. And he may well support this criticism of her character by adducing in proof of her weakness that singular episode in which before her judges she denies that she had even planned the crime, and disingenuously argues that if she had, she surely would not have neglected so trivial a precaution for her safety as the death of her creature, the assassin. Moreover, she shows no pity for the torture and death of Marzio, one of the assassins; but only indignation that he should have regarded her as a parricide. Indeed, there are moments in the play when her exaltation seems all too much a quibble glorified by passion. Surely, it would have been yet more magnanimous to have taken all the blame, immediately, as did Antigone? If she is fighting to shield brother and mother, she might well take all the responsibility to herself. It is difficult to see how, the circumstances being what they are, and she being what she is, she can do other than contrive or commit the murder. But it is also difficult to reconcile her high arguments with this disingenuousness, except on the grounds of an imperfect craftsmanship that failed to realize the inconsistency.

But this dilemma does not obscure the Shelleyan magnanimity, whatever its faults, which makes the greater part of Beatrice's character. Shelleyan it is, for it is nothing so much as a dramatic realization of Shelley's noble indictment of the antithesis between law and justice. This domestic tragedy results from the cold, savage, blind formalism of conventional justice against which Shelley had long since protested. His juvenile *Zeinab and Kathema*, as we have seen, was on the same subject. So, too, was *A Tale of Society As It Is*. But Beatrice, tragically caught in this antithesis, is more than a passive sufferer. She herself takes the initiative, executes the unwritten law as she understands it, and then pays the price of her greatness.

It is this activity of hers that makes the story a drama. It is the inevitability of the fatal conflict involved in the antithesis of law and justice with reference to such an action that makes the drama a tragedy. It might well have been entitled *Justice*. From Sophocles to Galsworthy the antithesis has been a subject prolific of tragedy. It bears a heavy freight of death — of tragic death — down through history.

In the death of Beatrice Cenci, Shelley achieves his most powerful handling of tragic death. Death in his early romances was mere play with fright. The death of the poet in *Alastor* is pathetic and sentimental. The deaths of Laon and Cythna are tragic to a certain degree. They arouse compassion for the blameless martyrs, and vividly remind us of the fearfulness of adventures in political idealism. But their tragedy is mediated by the blissful reunion of the lovers in the Temple of the Spirit. The deaths in *Rosalind and Helen* and *Julian and Maddalo* are not dramatically realized. The fall of Jupiter is an abstraction. The many references in many poems to the cruel death, or dysthanasia, inflicted by tyrants, are sermons, polemics, denunciations, lyrics of suffering, as the case may be. The going down of all beauty into the grave, and the summons of everyman by death, has been treated elegiacally, with more or less of hope and courage. But the death of Beatrice is truly tragic. It is inevitable, because legal justice can maintain its precarious balance only by remaining blind to that perfect justice which depends not from law but from wisdom. Once Beatrice were pardoned and her case become a precedent, where would be the end of such cases? The plea of the unwritten law is accepted always at the risk of the destruction of all law. And the deed for which she was punished was inevitable, under the circumstances. She would not have been Beatrice if she had not acted as she did. That action arouses at once admiration and fear. It is a noble

action of a magnanimous spirit. Lastly, the catastrophe arouses
intense compassion, or noble pity, according to the way one
interprets the character. If this dilemma in interpretation did
not exist, the play might be a greater play. But with the inevitability of the deed and the punishment, and with the effects of admiration, fear, and pity or compassion, the death
of Beatrice becomes tragic in the full sense of the term: not
meanly painful, but nobly and necessarily and fearfully and
pitifully and endlessly painful, because of the very constitu-
tion of things — or of our ignorance of the true nature of
things, which amounts to the same.

I think that the tragic quality of the play is deepened by
the repeated recognition of the equivocal character of death:
a punishment, a reward. This uncertainty, as in the case of
Hamlet, adds a fear and gloom of its own. The play would
not be Shelley's play were there not frequent addresses of
the soul to the mystery of death, alternating between depression and hope. Beatrice comforts her mother and brother
with the Christian hope, and in turn fearfully ponders annihilation, or wonders whether with death she will only meet
a repetition, on a greater scale, of the horrors she has met
here. After courageously hearing the inexorable sentence, she
wildly cries,

> My God! Can it be possible I have
> To die so suddenly? So young to go
> Under the obscure, cold, rotting, wormy ground?

Incidentally it may be remarked that in this, as in one other
passage of the tragedy, Shelley's beloved theme of the coffin-
worm at long last achieves a truly tragic expressiveness, instead of the more or less crude, macaberesque effect of all its
previous appearances. But again and again these various addresses of the soul to the grave occur. Hardly an attitude of
all those that have been traced in this essay is missing. At last,
Beatrice concludes it all on the three notes of speculation,

courage, and farewell, the while she summarizes this tragedy
of justice. She is speaking to her younger brother, Bernardo:

> One thing more, my child;
> For thine own sake be constant to the love
> Thou bearest us; and to the faith that I,
> Though wrapped in a strange cloud of crime and shame,
> Lived ever holy and unstained. *And though*
> *Ill tongues shall wound me, and our common name*
> *Be as a mark stamped on thine innocent brow*
> *For men to point at as they pass, do thou*
> *Forbear, and never think a thought unkind*
> *Of those who perhaps love thee in their graves.*
> *So mayest thou die as I do; fear and pain*
> *Being subdued. Farewell! Farewell! Farewell!*

Ah, as he reads those lines one cannot but see a double meaning — one for Shelley himself, another for Beatrice — in each
word, and believe they were written *in propria persona* —
Shelley's own valedictory to his own children, their num-
bers now thinned by death.

And once again, as at the close of the *Prometheus*, death
has been subdued to a moral struggle that culminates in a
realized higher beauty: the beauty of a tragic magnanimity.

IV

The second, third, and fourth Acts of the *Prometheus* were
written during 1819. In the same year *The Cenci* was begun
and finished, and several short poems were composed. From
the point of view of this essay, the short poems appear to fall
into three divisions. There is a small group of four non-
political pieces (*Ode to the West Wind, Medusa, Ode to
Heaven, Indian Serenade*), each of which in respect of death
displays some mood of defeat or victory. A larger, political
group is made up of seven pieces that develop the old theme

of the murderous tyrant, and curiously lead up to, or surround, the great non-political drama of the murderous tyrant
—*The Cenci*. There remain, outside the present view, only
three short poems and *Peter Bell;* these alone have little or no
relation to death.

The *Ode to the West Wind*, written several weeks before
the completion of the final act of *Prometheus*, is a lyric projection, or coruscation, of the drama. In it have been condensed, and fused into a new emblem, the sadness and personal grief of the poems of depression, which we have spoken
of as clustering about the *Prometheus*. And as in the latter the
story of that suffering, and of the triumph over it, is idealized,
so also in the *Ode* the pain, although it is permitted an intensely personal utterance, is nevertheless idealized, and then
resolved in a splendid appeal to conduct, which recalls the
exhortation at the close of the play.

These emotional and ideal elements, then, and many a
Shelleyan *cliché* besides, are ardently fused in a new emblem.
The emblem is taken from nature: the tumultuous autumnal
wind, at once destroyer and preserver, a symbol both of
death and of the new life that is hidden in death. The first
three stanzas, in an almost classical mode of impersonal objectivity, describe the effect of the wind upon leaf, cloud,
and wave.

The wind, which with a powerful animism is named the
very breath of Autumn's being, in a splendid spondaic chaunt
is described as driving the dead leaves, " yellow, and black,
and pale, and hectic red, pestilence-stricken multitudes,"
which flee like ghosts from an enchanter. Here are all the
old properties: the ghosts and the enchanter, from the juvenilia and elsewhere, almost everywhere, in his poetry; the
pestilence, the autumnal flight of the winged seeds, and the
recovery of spring from *The Revolt of Islam* (see IX. xx,
xxi); the dead leaves and the deathful gloom of autumn,
from many a previous poem; and the very idea of plasmic

persistence from a line in *Mab*, " Catching new life from
transitory death " (VIII. 22). And other often used properties follow. Again and again in reviewing previous poems we
have had occasion to anticipate the *Ode*. But now all these
former properties and ideas are clothed in a new splendour
of verbal beauty, and imbued, perhaps, with a greater meaning than Shelley has ever achieved, in equal space, from previous management of them. For the wind not only drives
dead leaves — a symbol of destruction; but also chariots the
winged seeds to their dark wintry bed, where they lie like
corpses in their graves, until spring, with her clarion, calls
forth their life upon plain and hill — a symbol of the constructive forces in nature. Then the commotion of the great
destroyer and preserver in the steep sky is imaged. The clouds
are scattered by the wind like the dead leaves of the earth;
but they are " angels of rain and lightning," and they are
driven together in life-giving storm. The music of the vital
storm-wind is, too, a " dirge of the dying year," the old year

> . . . to which this closing night
> Will be the dome of a vast sepulchre,
> Vaulted with all thy congregated might
>
> Of vapours, from whose solid atmosphere
> Black rain, and fire, and hail will burst.

So the panorama of autumn and death and new life unfolds.
Then the contrast of summer isles in a bland Mediterranean is summoned; much as Homer turns from the storm of
slaughter to picture for briefest moment the spring-ploughing
in far-away Attica. But, while the " sense faints picturing "
the fertile beauty of a " pumice isle in Baiæ's bay," suddenly
the level waves of the Atlantic are chasmed by the mighty
wind, and the sapless foliage of the ocean, far below, hears
the voice of the storm-wind, and grows grey with fear, as
Aïdoneus had terror in hell lest the world and waters above
be cloven by Poseidon raging in storm.

Now, in this diapason of the autumnal wind the melancholy music of death is forgotten, or transcended. Caught up into powerful communion with this emblem of the destructive-preservative force in natural change, the death-filled mind of the poet escapes from its depression. The meaning of death is inverted. For when the spirit is tranquillized and solemnly deepened by contemplating the balance of the seasons and the saving power of the destroyer, it realizes that nature itself scarcely could use the word " death," except vaguely as a name for one of the many changes of form that prove its life. This inversion, doubtless, is what Shelley had in mind when he said, more than once, in the *Prometheus*, that the gods cannot understand the language of things that die. To a mind tumultuously instinct with faith in the renewing power of life, " death " becomes but a frigid figure of speech. Nine tenths of what meaning it has for most of us is derived from human egotism, blindness, and pain. But the soul that has breathed this " breath of Autumn's being," this Brahma back of Vishnu and Siva, in its faith in a vaster renewal cheerfully makes its preparation to depart.

But, implicit as are these inspiring deductions in the first section of the poem, the fourth stanza leaves them unspoken, while it turns suddenly from impersonal description to a piercing lyric cry of pain and defeat. The contrast is dramatic. Quite in the way of Calderon, in whose work he took such joy, Shelley now briefly resumes in a new, intenser theme the symmetrical arrangement of the figures of leaf, cloud, and wave:

> If I were a dead leaf thou mightest bear;
> If I were a swift cloud to fly with thee;
> A wave to pant beneath thy power, and share
>
> The impulse of thy strength, . . .
>
> . . . I would ne'er have striven

The Burden of Life and the Moral Victory

As thus with thee in prayer in my sore need.
Oh! lift me as a wave, a leaf, a cloud!
I fall upon the thorns of life! I bleed!

A heavy weight of hours has chained and bowed
One too like thee: tameless, and swift, and proud.

After all, the inspiring deductions are here — in the form of
prayer. Here, too, is the personal depression; that depression
we have traced in its long history, from youth's faintness in
the presence of the grave — the ugly change that follows
every beautiful thing — through youth's impatient grief for
all the ugly murders of body and spirit that are done in the
name of the state and religion, and through youth's sorrowful
attempt to erase the loathsome, painted mask of human fears
and cruelty, until in its failure youth finds itself beguiled to
the grave of its own high hopes and its own loved ones. The
prayer is a cry to be lifted up from the slough of this despond.
In prayer the symbol of power and his own soul's need are
fused.

But, along with the figure of the prayer pressed out from
sore need, he has used the figure that dominated his imagination through the year of 1819 — that of the chained spirit.
The unbinding from the chain, in the last stanza, is the answer to the prayer. Once again, as in the *Prometheus*, the
spirit answers its own prayer, unbinds itself. The first four
stanzas have themselves delivered the re-creating spell that
untangles the doom. Strengthened by the solemn harmony
of autumn, " sweet though in sadness " — that healing harmony with which the *Hymn to Intellectual Beauty* had concluded, and then it was lost awhile in the intensity of grief,
to reappear here — strengthened again by its spell, he summons his own will to re-create hope from the wreck of his
hopes. Behold! His dead thoughts, like the withered leaves,
shall quicken a new birth, and the incantation of his verse
shall scatter them like sparks among mankind. They shall

The Pursuit of Death

Be through my lips to unawakened earth

The trumpet of a prophecy! O wind,
If Winter comes, can Spring be far behind?

Influential immortality? The persistence of the influence
of printed words? Yes, one might coldly aver it to be the
solution of this heart's desire to avoid the ugliness of death.
But the vision and passion amount to more than that. The
egoism and the blindness and the pain have been taken out of
death. Death has been purified of them by the individual
soul's perception of the soul of nature, the destroyer and
preserver. And the purified soul has asserted its will to display an individual conduct patterned on its vision of a universal process. Once again, as at the close of the *Prometheus*
and the close of *The Cenci*, " death " is assimilated to a moral
struggle that culminates in a realized higher beauty. Can man
that is mortal win from the tutoring of his suffering any ethical attitude toward death that is more victorious than
this? Magnanimity converts death. The sting of death is
destroyed.

Certainly there is in the *Ode* neither argument nor even
suggestion concerning personal immortality. On the contrary,
the figures of persistence — the winged seeds, the waning
clouds, the storm, and the destroying-preserving breath of
them all, the west wind — are held analogous not to personal,
but to plasmic immortality: the immortality of the plasmic
germ-cell. Therein Shelley reads the analogy more carefully
than it is read in the Pauline argument: " That which thou
sowest is not quickened, except it die. . . . It is sown in corruption; it is raised in incorruption "; or in the Johannine
argument: " Except a grain of wheat fall into the earth and
die, it abideth by itself alone; but if it die, it beareth much
fruit." What real analogy to a spiritual, glorified, personal
survival can be discovered in the propagation of ever different yet always mortal plants by seeds of the old? Paul's teach-

ing, like John's, is a metaphor rather than an analogy. Shelley's poetry is better based than Paul's argument. The spring that cannot be far behind is not personal immortality, but the glad renewal of the moral struggle after a dejection as of death. And this renewal is comparable to the preservation of life by its own death.

And how Aristotelian it is! The poem reads like a parable of Aristotle's central doctrine, and a summary of the doctrine reads like an exposition of the poem. Fundamental in both is the insight into a nature that is not appearances but the force working in appearances, destructively and constructively, from form to form, every form the matter for other form. And of the operation of mind the poem implies what is explicit in the doctrine: that mind, conceiving nature, makes indeed a continuous effort to conceive ever higher forms, patterns its own wisdom upon that effort — making its constructive poetry a creative picture, or " imitation," of idealized forms, and its ethics an exhortation to a generous rivalry among men and with nature in achieving excellent forms of conduct. In this poem, for a moment, at least, Shelley has advanced from the dream of Plato to the greater vision of Aristotle, from a retrospective dream of appearances as declensions of reality to a forward vision of becoming. In this great figure of the destroying and preserving wind — the power with two heads, as Aesop might have put it — he has now resolved the superficial dualism of good and evil, death and life, shadow and being, which he inherited through Christianity from Plato, as well as directly from Plato, and which again and again, hitherto, has infected his vision of poetic truth; though again and again he has had incomplete prevision of the constructive monism of life and death. And now, has he seen so clearly that the rest of his poetry will rise to the vision? Or, with his curious method of mental development, must he drop away from it for a while, only to come up to it once again, to express it again in yet more beau-

tiful and compelling fashion — as also is his wont? Ah! Time
grows short. His own death is not far away.

With this moral victory over the ills of life it is not inappropriate to compare an aesthetic victory over power, or,
rather, a merging of beauty and power, which Keats shadowed forth in *Hyperion*. In the third book of that fragment,
the young Apollo, like Keats, is oppressed with the antithesis
of the ugly and the beautiful; of love unselfishly revelling in
beauty, " full ankle-deep in lilies of the vale," and power forever realizing itself in a conflict and agony like that of un-
sceptred Saturn. Apollo, so marvellously gifted, like Keats,
with the gladness of song, finds himself weeping at Delos.
But Mnemosyne appears, with her history of all the wrongs
done under the sun, and passes into his mind. Then he cries
aloud his question, What is this terrible power in things that
makes me feel ignorant, cursed, and thwarted?

> . . . Where is power?
> Whose hand, whose essence, what divinity
> Makes this alarum in the elements,
> While I here idle listen on the shores
> In fearless yet in aching ignorance?

Suddenly a wondrous learning leaps in him, an enormous
knowledge that indeed makes him a God: somehow, he sees,
all destroyings are swallowed up in a process that, as a whole,
is beneficial and beautiful — the process, Shelley would
say, of nature as both destroyer and preserver. With that
reconciliation of the ugly and the beautiful in the higher
synthesis of the nature-process, Apollo feels he has conquered
his dilemma, has escaped his conscience-stricken luxuriating
in a superficial sensuous beauty, and has found the true, complete beauty for his singing. It is as though he had taken leave
of pale death itself to die into vivid life! His new song will
be one of struggle and beauty merged in a strong aesthetic
victory, taking the place of his former aesthetic dream, so

oblivious of reality. But just as Apollo is about to open his lips to sing this " new " poetry — the highest poetry, long since sung, by none better than by that poet who in the *Iliad* converted fierce conflict, agony, and death into tragic beauty, but a poetry always " new " — the fragment breaks off:

> " Knowledge enormous makes a God of me.
> Names, deeds, grey legends, dire events, rebellions,
> Majesties, sovran voices, agonies,
> Creations and destroyings, all at once
> Pour into the wide hollows of my brain,
> And deify me, as if some blithe wine
> Or bright elixir peerless I had drunk,
> And so become immortal " . . .
> Soon wild commotions shook him, and made flush
> All the immortal fairness of his limbs:
> Most like the struggle at the gate of death;
> Or liker still to one who should take leave
> Of pale immortal death, and with a pang
> As hot as death's is chill, with fierce convulse
> Die into life.

Thus the essence of tragic power is to enter his song and be merged with beauty. From a similar awareness of the higher synthesis of the ugly and the beautiful Shelley passed to a moral victory; *his* aesthetic victory, gathering up and carrying further the moral triumph, came a little later. In Keats's poetry, though not in his life, the special stamina of the moral victory over " death " is lacking.

The *Medusa* and the *Ode to Heaven* are not great poetic performances; but each touches rather powerfully upon a fairly common reaction to death. The former is Shelley's impression of Leonardo da Vinci's *Medusa* — of the terrible loveliness of that tragic head lying on the mountain's crest — which he saw at Florence. Da Vinci's sympathetic study subtly intensifies human horror by joining it with divine beauty. Shelley is fascinated by this union of loveliness and agony, finding therein a shocking symbol of his own suffering. The " tempestuous loveliness " of her terror " turns the gazer's spirit into stone." The " lineaments of that dead face " — its stony despair where thought no longer moves — seem suddenly to be engraved on his own dead spirit. Yet, in the same moment that he reads his own grief there, with an artist's eye he enjoys the picturesque treatment of suffering, and with a questionable intuition and defective grammar observes that the pathetic loveliness of the doomed maiden somehow harmonizes her pain:

> 'T is the melodious hue of beauty thrown
> Athwart the darkness and the glare of pain,
> Which humanize and harmonize the strain.

" Heart-easing " beauty of treatment! One is reminded of the mirage with which Keats loved to veil ugliness. A common enough reaction, as every heart knows; but the least Shelleyan part of the poem. His own special race is in his intense sympathy with the hideous pain cruelly imposed upon a beautiful spirit. A mutely accusing emblem of the savage jealousy of an anthropomorphic god, she lies there on high,

> Gazing in death on heaven from those wet rocks.

The *Ode to Heaven* is an ascension in contemplation, making use of the oft treated theme of astronomic sublimity. From meditating on the glory of heaven, the mind rises to behold, first, the greater glory of untold island-universes, and then the supreme splendour of the eternal Spirit, of which the universes are but atoms. As the heavens, and even the heavens beyond heavens, become diminished at the feet of Reality, the soul passes through them, as through the portal of the grave, and awakes in the unimagined. Thus death dwindles to a little step into immensity.

An essential operation of verse is to supply in the subtlest of verbal methods the intense feeling of an experience. This function is accomplished with amazing perfection in *The Indian Serenade*. But exactly what in this case the experience is — other than that it is one of sinking through love and beauty into deepest dejection — is uncertain. Whether the lover in the ecstasy of love is swooning toward an imagined death, like the draining delight of listening to Constantia singing; or with the doom of an actual death close upon him. is taking his farewell of the beloved — can scarcely be determined. Each reader must be his own oracle. It is especially tempting to discover here an analogue in love to the intellectual passion of the *West Wind*, for as there the poet cries to the destroyer and preserver to lift him from the thorns of life, where he bleeds in death, so here he begs the beloved to raise him from the ground, where he fails, and faints, and dies. Certainly both lyrics are woefully expressed from the poet's own suffering, and the *Serenade* is less a song of Mediterranean love than of the failure of love itself in this cruel, cold, and selfish world. It is no more an ordinary romantic tribute than that perfect lyric of Platonism in the *Posthumous Poems:*

> One word is too often profaned
> For me to profane it . . .
> I can give not what men call love,
> But wilt thou accept not
> The worship the heart lifts above
> And the Heavens reject not, —
> The desire of the moth for the star,
> Of the night for the morrow,
> The devotion to something afar
> From the sphere of our sorrow?

In the *Serenade* I like to see the elegy of the temporary failure, or set-back, of this devotion to " something afar from the sphere of our sorrow," the failure that, romantically, was the poet's in *Alastor*, and that is now, really enough, Shelley's own. Indeed, the *Serenade* might be regarded as the very reverse of those comforting songs of love with which Prometheus was healed; though both those and this alike spring from the sense of failure, as loveliest wishes are the children of desolation. But whatever be one's thought about the situation that has been translated into this exquisite music, the faintness of the poet, as he breathes the failing champak odours and listens to the dying plaint of the nightingale, is clearly a faintness as of the tired sleep that insensibly passes over into death. One cannot but recall the tired child in the *Stanzas Written in Dejection*. Even the opening lines have a mortal languor —

> I arise from dreams of thee
> In the first sweet sleep of night,
> When the winds are breathing low —

and every slightest nuance of the melody subtilizes the successive images of failure and cessation. The poem is a serenade sung " while the stars are shining bright " above a fatal sadness.

The group of seven political poems consists of: *Lines Written during the Castlereagh Administration, Song to the Men of England, To Sidmouth and Castlereagh, England in 1819, National Anthem, An Ode Written October, 1819, before the Spaniards had Recovered their Liberty*, and *The Mask of Anarchy*. They may be dismissed in few words, for they are of little poetical worth. They develop the Shelleyan theme of the murderous tyrant without remarkable addition. Indeed, the crude, popular style in which they are written, obviously in the hope of stirring the masses from their lethargy, gives them the effect of throwbacks to the juvenile period. But they achieve a mordant sincerity from the fact that they are expressions of revulsion from actually existing tyrannies, especially the repressive acts of Lord Liverpool's administration. Shelley's hatred of Sidmouth, the Home Secretary, and Castlereagh, the Foreign Secretary, is the motive of most of these ballads. In fact, they might well be called

songs of hate, so virulent is their vituperation. To impress
the popular mind he has employed an unusual realism in depicting suffering and death, which intensifies the mood of indignation and hatred. Over against Prometheus's repentance
of the curses he had flung upon the great heavenly minister
of evil, these songs of hate make strange, if not unwelcome,
reading.

But they remind us again of the grim realities of death-
in-life and death itself that constitute the problems of the
more important poems of this, as of every period, of Shelley's
life. In these lesser poems the practical burden of life — all the
evils men do under the sun — grows real, ugly, insistent.

In the greater poems but just now considered the poet has
wrestled again with these evils. First he elevated his old political theory of a realizable perfectibility into a dream of the
unbinding of the spirit of man and the advent of a real Utopia.
But, as he worked, the problem of unbinding the spirit revealed itself so indubitably as the moral problem of each individual, that Prometheus came to stand less for society and
more and more for the individual; until, at the close of the
poem, the final victory over the ugliness of death, whether
as a social symbol or a physical fact, is realized in a perfect
subdual of the fear and the pain and the ugliness to the moral
struggle of the individual. Utopia is spiritualized. It becomes
in effect a state of mind. Then, in the tragedy of *The Cenci*,
a drama more literal than symbolic, an extreme and particular
problem of evil and its accompaniments of death is resolved
by the same moral beauty. Finally, in the *Ode to the West
Wind*, Shelley, speaking in his own person, attains victory
over his own ills and his own dejection by the same summons to high ethical adventure. The burden of life, which is
" death," is carried bravely and gladly in the moral struggle it both demands and initiates. Moral sublimity conquers
death.

Chapter Five

BEAUTY AND LOVE:
THE AESTHETIC VICTORY

In the Letters of 1820 despondency bulks large. In the poems of the same year, there is comparatively little of despondency, and less of the distress of death. In no other year in all his writing life did Shelley write so little about death. It is the year of *The Witch of Atlas*, *The Cloud*, *The Skylark*, and the *Hymns* of Apollo and Pan, all of them poems of joy, in which death yields first place. It is the year of experimental poems on flowers — *The Song of Proserpine*, *The Question*, and *The Sensitive Plant* — in which loveliness takes precedence of death. It is the year of the two great political odes, the one to Liberty, the other to Naples; both spurning " the chains of dismay," and celebrating hopefully and happily political events that seemed advances toward freedom: in neither does the death-theme sustain a tragedy of tyranny. For his despondency, perhaps these were comforting songs.

But this very access of joy in life is the most significant moment so far in his pursuit of death; for now, after the unbinding from his *Weltschmerz*, he begins — as in the comforting songs of the fourth Act of *Prometheus* — to put the beauty of life above its ugliness. The aesthetic conquest of death there begun, then overshadowed by the moral conquest, is now carried forward joyfully. Indeed, in one of his letters, remarking of the projected *Julian and Maddalo* volume that it is made up of " all my saddest verses raked into one heap," he goes on to promise more smiles for the future.

The great act of disillusion has been played. Life, he now

realizes, is not what he had thought it, not what he had hoped. He had conceived human nature to be nobler than it is. He had confused possibility with fact. But at last the shattering surprise has run its furious course. Like his Prometheus, however, he has stood true to his visions, and they have brought him through, tortured, but master of himself. Now, accustomed to life as it is, he is ready to carry on steadfastly. He has learned the tragic spells to reassume the empire over himself. And if the stage of the struggle is now somewhat less grandiose — the innocent hopes of the eleutherarch having been adjusted to reality; if the glorious hopes for a world-change have been dashed against the helpless immobility of human custom: the fight is carried into the truer, deeper, more realistic world of the individual self. And there, when beauty of spirit is so perfectly achieved that the power of the world cannot change it, the aesthetic conquest of all ugliness — and of its Shelleyan symbol, death — is at last consummated. Thus change and death are swallowed up in the realized, indestructible beauty of one's own spirit, as at the close of *Prometheus* they had fallen before the moral victory over one's own weakness of spirit.

It is worthy of special remark that in this cycle of hope, disillusionment, and reconciliation, through which all who are greatly aware of life must pass, as by a natural law of the spirit, Shelley never completely sank into an Everlasting No, as did Teufelsdröckh, or into despair and cynicism, as did Byron's Cain, or into the pursuit of the senses, as did Faust. For he seems to have begun, in the untutored hopes of his youth, with the very visions that eventually liberated Teufelsdröckh and Faust. These were his intuitions of a unified world-order which, following Plato, he called intellectual beauty; and of the paramount duty of losing selfish desire in the higher desire to aid one's fellow-creatures, which, following Godwin, he miscalled perfectibility. His visions and vows which he narrates in *The Revolt of Islam* and dithyrambically, if inchoately, sings in the *Hymn to Intellectual Beauty* — the religious vision of a divine world-order and the ethical vow to human service — these keys to adjustment and reconciliation were his at an early date by right of discovery. The history of his maturing thought is not so much the gradual discovery of these, which open the one way out from despair, defeat, or mere animality, as the gradual adjustment of his early, sudden visions of them to the proper sphere of self-culture. He had begun by attempting to remake the world. But the world, as is its usual way, remade him; remade his vision into a finely and tragically tempered adjustment. But the vision was there from of old. Therefore, in spite of all suffering and dismay, he never sank into the abyss of inanity. He explored deepest Hell, but his vision never completely failed him. As Krishna taught Arjuna, so, almost identically, his visions taught Shelley.

And now he is on the last upward road to his supreme vision, which, characteristically, is to be a vision of death — of its conquest through aesthetic reconciliation with it. The *Adonais* is this vision. It is the inevitable conclusion of all the adventure. Now, the songs of sadness having been raked into one precious heap, Shelley pursues death through a poetry of tempered hope and joy, and masters it once for all.

It is a fascinating study to explore the preparation for *Adonais* in the poems of 1820 and 1821.

I

The Sensitive Plant is a beautiful but curiously imperfect parable of life and love and death. The imperfections affect both the outer form and the inner meaning.

The outer form parallels the seasonal changes, which have repeatedly been used by Shelley as symbols of life and death. This drama of change is performed within a garden. During spring and summer, the garden flourishes with beauty; in autumn and winter, it withers into the ugliness of death. The action is in three main parts and an epilogue.

The first part, which might be called Spring in the Garden, or Love in the Garden, is a marvellous description of flowers. It is a delicately luscious thing of the senses; a luxuriant blending of sights and sounds and odours, anticipating the synaesthetic loveliness of Rossetti's imagery. But it is more than a description. It is a romance, of rose and tulip, hyacinth, narcissus, and jessamine; and of plumed insects which float over the gleaming grass like " golden boats on a sunny sea." It is a creation of poetic animism. Every rose, lily, and other flower, every lovely living thing, is tremulously animate with passion. The garden is redolent with " love's sweet want." Longing is made as delicate and beautiful as a flower; in pagan innocence and freedom, as in Blake's *Garden of Love*.

In the second part, which might be called the Soul of the Garden, spirit is added to sense. A lovely lady, or witch — another anticipation of the Witch of Atlas — tenderly ministers to this paradise, scattering love wherever she moves. She is the sustaining spirit of the flowers, the Platonic Idea of their beauty. She visits, consecratingly, each herb and shrub, as the Spirit of Beauty in the *Hymn* visits, though unseen, all parts of this various world. Then, again like the Spirit in the *Hymn*, she passes away, leaving the garden vacant and desolate. With the seasonal change to autumn and winter, the lady dies.

Part three might be called Death in the Garden, or Death's Ugliness. It is the story of the garden's passing. It is the tragedy of beauty gone down into the grave: a tragedy of pity for all this innocent loveliness suffering into nothingness, a flower-analogue of Ophelia and Juliet and Desdemona; a tragedy of fear of the darkness and dankness of death, of the obscenity of decay. The flowers fade and are gone. There are autumnal leaves,

> brown, yellow, and grey, and red,
> And white with the whiteness of what is dead;

and on the dry wind, as in the *Ode to the West Wind*, they pass like troops of ghosts:

> Their whistling noise made the birds aghast.

Then there is a pestilence of loathliest weeds: thistles, nettles and darnels, dock, henbane and hemlock.

> And agarics and fungi, with mildew and mould,
> Started like mist from the wet ground cold;
> Pale, fleshy, as if the decaying dead
> With a spirit of growth had been animated!

The usual theme of the ugliness of death — the usual reverse of Shelley's heavenly animism! Nor is there lacking the coffin plank and the corpse — the coffin of the lady, and her corpse

> Which at first was lovely as if in sleep,
> Then slowly changed, till it grew a heap
> To make men tremble who never weep.

The imperfections of this outer form of the parable lie in the technique of the verse. There are several signs of careless-ness. Some of the rhymes are awkward, imperfect, or inexpres-sive; making not for harmony, but only a disturbing tinkle. There is a dullard footing in some lines, especially an eking of the metre with ineffective, unrequired monosyllables, such as *did*. Some of the anapaests drop into sing-song in spite of no little success in fingering the pauses. Moreover, the com-bination of these defects, so well known to the reader of Shelley's earliest anapaests, with the inappropriate throw-back to Gothic horrors, as in the lines cited above, leaves the reader incongruously reminded, in the midst of much beauty, of the juvenile exercises. In passing, it is worth remarking that similar throwbacks in rhythm and horror are found in another and indubitable experiment written at this very time, the quite uneven *A Vision of the Sea*. At any rate, *The Sensitive Plant*, powerful as it is, leaves one reader, at least, with an impression as of an unfinished experiment.

The imperfection of the inner meaning develops with the epilogue, and is of the nature of a technical *non sequitur*. Once more the poet's extreme sensitiveness to ugliness entails the need of reconciliation with death, and once again he has recourse to the doctrine of the illusory character of appearances, which he had inherited from some of the classical philosophies. In actuality, he cries, all things are only a seeming — the shadows in a dream; and it is a modest and comforting creed to consider that death itself, like all the rest, is a mockery. What is real is the unchanging Idea back of the changing appearance. Reality is in the rational concept. The Ideas of love and beauty and delight suffer no change or death, exceeding in their nature our obscure organs of perception. It would follow, then, one might suppose, that the beauty of the garden persists as an unchanging Idea, while various incorporate appearances exist, pass, re-exist, and re-pass, in endless change, or *samsara*. What Shelley actually avers is the *non sequitur* that

> That garden sweet, that lady fair,
> And all sweet shapes and odours there,
> In truth have never passed away:
> 'T is we, 't is ours, are changed! not they.

But, by the argument, it is precisely the sweet shapes and odours that would pass away, and we, too: all alike, the shadows in the dream. Shelley would have been truer to his doctrine had he even taken comfort, as Wordsworth did, in that inward eye, of memory and idea, " which is the bliss of solitude." But his intense love of the actual form, or appearance, of beauty persuaded him to assert that the " sweet shapes " themselves have never passed away.

The Pursuit of Death

The anguish caused by the death of his children, particularly by the death of William in June of 1819, could be rendered bearable, perhaps, only by denying the reality of death. In Plato's Ideas he found some ground for that denial — but of it he made not a firm ground: only the instability of a *non sequitur*.

The fallacy, it may be admitted, is only technical; for the passage that has just been quoted may properly be taken to be a poetic, or figurative, way of asserting that in deep truth the shapes forever exist unchanged in their proper reality as Ideas. But then we are reduced to the absurdity of admitting that death, like the sweet shapes, is a mockery-appearance, and denying Idea-reality to death while asserting it for the sweet shapes. If Shelley is pressing toward that alleged Mahayana consciousness in which death and pain, on the one hand, and life and joy, on the other, are realized in a higher, harmonious synthesis, he has yet to conquer the deep-rooted aversion to death and pain which makes him except them from reality.

Indeed, one can conceive a far nobler epilogue to the poem: a splendid synthesis of the beautiful and the noxious in their harmonious interaction — their dualism annihilated in a realization of their mutuality. Here would have been an appropriate place for realizing poetically Hegel's optimistic conception of the end of tragedy — the harmonizing of opposed forces by destruction, or, to use the Hegelian jargon, the reconciliation of imperfect subjectivities of the good with the good itself by their necessary destruction. It may be true that few tragedies have been so composed that the actual victim, an Othello or an Oedipus, has realized at the moment of destruction this salutary vision, however much the philosophic reader may approach it. But the present tragic antithesis of beauty and death is potential with a confession of imperfect subjectivities, and it would have been so deeply appropriate to realize the imperfections explicitly in the Conclusion, by bringing forward their reconciliation in a higher synthesis. A less ambitious conclusion might have been managed by realizing that death and beauty are not a perfect antithesis, and that for liberation it is only necessary to find the beauty in death. The truer antithesis of life and death, however, is essential to the poem, and that each member of this antithesis is an imperfect subjectivity is apparent as soon as they are synthesized in the concept of the all-inclusive nature-force — say the *physis* of Aristotle, or the *natura naturans* of Spinoza — which works imperturbably through both life and death. Death, then, so far as it is anything more than mere subjectivity, becomes only a name for the most obvious of those continual changes whose process we variously hypostatize; and the ugliness of death is revealed as entirely subjective, based in egotism, ignorance, pain, and common-sense. Either Aristotelianism or Spinozism or Hegelianism, to say nothing of the release of life-supporting nitrogen through vegetable-decay, would have supplied Shelley with this truly liberating concept, or attitude. And how superior it is rationally to the one-way idealism of the *Symposium*, which neglects the reconciliation of opposites to idealize one term (beauty) at the expense of its anti-type! How such a reconciliation purges death of ugliness, pain, and fear! And how splendidly, in the poesy of some great concreting imagery of the synthesis, might the tragedy of this garden-parable have been resolved by such a mythopoeic imagination as was Shelley's!

Toward this realization Shelley seems to have been moving in parts of the *Prometheus* and especially in the *West Wind*. *The Sensitive Plant* is, indeed, such a step backward into the abysm of his painful antithesis of the ugly and the beautiful, as was anticipated in our study of the *Ode*. Perhaps the very imperfections, alike of its outward form and inner meaning, are signs that *The Sensitive Plant* was more a superficial exercise, lightly undertaken to see how well he could describe living and dead flowers, than a true expression of the moods that were deepest in him at this time. And the epilogue has the effect of an insufficiently considered afterthought. In fact, is it not this very superficiality, this easy throwing together of old ideas in specious and erratic relation, and the dressing of them in a parable at once seemingly simple and undeniably beautiful, that has made the poem one of his few *popular* compositions?

But the sensitive plant itself? What of *it?* What, except that it is Shelley himself, in a way, and so the key to the poem. If that proposition be true, the key should fit our interpretation, if the latter, in turn, be true. And, indeed, does not one discern in the description of the plant that very extraordinary yet misleading sensitiveness to love, beauty, and ugliness which we have come to associate with Shelley himself, and in which also we have found at once the source of the beauty of the outer form of the parable and the imperfection of its inner meaning? The plant is described as one

> . . . which could give small fruit
> Of the love which it felt from the leaf to the root, —

> For the sensitive plant has no bright flower;
> Radiance and odour are not its dower;
> It loves, even like Love, its deep heart is full,
> It desires what it has not, the beautiful!

If these lines be not confession, the same confession of love for " something afar from the sphere of our sorrow " that occurs elsewhere, the same picture of the stricken poet that we find in *Adonais;* if their mood be not the mood of all the latest saddest songs he had " raked into one heap," to be done with; if they be not another expression of Shelley's own ever-recurring tragic sensitiveness in the face of beauty and death — the careful reader of Shelley's poetry will be amazed. They are all compact of the Shelley we have learned to know. And it is this very acuteness of emotion that has again and again, and once again here, rather unexpectedly, prevented

Shelley from attaining the serenest insight into his premises of life and death.

A true step forward, however, is taken in one of the most popular of all his lyrics, the next to be considered.

The Cloud succeeds where *The Sensitive Plant* failed. The agonizing contradiction of life and death is surmounted in the optimistic synthesis of a *natura naturans*. The poetic, or mythopoeic, imagery is a cloud in mutation. The exhalation of the seas, the growth of the cloud, its processional thunder and lightning, its beautiful reflection of sunrise and moonlight, its precipitation in dew and rain, hail and snow, its dissipation, and the re-continuation of the whole process, are vivified in rapid succession. The shifting beauty of these changes produces no mood of pensive sadness in the poet, but intoxicates him with gladness. The vitality of the life-process takes hold of his imagination, as, really, it had informed Keats's when he spoke of life as " a pigeon tumbling in clear summer air." It energizes his susceptibility to impressions, and then exalts his intuition of the everlasting vitality of nature. Each loveliness passes, but only to yield place to its successor; and the anguish of each departure is absorbed into the glory of each advent. Death is swallowed up in the victory of a persistent and beautiful, beneficent process. This is that intuition of change, or of an *élan vital*, that comes to one contemplating the procession of nature: the realization that nature itself cannot use the word death with our egotistic, sorrow-bred meaning, for death is but the gate through which the procession passes on. *Mors janua vitae est.* This is that Apollonian intuition and aesthetic victory over conflict and agony which in *Hyperion* makes Apollo a veritable god. The thoughtful and imaginative vigour of Shelley's development of the idea is strikingly apparent if we contrast *The Cloud* with Tennyson's moody approach to the theme in his *Nothing Will Die,* or with Christina Rossetti's characteristically desolate commentary in her *Mirrors of Life and Death.*

Years before, this classic intuition had marked the culmination of Shelley's poetic cosmogony, in *Queen Mab*, where mention is made of the bickering wheel of life flashing forever into successive vitalities. But that young view of life had not been disturbed by the intrusion of personal misfortune and deep, irrecoverable loss of hopes and persons dearer than hopes. Youth's vision of the general life-process is impervious to the effect of unexperienced particular sorrows. Youth stands ready to give up everything for its vision because as yet it has so little to lose. With the actuality of misfortune, the theoretic vision collapses. There supervenes the long purgatory of becoming accustomed to sorrow. But, the adaptation to sorrow once achieved, the young vision is resurrected by sadness to a far more real, far less theoretic, understanding. An idea has passed through experience and become understanding. Joy impregnates, sorrow brings forth, as Blake said; and the chastened, immeasurably surer joy of the new birth succeeds. Nor is there any more comforting and inspiring attitude toward change than this classic synthesis of life-in-death. For in the presence of personal bereavement of all sorts, alike of beloved ideas and beloved causes and beloved persons, it rationally validates our desire-born conviction that all bright and lovely things exist in each other. In place of an egotistic sorrow, concerned with the loss of particulars, it substitutes a magnanimity developed by a perspective of many sorrows. Nor is the substitution an arbitrary exchange of one thing for another that is unrelated to the first. Instead, the magnanimity is a drawing out, or education, of the susceptibility in us for realizing the architectonic of life, the deep somehow-oneness of all particulars in their ordered relation to a splendid whole. One of the most sublime poetic images of this intuition is Dante's vision of the redeemed, rank above rank, as the petals of a divine rose, adoring without envy of place the whole that is God.

But in *The Cloud* the figuration joyously parallels the time-changes of physical apparitions, adding beauty to beauty, and marching to the splendid accompaniment of the elaborately harnessed anapaests, until the meaning of the whole procession breaks out in a kind of *in excelsis* with the last stanza:

> I am the daughter of earth and water,
>> And the nursling of the sky;
> I pass through the pores of the ocean and shores;
>> *I change, but I cannot die.*

"*I change, but I cannot die*": there, in a reference to death, is the culmination of this lyric of what I should like to call cosmic gladness, were not such a phrase long since spoiled by cheap usage on the part of superficial mystics. This gladness, no longer the theorem of inexperience, but the tragically achieved attitude of a man of sorrows — rendered necessary by the logic of events, in part validated by the best guess of reason — this gladness in death repairs the inadvertent failure of the conclusion of *The Sensitive Plant*. It is the more acceptable statement of what, doubtless, Shelley meant to say in that conclusion.

And it is, too, the authentic note of the poems of this year, 1820. It reaches back to the destroyer-preserver theme of *The West Wind*. It anticipates the profounder, lovelier, and more personal treatment of the same theme in *Adonais*. Here, it reinforms, with a new gospel, the old Shelleyan paraphernalia of caverns, tombs, and ghosts:

> I change, but I cannot die.
> For after the rain, when with never a stain
>> The pavilion of heaven is bare,
> And the winds and sunbeams with their convex gleams
>> Build up the blue dome of air,
> I silently laugh at my own cenotaph,
>> And out of the caverns of rain,
> Like a child from the womb, like a ghost from the tomb,
>> I arise and unbuild it again

Thus, at long last, the Gothic horrors of *Zastrozzi* have become the glad mysteries of *The Cloud*. Our Richard of St. Victor, with his genius for seeing invisibles, born with ghosts in his eyes, has exchanged raucous make-believe for poetic insight.

Even that poem of " an unbodied joy whose race is just begun," *To a Skylark*, with its symbolism of spiritual desire and exultation, ascends a climax to death, or, rather, to this classic synthesis of life-in-death. For, after piling figure on figure to suggest the impression the bird's high carolling has made upon him, Shelley reaches an acme by alluding to this synthesis in a poetic fable:

> Waking or asleep
> Thou of death must deem
> Things more true and deep
> Than we mortals dream —
> Or how could thy notes flow in such a crystal stream?

The whole idea is not there. But surely one may be justified in finding in this stanza of *To a Skylark* an allusion to " the true and deep " intuition in which *The Cloud* culminates. Moreover, the very next stanza is Shelley's best known and most perfect expression of the human sadness from which this deep truth is born. Indeed, if the two stanzas are read in reverse order, the one quoted above will immediately read as a poetic truth, or imaginative possibility, suggested by the following lines:

> We look before and after,
> And pine for what is not;
> Our sincerest laughter
> With some pain is fraught;
> Our sweetest songs are those that tell of saddest thought.

But it is the nature of the poet, certainly of Shelley, to vere from mood to mood; and even in this year that is so distinguished by the comparative absence of despondency from his

verse and by the presence therein of an unwonted accumulation of joy, there are several short poems that recur to the
darker mood. Over against the liberative synthesis of life and
death attained in *The Cloud* and *To a Skylark*, and curiously
fumbled in *The Sensitive Plant*, they stand in striking contrast.
There is a little dirge, *Autumn*, reminiscent in its address to
the winter months, *Come, months, come away*, of Shakespeare's *Come away, come away, Death;* and delicately allu-
sive to paling flowers and dead leaves, " the saddest array . . .
of the dead cold year." Yet in the last line, in a reference to the
wintry rain making the grave of lost beauty green with its
tears, is a faint touch of the more liberative idea. Again, a
passing but dismal impression is caught in six lines that compare the waning moon to

> . . . a dying lady, lean and pale,
> Who totters forth, wrapt in a gauzy veil,
> Out of her chamber, led by the insane
> And feeble wanderings of her fading brain.

Is there a reminiscence here of Keats's Angela feebly laughing
in the languid moon? Another six-line stanza on the lessening
moon, beginning

> Art thou pale for weariness
> Of climbing heaven,

recalls in its adaptation of languid sound to the weary sense of
the passing of time, Sidney's most famous line,

> With how sad steps, O Moon, thou climb'st the skies.

Shelley makes this plaintive image of world-weariness a symbol of his dissatisfaction with change, comparing the ever-
changing moon to

> . . . a joyless eye
> That finds no object worth its constancy.

The Pursuit of Death

What a history of disappointment is packed into those two lines! And into the three stanzas of *The World's Wanderers,* where star and moon and wind become types of the restless soul, has been distilled once again the emotions of the failing quest that were storied in *Alastor.* Then there is *The Two Spirits,* an allegory of the idealist's removal from earthly struggle only to find that he is overtaken in his regional heaven by whirlwind, stormy rain, and inevitable night, whose terrors he must ride with a calm heart if he would remain true to his aspirations. But in a fragment called simply *Death* and in a sonnet beginning, *Ye hasten to the grave,* the elegiac mood comes out most starkly. Death is everywhere, he cries in the fragment, and we are death:

> Death hath set his mark and seal
> On all we are and all we feel,
> On all we know and all we fear.

There may be some relief in the concluding, half-cryptic suggestion that did not all things else die, love itself would perish. But there is unrelieved regret in the sonnet — a tired, dejected heart wondering why all its life it has pressed with swift feet green and pleasant paths in the pursuit of death,

> Seeking alike from happiness and woe
> A refuge in the cavern of grey death?
> O heart, and mind, and thoughts! What thing do you
> Hope to inherit in the grave below?

Finally, in another allegory, the dejection swallows all besides. Death is a portal, shadowy but adamantine, yawning on that highway of life we all tread, leading into " a cavern huge and gaunt." About it rages an unceasing strife of shadows, like restless storm-clouds about the cleft in a great mountain. Many pass by carelessly, indifferently. But others,

> . . . by more curious humour led,
> Pause to examine, — these are very few,

Beauty and Love: The Aesthetic Victory

And they learn little there, except to know
That shadows follow them where'er they go.

Thus the poet of *Prometheus Unbound* and *Ode to the West Wind*, of *The Sensitive Plant*, *The Cloud*, and *To a Skylark*, turns away from the optimistic synthesis of life and death in those poems of gladness, and, remaining true to the inescapable emotional antitheses of human experience, restates the moods of gloom and dejection, all the more powerfully for his success in rendering the more expansive and heartening moods. Side by side with the two joyful dithyrambs to liberty — the *Ode to Liberty* and the *Ode to Naples* — in which his " soul spurned the chains of dismay," is this little collection of brief but intense lyrics of reluctance and dismay.

And now we come to the brightest coruscation of this *annus mirabilis poetae*, and with it turn again to the poems that spurn despair. Like the fourth Act of the *Prometheus*, it voices the gladness of a soul unbound from too much pain of living. But, like all our poet's greatest poems, it is born of the antithesis of life and death and reaches its crisis in a gesture of victory over the latter.

The Witch of Atlas is, perhaps, the most characteristic of Shelley's compositions. At any rate, of all his poems it seems, at first sight, the most susceptive of the common charge that his work is thin sown with thought. There is a charming story of an encounter between a Shelley enthusiast and James Russell Lowell. Edward A. Silsbee had secured from the hands of Claire Claremont, in Italy, a notebook into which Shelley and Mary had copied a number of his poems, including *The Sensitive Plant*, *To a Skylark*, and *A Vision of the Sea*. Mr. Silsbee brought the treasure to Harvard, and, after showing it reverently to several friends, whose breathless enthusiasm matched his own, determined to surprise Lowell with the marvellous find. From the interview Mr. Silsbee returned stunned and disgusted. Lowell, not too much impressed, had asked him whether he found any thought in Shelley's poetry! Lamb, Arnold, Stopford Brooke, and many others of less note, have made the same criticism. What better example, at first sight, of their contention is there than *The Witch of Atlas?* Better even than *The Cloud* or *To a Skylark*, for their brevity minimizes the charge of unprofitableness; whereas the prolonged play of alleged meaningless, merely beautiful, imagery and music in the *Witch* has made it the tip-top example of Shelley's ineffectuality. Mary herself thought it a visionary rhyme, lacking human interest. Many a critic has luxuriously praised its inconsequentiality, deeming that here Shelley has cut loose entirely from all responsibility for meaning, to follow in sheerest dream wherever his fancy led. One is reminded of Francis Thompson's too eloquent description of Shelley's rapturous toying with imagery — too eloquent, because the imagery is praised at the expense of its meaning.

But is there not something more to the *Witch* than opulent imagery? Has it not a perfectly developed, consistent meaning? Mr. Yeats and Mr. Kellett think it has. Thompson himself, noting Shelley's " well-known power to condense the most hydrogenic abstraction " into concrete imagery, declares that in the *Prometheus* " the very grass is all a-rustle with lovely spirit things." But the Witch herself is compact of all these lovely spirit things, and is the very soul of their soul; for she is indeed the incarnation of the fundamental abstraction whence they all derive. She is that Platonic Idea of beauty, that " Intellectual Beauty " of the *Symposium*, which constitutes both the meaning and inspiration of so much of Shelley's poetry. With that interpretation, to which Mr. Yeats inclines, or with Mr. Kellett's (that the Witch represents poetry), the meaning of the poem becomes fairly clear and certainly remarkable. Indeed, the virtual synonymity of these terms, beauty and truth, along with imagination, so far as the meaning of the Witch is concerned, corresponds to their intimate inter-relation in Shelley's *Defence of Poetry*. But these words are cold. To feel and see, as well as conceive, the meaning of the poem, one should first remind himself of the deepest passions of beauty he has himself known, when the mood of the beautiful was raised to the religious sublime and he seemed to feel his way, so to speak, almost into heaven itself. The incommensurable beauty of Beethoven's *Pastoral Symphony*, of the Taj Mahal, of Shakespeare's sixtieth sonnet, of the Parthenon sculptures, of the Kanchenjunga at sunrise! Those well-nigh ecstatic moods, with their " instinctive perception of the underlying analogies, the secret subterranean passages, between matter and soul "! Remembering those intense, beautiful experiences, and the deep feeling of their unique meaning, one may turn to find a subtly exact description of them in the beauty of the Witch herself, for she *is* all those experiences condensed into an appropriate, symbolic — by no means arbitrary, allegorical — image:

> A lovely lady garmented in light
>   From her own beauty; deep her eyes as are
> Two openings of unfathomable night
>   Seen through a temple's cloven roof; her hair
> Dark; the dim brain whirls dizzy with delight,
>   Picturing her form; her soft smiles shone afar,
> And her low voice was heard like love, and drew
> All living things towards this wonder new.

As a description of a mortal woman, of any piece of complicated pink and white protoplasm, this stanza is unbearably extravagant, sentimental. But as an animation of deepest beauty and its feeling-tone — what it seems to mean — the figure is perfectly expressive: " garmented in the light of her own beauty " — this abstract or naked, intensest beauty, with no garment of sensuous apparition, but effulgent with its own intelligence; her deep eyes, like " two openings of unfathomable night seen through a temple's cloven roof " — the unfathomable sacredness of the beauty; " the dim brain whirls dizzy with delight, picturing her form " — the ecstatic, swirling mood; " her soft smiles shone afar " — the intuition of the all-pervasiveness of the beauty; " her low voice was heard like love " — the sense of an universal harmony; " and drew all living things towards this wonder new " — the conviction, at least temporary, that this beauty is a revelation of a some-how-oneness of all things. More direct, less symbolic, descriptions of a human mind undergoing this passion are to be found in *To Constantia Singing* and in the closing stanzas of the *Hymn to Intellectual Beauty*. Parallels from other writers are not far to seek. There is Rossetti's *Soul's Beauty* and Spenser's *Hymne in Honour of Beautie*. In some of their sonnets, Sidney, Spenser, and Shakespeare praised their beloved ones by representing them as participants of absolute beauty. Mr. Kellett has suggested that the idea of the Witch was found in Dido's description of a priestess, one of the Atlantides (*Aeneid*, IV). But I like, also, to juxtapose this description of beauty from the *Phaedrus:*

> But of beauty, I repeat again that we saw her there shining in company with the celestial forms; and coming to earth we find her here too, shining in clearness through the clearest aperture of sense. For sight is the most piercing of our bodily senses; though not by that is wisdom seen; her loveliness would have been transporting if there had been a visible image of her, and the other ideas, if they had visible counterparts, would be equally lovely. But this is the privilege of beauty, that being the loveliest she is also the most palpable to sight. (*Phaedrus,* 250; Jowett's translation.)

The Witch, then, is the " visible counterpart " of the subjectivity of a supreme beauty; or, more truly, the poetic incarnation of it — a poetic personification of a special movement of the mind.

Every detail of the description of the Witch furthers the

account of the intuition called spiritual beauty. For example, one aspect of this mental experience is that by its extreme vividness the intuition makes all objects seem, in comparison, unreal — " mere things." If we translate this feeling into a proposition, we obtain Spinoza's theorem that all phenomena in time are phantasms, whereas essential truth, or noumenon, is beheld only by the imagination. Now, the poetic counterpart alike of the feeling and the related proposition, is the following description of the effect of the Witch's beauty upon the beholder:

> For she was beautiful; her beauty made
>   The bright world dim, and everything beside
> Seemed like the fleeting image of a shade;
>   No thought of living spirit could abide,
> Which to her looks had ever been betrayed,
>   On any object in the world so wide,
> On any hope within the circling skies,
> But on her form, and in her inmost eyes.

Such half-mystical, religious experiences as this find an intellectual interpretation in idealism and transcendental realism. With what glad recognition, then, Shelley must have read the propositions of Spinoza and the myths of Plato, finding therein an even startling community of experience! With Dante, too, he must have communed in this very intuition, as witness these lines from the thirty-third book of the *Paradiso*, confessing an effect of the vision of God:

>   It may not be
> That one who looks upon that light can turn
> To other object willingly his view,
> For all the good that will may covet, there
> Is summ'd; and all, elsewhere defective found,
> Complete.

Although one should indeed be on his guard against assuming too metaphysical an implication of such poetic intuitions as these of Shelley and Dante, and should, also, consider them as primarily expressive of the intensity of the poet's aesthetic experience, yet both poets were well read in idealism and confessedly were conscious in their poetry of metaphysical intention.

At any rate, in the next stanza, the thirteenth, a metaphysical intent is perfectly clear. The relation of phenomenal to ideal beauty is symbolized. The Witch weaves herself a garment.

> She took her spindle
> And twined three threads of fleecy mist, and three
> Long lines of light, such as the dawn may kindle
> The clouds and waves and mountains with, and she
> As many star-beams, ere their lamps could dwindle
> In the belated moon, wound skilfully;
> And with these threads a subtle veil she wove —
> A shadow for the splendour of her love.

A shadow for the splendour of her love — that is, the creature-veils of the Idea of beauty. The three threads of fleecy mist, the three kindling lines of dawn, and the three star-beams stolen from the dimming radiance of the belated moon, entwined to make her subtle veil, are symbols of phenomenal beauty. What exquisite mythopoesy of a metaphysical concept! Shelley's mythopoeic genius, it seems to me, shows nowhere more clearly or more beautifully than in this story of the Witch weaving her tenuous life-garment, so that men, as it were, may not be blinded and maddened by her naked beauty. Even Goethe's famous poetizing of a similar concept is, in comparison, itself lacking in the sensuous beauty it celebrates:

> In Lebensfluten, im Thatensturm
> Wall' ich auf und ab,
> Webe hin und her!
> Geburt und Grab,

Beauty and Love: The Aesthetic Victory

Ein ewiges Meer,
Ein wechselnd Weben,
Ein glühend Leben,
So schaff' ich am sausenden Webstuhl der Zeit
Und wirke der Gottheit lebendiges Kleid.

Shelley's poetry repeatedly illustrates by its nature-sensuous-
ness the beauty of the idea that it presents, so that nature
seems to utter his moods and ideas with its own voice. His
moods and ideas are completely identified with things, becoming the soul of their soul, as he would say. Thus he carries
poetic animism to its loveliest and most significant limit, as
far beyond the reach of Hafiz as Hafiz carries beyond Rück-
ert or even Goethe.

Next, the arts and philosophy are brought into relation
to the Idea. The most ideal delights of the senses and the
imagination, such as music and poetic vision, and the craftsmanship of beautiful objects, are the treasures of the Witch,
fulfilled of her spirit. The highest reaches of the intellect —
such as speculation on the nature of the ideal state — the " inmost lore " of love, the wizardry of the ordering power of
mind, are also her treasures, participating of her power.

Thus, successively, the noumenal beauty has been related
to phenomena, the senses, and the mind, in a sort of crescendo.
But when was a Shelleyan cosmogony complete without a
cry of pain for the mutability of beautiful things? The melancholy problem makes its advent in the form of spirits of beautiful things, ocean nymphs, hamadryads, oreads, and naiads,
who beg to live forever in the light of the lady's sweet presence. But it may not be, she replies:

" This may not be," the Wizard Maid replied;
  " The fountains where the Naiades bedew
Their shining hair, at length are drained and dried;
  The solid oaks forget their strength, and strew
Their latest leaf upon the mountains wide;
  The boundless ocean, like a drop of dew,

Will be consumed — the stubborn centre must
Be scattered, like a cloud of summer dust;

" And ye with them will perish one by one.
    If I must sigh to think that this shall be,
If I must weep when the surviving Sun
    Shall smile on your decay, oh, ask not me
To love you till your little race is run;
    I cannot die as ye must — over me
Your leaves shall glance — the streams in which ye dwell
Shall be my paths henceforth, and so — farewell! "

The Idea remains; the shadows of it come and pass, to come
and pass forever. But the Witch herself weeps most humanly
at the change, and a " knell of sobbing voices came upon
her ears from those departing Forms." Again, the elegy of
change. Here it brings the first part of the poem to its
close.

So far, the meaning of the poem can best be summarized
in a sentence from Shelley's own translation of the *Banquet*
of Plato:

> Nor does it [i.e., Intellectual Beauty; here, the Witch]
> subsist in any other that lives or is, either in earth, or in
> heaven, or in any other place; but it is eternally uniform
> and consistent, and monoeidic with itself. All other
> things are beautiful through a participation of it, with
> this condition, that although they are subject to produc-
> tion and decay, it never becomes more or less, or endures
> any *change*.

Yet this is the poem that is supposed to be without thought,
a mere fantasia of loosely connected images!

Now, the poem, after this climax through beauty to a moment of pain for the mutability of all fair things, begins another ascent toward a yet more definite facing of death, this
time not elegiacal, but contemptuous.

From her sadness the Heliad takes refuge in poetry, and,

in turn, it is the splendour of her sweet smiles that makes the shining beauty of poetry. She fashions a marvellous boat, beautiful and passionate as a panther, swift as " a wingèd thought on blind Homer's heart." In it she places the sexless spirit of pure poetry, which she herself has created by kneading, or synthesizing, fire and snow with love. Then begins the voyaging of poetry, the visiting in imagination of the wonders of the universe, past, present, and future. This part of the poem, indeed, might be entitled " The Pleasures of the Imagination "; for the sheer joy of imaginative enterprise is its theme and spirit. It is no Endymion-search or Alastor-quest for a satisfying, perfect beauty in the sense-world, tragic in an initial mistake of trying to realize the ideal; but the testament of the beauty that lies everywhere for the exploring imagination. Many of the sights that have bewitched poets of all the ages are — I was going to say — passed in review. It is more accurate to say the things themselves are here, in their own beauty, like a fire itself, instead of a painted fire. Here are amazing rivers, boring the Caucasus; the awful gloom of forest wildernesses; unfathomable caverns; a " star-surrounded pyramid of icy crag cleaving the purple sky "; deep, shadowed pools, and " the shallow road of white and dancing waters," as lovely as Spenser's Idle Lake; earthquaking cataracts, shivering " their snow-like waters into golden air "; darkness, and stars speeding up the torrent of the night; the infinite reaches of space, and their island universes; thought racing " on the platforms of the wind "; the music of the spheres; the vapour-belted pyramids of the Nile; and the beautiful arrogance of ancient Egypt, in temple, labyrinth, and Osirian feast:

> But her choice sport was, in the hours of sleep,
>   To glide adown old Nilus, where he threads
> Egypt and Œthiopia, from the steep
>   Of utmost Axumé, until he spreads,
> Like a calm flock of silver-fleecèd sheep,

His waters on the plain, — and crested heads
Of cities and proud temples gleam amid,
And many a vapour-belted pyramid;

By Mœris and the Mareotid lakes,
  Strewn with faint blooms, like bridal-chamber floors,
Where naked boys bridling tame water-snakes,
  Or charioteering ghastly alligators,
Had left on the sweet waters mighty wakes
  Of these huge forms — within the brazen doors
Of the great Labyrinth slept both boy and beast
Tired with the pomp of their Osirian feast.

These, and many more, are the pleasures the Witch pursues. Although they rush fast upon each other, in bewildering and untired imagery, until they seem indeed a veritable Mozartian fantasia, they are, nevertheless, integral parts of the central theme: the Idea of beauty as imaged in poetry. The meaning is never lost, however amazing the virtuosity.

These pleasures amply justify calling this the supreme poem of joy of this year. Shelley himself calls it, with this sense, a " holy song." But imagination bodies forth, too, the other side of beauty — the ugliness of life, especially human life. Of course, the usual evils reappear: foul religious superstitions, cruel custom and law, the stupidity of priests, the persecution of the weak, shipwreck and war. It is best not " to mirror these in a holy song," he says; so their treatment makes only a small part of the poem. But that small part is placed toward the end, and the culminating effect is that of a defeat of evil by the Idea of beauty and by the dominating spirit of joy. First, the Witch herself minimizes evil by calling it the contention which merely stirs " the liquid surface of man's life " — a demotion that depends from wishful, romantic thinking under the control of a joyful mood, rather than from a consistent philosophy. For, if there is an Idea which renders things beautiful by participation in it, is it not logical, at least, to assume an opposite Idea which renders things ugly by participating in it? Or, if it is matter that dulls the Idea, whence matter? We are back to the *non sequitur* of *The Sensitive Plant*. Second, death itself is faced, here at the end of the poem. Beneath many an outer, ugly form the Witch beheld the " naked beauty of the soul," and to those most beautiful she gave strange panacea in a crystal vessel — a symbol of their awareness of ideal beauty. These drank in their deep sleep, i.e., in their deep poetic dream, of that fair panacea of evil, ideal beauty,

> And lived thenceforward as if some control,
> Mightier than life, were in them; and the grave
> Of such, when death oppressed the weary soul,
> Was as a green and over-arching bower
> Lit by the gems of many a starry flower.

They lived " *as if some control, mightier than life, were in them* " ! In other words, death was swallowed up in the inde-structible beauty of their own vision. Marvellously intoxi-cated, or, as the Greeks would say, maddened, by their in-sight of beauty, these seers find release from ugliness while they live. But death is not welcomed as the preserver of beauty: it *oppresses* the weary soul.

The next stanza, however, reaches a higher mood. The ec-stasy rises superior to death, overmatching it with contempt. In an hyperbole, the Witch is represented as scornfully cast-ing away the cerements of the grave and preserving the beau-tiful souls in an ideal, sequestered life forever, while the blind generations of mankind fleet onwards through life and death. On a night when beautiful souls were buried, she

> Restored the embalmers' ruining and shook
> The light out of the funeral lamps, to be
> A mimic day within that deathy nook;
> And she unwound the woven imagery
> Of second childhood's swaddling bands, and took

The coffin, its last cradle, from its niche,
And threw it with contempt into a ditch.

And there the body lay, age after age,
   Mute, breathing, beating, warm, and undecaying,
Like one asleep in a green hermitage,
   With gentle smiles about its eyelids playing,
And living in its dreams beyond the rage
   Of death or life, while they were still arraying
In liveries ever new the rapid, blind,
And fleeting generations of mankind.

This hyperbole is the final symbol in the poem. It is a symbol of that self-realized beauty of an individual spirit which nothing in the world can defeat. The undefeated soul is poetized as immortal, living on in the Idea. Yet, even so, death is not welcomed, equably and strongly, as one phase of the Witch's power. A contempt of death concludes the poem with an attitude of aesthetic victory, or aesthetic *quasi* victory. But this contempt of death does not involve a contempt of life. Shelley never cries with Rabelais, " Ring down the curtain; the farce is over."

II

O world! O life! O time!
On whose last steps I climb,
   Trembling at that where I had stood before;
When will return the glory of your prime?
   No more — oh, never more!

Out of the day and night
A joy has taken flight;
   Fresh spring, and summer, and winter hoar,
Move my faint heart with grief, but with delight
   No more — oh, never more!

The next year, 1821, is the year of Shelley's holiest poem on love, *Epipsychidion;* his most lyrical political poem, *Hel-*

las; and his greatest poem on death, *Adonais:* long poems all, each devoted to one of his three favourite subjects. It is, moreover, the year of his deepest dejection, which breaks forth in several shorter compositions. Close upon the many poems of joy, of the previous year, come now a company of sadness. As so often, in so many years, the short poems are the immediate expression of personal experiences; the longer poems, the expression of the same experiences mediated by being brought into agreement with the major controlling ideas of his genius.

He who wishes may read in the biographies the private history of this year, told with or without innuendo, as may be the habit of each biographer; and there he may find facts that will allure him into offering " explanations " for all these poems, both long and short. But even if one could be sure, beyond a shadow of doubt, that some special phase of the poet's intercourse with Mary, or Emilia Viviani, or Jane Williams, lay behind a given poem, or a part of it, this finding would be an " explanation " of the poem only if one were to assume that the poem is bare reporting, or only disguised repression, or mere wishful thinking. Is the poem little more than a self-beguilement with beautiful words, or is it an eloquent and significant utterance of a momentous experience? From his sorrow has the poet learned something of general value, which he teaches in song? Or has he deceived himself with a dream-disguise of his thwarted passions?

The longer poems, as I read them, very clearly involve the adjustment of current experience to a considered, let alone an intuitive, philosophy. But some of the shorter poems, too, though they seem rather obviously the lyric cry of the moment, are nevertheless such deeply poetic renderings of representative experience that they cannot be " explained " sufficiently by paralleling them with fragments of biography. An example will make this contention clear. The following song has by innuendo been attributed to each of two different experiences of the year. There is not enough evidence to prove which experience is the contributing factor: a typical difficulty in this kind of interpretation. It is said that the poem confesses Shelley's disappointment at Mary's cooling passion; also, that it confesses Shelley's disillusionment after some passionate encounter with Emilia Viviani.

> When passion's trance is overpast,
> If tenderness and truth could last,
> Or live, whilst all wild feelings keep
> Some mortal slumber, dark and deep,
> I should not weep, I should not weep!
>
> It were enough to feel, to see
> Thy soft eyes gazing tenderly,
> And dream the rest — and burn and be
> The secret food of fires unseen,
> Couldst thou but be as thou hast been.
>
> After the slumber of the year
> The woodland violets reappear;
> All things revive in field or grove,
> And sky and sea, but two, which move
> And form all others, life and love.

Well may he have learned this lesson of cooling love from Harriet, or Mary, or Emilia. Who has not learned it? But does one testimony of one couple *explain* the experience, to say nothing of the poem? Real explanation must go far deeper, into psychology and philosophy alike. The task of explanation is far more compendious than the dilettante literary interpreter seems to realize. But no such thorough explanation is required to fathom the significance of the poem. The expression is at once general and intense enough to be true to human experience the world over; so piercingly eloquent that Everyman realizes himself in it, knowing himself, and mankind, more keenly than he had before; so musical that pain is purged of crude selfishness, beauty taking over the place of intemperate self-love. Sappho might have sung the experience much as did Shelley. In spite of a flaw in the thought of the last stanza, which a little more revision could easily have removed, the poem gives a new and beautiful form to a common emotional experience, and purifies it of all that is ignobly weak and selfish. Therein lies the poem's significance: and if explanation be yet required, it is an explanation of the poem's power, in mood and music and image, to interpret incommensurably a memory in the hearts of all men.

If this appreciation be acceptable, how much more emphatically in the same vein may one speak of the two stanzas at the head of this section. To anyone who has followed the story of Shelley's heart and mind, every line is a revelation of the poet's adventures. But a knowledge of the points of contact is not necessary to a worthy understanding of the poem; it only adds a special poignancy to the understanding. The world that knows nothing of Shelley repeats the lyric as its own. And the poets are able out of their own lives to speak universally just because they have the gift to recognize the representative quality of their individual experience.

As the less significant approaches to the poems of this year, I shall take leave herewith of the biographical, the gossipful, the Freudian. Instead, I am concerned to realize the dejection, the sense of loss and failure, which pervades so many of the writings of this year; and then, to see rising out of that low-spiritedness the more notable reflections on death; and finally, to study in *Adonais* the most notable poetizing of the most common of Shelley's subjects.

One might appropriately single out as an introduction to the lyrics of sadness, a little song of farewell to delight, beginning

> Rarely, rarely, comest thou,
>   Spirit of Delight!
> Wherefore hast thou left me now
>   Many a day and night?

A simply told regret for that mood of gladness which had lifted its head in the previous year, the poem consists of an enumeration of the beautiful things which make, or had made, him glad: spring, starry nights, a golden morn, an autumnal evening, snow and radiant frost, waves, winds and storms, and solitude, and love, and everything which is " untainted by man's misery." Delight in these has for a while deserted him. When will it come again?

But the prevailing moods of sadness are darker and more definite. There are two overlapping moods which appear repeatedly: grief for dead love, and dejection, verging to despair, in the face of the infinite misery of life, change, and death. The most personal example of the former is the epistolary poem, *To Edward Williams;* the saddest, *Remembrance,* in which he speaks of himself as a living grave of sorrows; the most poetically impressive, the last two quoted above. But in the midst of these fragments of grief occurs one of Shelley's best-known lyrics, which, by the very restraint it places upon pain and by its idealization of love, adds a welcome effect of moral strength. It has already been compared, above, to the *Indian Serenade;* but its beauty, and its importance for an understanding of Shelley, justify further quotation and comment.

> One word is too often profaned
>   For me to profane it,
> One feeling too falsely disdained
>   For thee to disdain it;
> One hope is too like despair
>   For prudence to smother,
> And pity from thee more dear
>   Than that from another.
>
> I cannot give what men call love,
>   But wilt thou accept not
> The worship the heart lifts above
>   And the Heavens reject not, —

Beauty and Love: The Aesthetic Victory

> The desire of the moth for the star,
>   Of the night for the morrow,
> The devotion to something afar
>   From the sphere of our sorrow?

Simply imaged, clear and definite in thought, perfectly phrased, the mood constrained to its natural musical form, this is one of Shelley's finest poems in his more classical mode. It says much for the essential integrity of Shelley's will that this poem should appear among these lyrics of lost or defeated passion. Indeed, the last two lines sum up as well as any other short passage in all his work, or better, both the major impulse of his life and the chief source of his sadness — that incurable devotion " to something afar from the sphere of our sorrow." The " something afar " is that " awful Loveliness " to which he had taken the oath of allegiance in the next to the last stanza of the *Hymn to Intellectual Beauty*. Clearly, the old devotion will bring him triumphantly through this valley of the shadow of death. Out of such emotional immediacy as is revealed in this group of short poems grew the *Epipsychidion*.

In the yet darker and more tragic mood, the most notable achievement is the solemn cry of despair, already noticed, which has been placed at the head of this section because it so well sets the key for this melancholy year. It, too, fixes personal passion in a perfect form, and by its controlled intensity in a significant mood attains universality. But the most sensational example of this hopeless mood is the ten-line poem called *Time*.

> Unfathomable Sea! whose waves are years,
>   Ocean of Time, whose waters of deep woe
> Are brackish with the salt of human tears!
>   Thou shoreless flood, which in thy ebb and flow
> Claspest the limits of mortality,
> And sick of prey, yet howling on for more,
> Vomitest thy wrecks on its inhospitable shore;
>   Treacherous in calm, and terrible in storm,

The Pursuit of Death

> Who shall put forth on thee,
> Unfathomable Sea?

True, these lines may be nothing more than an adventitious exaggeration of the depression of this period, called into being merely by a sudden realization of the splendid opportunity to use the sea as an image of misery. But, even if this be so, the poem continues to take its place in the present group, as well as in all Shelley's work, as the most pessimistic of his reactions; so pessimistic, indeed, as to be out of character with the fundamental enthusiasm of his nature. If Shelley were no more than an ordinary example of the manic depressive type, passing erratically from egregious exaltation to egregious prostration, without any ethical and philosophical management of himself, we should expect many poems of this kind, instead of being surprised at one or two. In *Ginevra*, which had better been called The Death of Ginevra, there is an almost equally bitter, un-Shelleyan observation: " life's great cheat — a thing bitter to taste, sweet in imagining "; and an actual echo of the seventh line of *Time:*

> In our night
> Of thought we know thus much of death — no more
> Than the unborn dream of our life before
> Their barks are wrecked on its inhospitable shore.

Strange language this for the idealist who in the same year wrote more than once of the immortal deity " whose throne is in the depth of human thought "! But it is a language that is repeated toward the beginning of *Epipsychidion* — another emotional immediacy out of which that poem grows.

In some way, perhaps, these passages mark the nadir of spirit in Shelley's work: some very temporary weakening of that stern resolution which continually dictated an heroic resistance to the ills he knew so well — as in the courageous closing lines of the *Prometheus* and the *West Wind*. Indeed, even in this little collection of 1821 he soon repeats the spells

by which he reassumes an empire over his misery. In a sonnet, *Political Greatness*, we find the noble iteration of the
ethical ideal:

> Man who man would be,
> Must rule the empire of himself; in it
> Must be supreme, establishing his throne
> On vanquished will, quelling the anarchy
> Of hopes and fears, being himself alone.

In this spirit he himself goes forth in his longer poems to build
another gospel on the vanquished will and emotional anarchy
he has revealed in these lyrics. But in the lyrics, too, there is
further trace of the audacity with which, at length, he always
faced life — and death. In *Dirge for the Year*, usually printed
first among the poems of 1821, he repeats the optimistic message of the *West Wind;* and also in a fragment on Keats,
where he splendidly addresses death as " the immortalizing
winter." This is that hopeful idea of death as both destroyer
and preserver which has been one of the noblest attainments,
so far, in his study of death.

From this lyric underbrush rises the most un-English
growth of English poetry, the *Epipsychidion*. Its exotic, trop-
ical Platonism is amazing: as though it were a tree, white of
trunk and branch and twig, yet so transparent that scarlet sap
could be seen pulsing in every stem and entirely incarnadining
its countless leaves. I sometimes believe no stranger love-poem
exists in any language. It is not a poem solely filled with
double-distilled sensuousness, like Sappho's *Anactoria;* or
with artfully impassioned adoration, like Petrarch's sonnets
to Laura. It is not " the laughing glory of an amorous boy
and girl," like Catullus's *Septimius and Acme*. It is not the
Anacreontic mysticism of Hafiz. It is not the definite religious
allegory of Dante's Beatrice in the *Paradiso*, nor yet the tense
love-of-love of *La Vita Nuova;* nor the guilty love of Guine-
vere, nor the sheer passion of Tristan and Iseult. Yet it has

something of all of these; and, besides, a smashing defence of free love, a tragic retrospect of love's failure, and a continual interweaving of love and death, ending in their mutual assimilation. It is a unique, paradoxical composition of Platonic transcendental realism, uninhibited sensuousness, prohibited Puritanism, exalted passion, and poignant pain. It is one of the loveliest of English poems, and its loveliness is repeatedly beset with the remembrance of a terrible ugliness. And it is written, *mirabile dictu*, in the heroic couplet!

Indeed, I cannot resist a digression, at this point, on the metrical achievement of the poem. But I shall do myself the pleasure and honour of using Professor Saintsbury's words on the matter, thus paying tribute, in passing, to that most salient and contagious enthusiasm which lifts his remarkable work on the history of English prosody so far above most of its kind. These are his words:

> But that " going from strength to strength," which is so noteworthy in Shelley's last years, and which makes one lose himself in wonder as to what he might have done, is as noticeable in his mere prosodic aspects as in his general poetic quality. The enjambed couplets of *Epipsychidion* show an immense advance on *Julian and Maddalo*, entirely avoiding that limpness which . . . is the curse of the species, and attaining a rhymed verse-paragraph which, quite unlike *Lycidas* in particular effect, resembles it in belonging to the general class of " rhymed blank verse " — rhymed verse that acquires the power of blank, and blank verse that borrows the attraction of rhyme.

The moment we begin to interpret this poem by the " matter-of-fact history of the circumstances to which it relates " (the words are Shelley's) — its references to Harriet, Mary, the mysterious woman in Naples, and Emilia Viviani — we run the danger of turning its " sweet food into poison " (again, Shelley's words). For we are not given a literal transcript of fact, but an imaginative transfiguration of it; a confession not of his practical, but of his artistic experience — though Shelley was seldom able completely to divorce the two. It is not so much an allegory of his life as a symbol of what he found most significant in life. With literal life it has little to do. Browning said that its passions " never came into the real world at all." Shelley calls its passions " votive wreaths of withered memory "; the petals of the practical rose of love are become " pale and dead." There is no thorn of literal reference that could have wounded the living. It is a dream of ideal loveliness, veering off from the actual, and thereby achieving a deeper, aesthetic reality. The descriptions of the beloved are as inapplicable to a mortal woman as are those of Asia and the Witch. Shelley himself called it an " idealized history of my life and feelings." " Idealized " not in the sense of " disguised," but in the sense that he has generalized and aggrandized the particular.

We shall come closer to its special power, therefore, if, forsaking all attempts to reduce its magnificence to a *confession scandaleuse*, we follow sympathetically the part that death plays in the luxurious but ideal love which is the heart of the poem. Again we shall witness the ascension of Shelley's spirit out of dejection to an aesthetic and individual conquest of the causes of dismay. But it is no *quasi* victory, involving a contempt of death, that we shall now see; but a victory so much more real that death becomes " sweet death," its advent is welcomed, and its release is mystically conceived.

In no other of his poems is Shelley's way of interrelating love and death made so clear. In this respect *Epipsychidion* is to be regarded as the culmination of a long development, beginning in the juvenilia, and extending through the love-in-death themes of *Queen Mab, Alastor, Prince Athanase, The Revolt of Islam, Rosalind and Helen, Julian and Maddalo, The Sensitive Plant,* and *The Witch of Atlas,* to say nothing of many of the lyrics. In all these, two irreconcilable attitudes are discernible. First, death has been feared as the destroyer of love. Ruin has been " love's shadow,"

> Following him, destroyingly,
>   On Death's white and wingèd steed,
> Which the fleetest cannot flee,
>   Trampling down both flower and weed,
> Man and beast, and foul and fair,
> Like a tempest through the air.

But this idea is nearly always only the momentary product of an instinctive, passing fear; and from it Shelley reacts, in the second place, to an opposite, carefully considered, and permanent attitude. Love becomes one of the chief sources of a mystic faith in some sort of escape for beauty from the grave; for the poet's sensitive mind has not been able to admit that the intense beauty of love may cease altogether, and the exalted passion of oneness between two lovers has been for him as for so many poets a symbol, or promise, if not proof, of an all-unifying spiritual reality. This poetic faith he could not give up even in the period of his temporary fascination in French realism: it persists illogically in every page of *Queen Mab*. The failure of the quest in *Alastor* only intensifies the need of such a faith. The distinction between the common and the ideal love in *Prince Athanase* is an attempt to ground the emotional need in a rational ideal. The reunion of the souls of Laon and Cythna, after death, is a poetic figuration of the ideal. The confession of the madman in *Julian and Maddalo* is the tragic story of the failure of Pandemos, the earthly and unworthy Aphrodite. The epilogue of *The Sensitive Plant* reiterates a faith in the immortal, or, rather, unmortal, nature of love. *The Witch of Atlas* is a dithyramb in honour of the Platonic Ideas of love and beauty. Death has always been the shadow threatening love. But the impassioned beauty of love's union has always been a prefiguration of the soul of the universe. Moreover, love and its shadow, death, have been the intense centre of his own self, or soul. Now, in this culminating poem, he has tried fully to realize this central intensity of love and death, this " soul of his soul " — a phrase he may have borrowed from an epigram by Meleager of Gadara. And he has named the effort " a little poem upon the soul," *Epipsychidion*.

But this supreme love-poem is not shadowed by fear of death. It is a gleaming thing. It opens with burning praise of love as the most vivid and beautiful experience in this dark world, as an echo of a divine harmony. Within the first twenty-eight lines love is made both the living soul of the body of this death, and the seraph of Heaven — the

> Sweet Benediction in the eternal Curse!
> Veiled glory of this lampless Universe!
>   . . . living Form
> Among the Dead!

Yet a little further, and it is called the " violet-shrouded grave of woe," and the beloved is

> A lute, which those whom love has taught to play
> Make music on, to soothe the roughest day
> And lull fond grief asleep.

It is the " sweet lamp " at which his " moth-like Muse has burned its wings ": that ideal fire which has been his bliss and bane, for he has tried to live as though the ideal were actualized in the commonplace. Thence, from that misguided sincerity, that untutored fallacy, pathetic and tragic — all his deepest woes! But ideal love is still the " violet-shrouded grave of woe." He turns back to that. In spite of all failure in the fact he turns again, for comfort, for strength to live, to his dream. I am reminded of George Moore's Paul of Tarsus. Jesus had been taken from the cross in time to be resuscitated. For twenty years he has lived in a little cenobitic community of the Essenes, tending sheep. Paul, preaching the

risen Christ, finds the mortal and living Jesus. Jesus disclaims
the miracles of the resurrection and ascension. But Paul refuses to face and accept the fact. He continues to preach the
risen God — and the Essenes follow him, and his dream; for
the dream is the grave of their woe. They are romantics, like
Amiel, using the ideal to escape captivity.

But Shelley's romantic dream of love becomes a reasoned
faith in a kind of miracle — in love as the effluence of the
divine. His dream may indeed originate as a creative expression of an enthusiast's special need for sympathy. By the very
nature of their being, enthusiasts search for sympathy, and
according to the measure of their success they experience the
" sweet benediction in the eternal Curse." Shelley, by his
notable gift for finding beauty in passion, intensified both his
need of love and his response to it. Hence arose, as we have
seen repeatedly, an overpowering consciousness of death,
for death sunders lovers. Therefore he is impelled to conquer
death by finding an indestructible reality in love. And, first,
by brooding on love he comes to feel its more than mortal
nature. This has always been the way of enthusiasts. He who
prays much to God hears the voice of God. Dr. Masefield's
confession of faith is a case in point: " I believe that this
world is only a shadow of the real world, and I think that by
brooding on what is brightest and most generous in this world
the beauty and the bounty and the majesty of the real world
shine in upon the soul." Then, second, because he believes
in living by reason, Shelley assimilates this intuitive belief
to the conceptual form of a Platonic Idea: the Idea of love
is unmortal, and human love is what it is by its participation in the unmortal Idea. Death, therefore, does not destroy love, however much it may change the lover and the
beloved. And it is precisely this concept, I believe, that lies
behind the following description of the Aphrodite of the
Epipsychidion:

Beauty and Love: The Aesthetic Victory

See where she stands! a mortal shape indued
With love and life and light and deity,
And motion *which may change but cannot die;*
An image of some bright Eternity.

The key-words I have put in italics: they are an iteration of
the central idea of *The Cloud:* " I change, but I cannot die."
To romantic dream has been added the sanction of the Platonic theory of the concept.

But in *Epipsychidion* Shelley recapitulates the story of his
intellectual pursuit of this Idea-reality: his first vision of it in
an intense and beautiful abstraction, his naïve hope of discovering a physical embodiment of the abstraction, the failure
of that hope, the longing for death as an escape from despair,
the further search, the final success, and the new vision of
death. The same story is told in his prose allegory, *Una Favola.* From these parallel pieces, the poem and the fable, we
may reconstruct this ideal history of love and death, as distinct from any related sequence of matter-of-fact experiences.

In the poem, the story begins with the poet's adolescent
awakening to the spirit, or Idea, of beauty: " a Being whom
my spirit oft met on its visioned wanderings . . . in the clear
golden prime of my youth's dawn." This is that vision of ideal
reality which in his verse has taken so many forms, the most
notable being the " unseen power " of the *Hymn to Intellectual Beauty*, the " secret power " of *Mont Blanc*, the lady of
the Sensitive Plant, and the Heliad of *The Witch of Atlas*.
Now it is described as that Beauty

Which penetrates, and clasps and fills the world.

Like the Witch clothed in the light of her own beauty, this
spirit is said to be " scarce visible from extreme loveliness "
— " robed in such extreme glory that I beheld her not." But
her voice animated the woods and fountains, flowers and
breezes, the rain of every passing cloud, the singing of summer birds, all sounds, all silence. There is similar confession

in his prose fragment *On Love,* though it is couched in a more psychological, less mythopoeic mode:

> In the motion of the very leaves of spring in the blue air, there is then found a secret correspondence with our heart. There is eloquence in the tongueless wind, and a melody in the flowing brooks and the rustling of the reeds beside them, which by their inconceivable relation to something within the soul, awaken the spirits to a dance of breathless rapture, and bring tears of mysterious tenderness to the eyes, . . . like the voice of one beloved singing to you alone.

In all high poetry, and romance, too, and in the other arts, he divined the same spirit, as well as in " that best philosophy," which

> Makes this cold common hell, our life, a doom
> As glorious as a fiery martyrdom.

This vision has always been, according to his belief, the soul of his soul, the innate and originative principle of his imagination. Coleridge would call it the characteristic product of his " secondary," or all-unifying, imagination. It is his deepest knowledge, to which all experience must be assimilated: " to this we eagerly refer all sensations, thirsting that they should resemble or correspond with it," as the prose fragment says. Then the youth, impelled by the need for that companionship which our mating nature requires, even in respect of spiritual experience, searches for an incarnation of this soul of his soul in the form of woman. By the old law of our being, ideal beauty and sex coalesce in love.

With this quest youth enters the " gloomy valley " of matter-of-fact life, pessimistically called the " cold common hell," the dark wood where the straight way of the spiritual life is lost — " *selva oscura, che la diritta via era smarrita.*" In *Una Favola,* love abandons him in this " savage place," and he is beset, thereupon, by loathsome figures, mocking and threatening, until the fair heaven of his vision is hidden in earth's miasma. In the poem, the vision " passes into the dreary cone of our life's shade " — a highly symbolic image of the shadow cast by the earth. In his despair for the loss of his vision, death comes very near, at once the type of his dismay and a promise of release. So death had relieved the poet in *Alastor.* In *Una Favola,* this death is described as the lovely sister of life, a great enchantress, " sitting before a pale fire of perfumed wood, singing laments sweet in their melancholy, and weaving a white shroud upon which his name was half-wrought, with the obscure and imperfect beginning of a certain other name." The youth, begging her for aid against the hateful, tormenting figures of life, continually converses with her, and requires her love. Wherewith she, too, leaves him. " From that moment the youth pursued the track of Death."

Love and death, vision and failure, are the two poles of this typical story of the heart.

In the poem, a voice now says,

> O Thou of hearts the weakest,
> The phantom is beside thee whom thou seekest.

Into " the wintry forest of our life " the poet, " every gentle passion sick to death," enters again to find the veiled Divinity. Then, stumbling, and bewildered by the new forms of life, he finds the Venus Pandemos, the lower, physical love and beauty — the theme of *Prince Athanase* and *Julian and Maddalo:*

> One whose voice was envenomed melody
> Sate by a well, under blue night-shade bowers;
> The breath of her false mouth was like faint flowers;
> Her touch was as electric poison.

Pain and ruin followed. Thereafter, the quest was continued rashly, with new failures, until he stood at bay, weak and wounded, in mortal despair of beauty. Then, beside him, stood a cold, chaste shape, as like his glorious dream as the moon is like the sun. She made his wild heart sleep. At her silver voice both life and death grew weak, and became " unmindful of their accustomed strife." They left him, and there was nothing but a moon-world of cold dreams, in which his spirit lay frozen. But at last into the " obscure forest " — the *selva oscura* of the *Inferno* again — came the very living light of his vision, dissolving the dull cold:

> I knew it was the Vision veiled from me
> So many years.

Love revivifies his dying spirit. Again the mysterious voice is heard in every wilderness and bower of beauty, the storms " chaunt their thunder-psalm,"

> And every motion, odour, beam, and tone,
> With that deep music is in unison,
> Which is a soul within the soul.

As the lovers' joys grow perfect, death is swallowed up in aesthetic glory, in a realized subjective beauty. Their thoughts and joys may sleep, but cannot die, for they are " folded within their own eternity." Each moment of perfect passion is an eternity. Then, in its ecstasy, the imagination rends the curtains of time and space, and speaks a mystical faith no reason can prove. Death is no longer the " lovely death " of release from the gloomy valley and cold common hell. It is a " sweet death," for it is conceived as a phase of persistence, the very entry, perhaps, to a purer beauty. Love is said to lure one upon life's rough way toward " sweet death," as the day lures the night, spring the winter, hope sorrow — into " life, light, and peace." It is not the death that appeared so alluring to the young man who always carried laudanum with him and who made more than one attempt at suicide. This sweet death lures him not with a promise of a retreat from too much living, but with a promise of a yet more glorious realization of the Idea than can be offered by any mortal incarnation of it. With this faith in death the soul passes on to renewed vitality, finding its place in the infinite reality:

> Then call your sisters from Oblivion's cave,
> All singing loud: " Love's very pain is sweet,
> But its reward is in the world divine,
> Which, if not here, it builds beyond the grave."

On that exalted note the poem ends. *Una Favola* comes to a similar close. The wretched youth, after years of vain search for releasing death, meets a lady of surpassing loveliness. She is the very lady in quest of whom Love had led him through the gloomy labyrinth of error and suffering. At once his love for her becomes so potent that it overcomes every other thought, and now he hates death for her dear sake. Then Death stands before them, saying:

> Whilst, O youth, thou didst love me, I hated thee, and now that thou hatest me, I love thee, and wish so well to thee and thy bride that in my kingdom, which thou mayest call Paradise, I have set apart a chosen spot, where ye may securely fulfil your happy loves. . . . Ye mistrust me, but I forgive ye, and await ye where ye needs must come, for I dwell with Love and Eternity, with whom the souls whose love is everlasting must hold communion.

So the aesthetic trinity of Love, Death, and Eternity is faithfully and mystically set up and worshipped. Nor is one left with an impression that this love must fail in the event, after the enthusiasm of discovery has passed.

The more we document a dream the flimsier it becomes. Certainly the more the *Epipsychidion* is documented the more its poetic truth is sacrificed to fact. Dextrously to parallel its persons and parts with the circumstances of the poet's outer life, such as his disappointment in the actual Emilia, reduces its special power, viz., that idealization of matter-of-fact which we call symbolism. In every truth, behind each figure, incident, and phrase of the poem lurks not an isolated individual experience, stark and singular, but a universalized particular. Shelley's genius leans to seeing each particular *sub specie aeternitatis*. But the eternal species, or Idea, is always brought forward in an amazingly sensuous embodiment, which is its symbol. Thus Emilia, and every other character and every event in the poem, is made into a symbol, each standing for typical experiences and some incommensurable meaning in these typical experiences. These characters and events are not mere transpositions of the literal and actual. They are so much fictive biography, into which, indeed, have entered some details of the author's matter-of-fact experience; but those details in the process have been imaginatively transformed into symbols of largest possible meaning. They are examples of the ideal to which art attains, so well defined by Bosanquet as " the heightened expression of character and individuality which comes of a faith in the life and divinity with which the external world is instinct and inspired." Or, to put the same thing more briefly, in words borrowed from Shelley's *Defence of Poetry*, which he in turn had borrowed from Shakespeare, they are the result of that adding of spirit to sense which is the function of poetry.

That the poet himself was conscious of his habit of idealizing the fact into a symbol of spirit, we have seen in his Preface to *Prometheus* and in our review of that and many another poem. Moreover, most of his difficulties in practical conduct have derived from the reverse instinct to realize the Idea in the fact; for symbolism, though it makes for greater poetry than does allegory, makes for disastrous living just so far as it elevates persons and things to an ideality they can nowise support. It is more profitable, indeed, to interpret Shelley's biography by his poetry, than his poetry by his life. Neither Harriet nor Mary nor Emilia could attain to perpetual Witchhood. It is possible to understand how their natural failure to support the sublime role imposed upon them, inspired the poet to another symbol — that of the moth forever burning its wings at the flame of the ideal.

This symbolic habit had doubtless received a special impetus from Shelley's recent reading of Dante's three works, the *Vita Nuova*, the *Convito*, and the *Divina Commedia*. There are reminiscences of all three in the poem. Most impressive is the superficial contrast but profound similarity of Emilia and Beatrice. Emilia retains more of sensuous reality than does Beatrice even in the *Vita;* and far, far more than does the Beatrice of the *Paradiso*. For even the comparatively slight realness of description and adoration in the *Vita* Dante apologized in the *Convito*. The utmost of sensuousness in the spiritual portrait in the *Paradiso* is the splendour of Beatrice's smiling eyes — *lo splendor degli occhi suoi ridenti* — which, coming fast upon Dante's momentary forgetfulness of her while he concentrated his thought perfectly upon God, served to dispart his mind again amongst the objective multiformity of things. But Emilia's beauty again and again renders the page far warmer to the touch, far more voluptuously coloured to the eye, than even the pages that entranced Abélard and Héloïse, Paolo and Francesca. Now it has been suggested by one of the most sympathetic readers of Shelley — Professor Woodberry — that this intrusion of Emilia's physical allurement spoils the ideality of the poem; and that nowhere are the mortal woman and the ideal vision fused into one, as they are in Beatrice. To me it seems, rather, that Dante and Shelley, using opposite methods, have reached the same ideal end.

Dante has preserved the ideality of Beatrice in the *Commedia* by avoiding the sensuous. He is as intent upon averting the " infamy of having yielded to so great a passion," as he was when, in the *Convito*, he allegorized all the passions of his earlier odes. I am reluctant to believe that I must yield to any reader in enjoyment of those sacred but glowing eyes of Beatrice —

che sorridendo ardea negli occhi santi.

The Pursuit of Death

I like to believe that none can be more stirred than am I by that sweet and joyful beauty of the woman close by the throne of God. The very reticence in sensuous portraiture throughout the poem, renders this simple touch of physical beauty, in the moment of utmost idealism, extraordinarily vivid and sacred. The effect is at one with Dante's special gift for mixing the divine and the human very simply, without visible effort, with the least possible expenditure of debate: witness the whole plan of the poem, the intimate association of politics and the divine, or the assimilation to spiritual meaning of such ordinary details as a burning coal, or water in a bowl. Maurice Hewlett described this gift as " Dante's naked simplicity — that matter-of-fact statement of poetical truth in the terms of literal truth." Dante's complete absorption in his vision is again and again revealed in this identification of subtle ' soul ' experiences and heavenly splendours, with common and small things, the furrow of a ship, or a right triangle. Always conscious of the ideal unity of life, he must have taken a peculiarly artistic satisfaction in endowing these commonplaces with vast and subtle spirituals. This gift is, indeed, representative of the literal truth which once characterized Christianity, and which is impressed upon many of the allegories and romances of the Dark and Middle Ages — upon none more than upon Malory's *Morte d'Arthur*, with its " familiar clasp of things divine." But Dante's power is the perfect and sophisticated phase of this naïve fidelity.

The *Commedia*, by virtue of this power, became the epic of the Catholicism of the Middle Ages, the sufficient poetic interpretation of its highest truth. Christianity always needs poetic treatment of its verities, if they are to satisfy the cultured mind. It was Coleridge who remarked that " unless Christianity be viewed and felt in a high and comprehensive way, how large a portion of our intellectual and moral nature does it leave without object and action." Dante's vision of the spiritual order of the universe, with the hierarchy of souls, each in its appointed place, wrapt in perfect contemplation and unenvious love of the Whole, the one spirit pervading all, from the greatest to the smallest, supplied the requisite comprehensiveness.

Five hundred years later, eighteenth-century skepticism put the quietus to this pre-Raphaelite intensity of spiritual vision. Another hundred years, and a renascence of wonder became necessary. The esemplastic — or spiritually visioned — imagination, which reveals the hidden analogies of things and assembles them into an ideal unity, cannot long remain in eclipse. From Keats to Turner and Rossetti the revival of faith ran its course. But it was not the old course. Skepticism had undermined the simple realness of a spiritual universe. The later poets of faith turned again, like primitive man, yet with a vast difference, to the sensuousness of the physical world and to their own emotions and imaginative animisms, and discerned there vaguely but intensely the art of God. Where Dante, clear and definite in his theology, read the divine in the physical plainly and simply, with a great love of white light, the romantics perforce found their revelations in the highly and ingeniously coloured. They had to create a new faith out of the intensity of their aesthetic experience. Symbolism, with its feeling for a mystery lurking in all vivid beauty, was the inevitable outcome of such a renascence.

Now it was in this spiritual rebirth of the senses, of emotion, and imagination, that Shelley played what is in some ways the most significant of all poetic roles. For he, more daringly than any other artist in the movement from Wordsworth to Maeterlinck, united passion and colour with idealism. In no other of his poems did he carry this daring further than in *Epipsychidion*. In no other of his idealizations of women did he carry it further than in that of Emilia Viviani. Embraces and kisses, indeed, are in each of his holy of holies. Prometheus has his Asia. They unite in a bower of bliss. The poet feeds on the " aërial kisses of shapes that haunt thought's wildernesses." The Heliad herself " knew what love was." But the physical transports of Emilia and the poet are the frankest of all. Indeed, they shock even the Shelley enthusiasts — or most of them.

But it is this final fusion of the real and the ideal that is at once a supreme example of Shelley's special genius, the most remarkable of romantic symbolisms of its kind, and the most striking contrast to Dante's Beatrice, though Emilia and Beatrice are fundamentally akin. To ask that Emilia be remade in the spiritual simplicity and definitiveness of Beatrice, merely personal preferences aside, is to become forgetful of the intellectual history of five centuries. Emilia is to the romantic movement what Beatrice is to the first twelve hundred years of Christendom. In sensuous reality she is closer to Goethe's Marguerite. In the exploring efforts of the idealizing imagination all three are equally daughters of one mother.

Nor will any superficial talk of repressed wishes, or disguised animality, or dream-transferences, for long take precedence over a more sympathetic appreciation of the poem. For animalistic determinism is oblivious of the simple fact that the humane life consists of nothing so much as the intellectualization of the passions — not their ascetic renunciation, but their completest re-formation by the mind's loveliest and noblest abstractions. Fanatical asceticism has been tried repeatedly. It has nearly always been found wanting. It leads to hypocrisy and mischief. By its very neglect of the humane method it, for a fact, does fall back into the arms of Freudian determinism. But *Epipsychidion*, this most daring of fusions of realism and idealism, cannot be compassed by an incomplete psychology. Herein is implicit a frank recognition of what man and humanism are, or, at least, of what constitutes the essential principle of their struggle, or history: the ever renewed attempt to translate the lower into the higher passions, without ever denying either or sacrificing the one to the other. Read the *Epipsychidion* as a poem of prostitution, and its transports become ridiculous exaggerations of the intoxications of lust. The " sweet food " is turned into poison. Shelley said the reviewers turned it into something like the love-affair of " a servant girl and her sweetheart." Read it as the intensest of all romantic fusions of physical and ideal love, and its ecstasies approximate the most potent of human experiences — known, after all, to but few men and women. Perhaps the time has not yet come when the meaning of the poem can be readily understood. Fear yet sanctifies the old taboos the poem itself holds in disdain.

The measure of the potency of this experience in Shelley's life is that it overcame his aesthetic distaste of death, and ratified for him, as it does for most romantics, the incurable devotion to " something afar from the sphere of our sorrow." It is when the fusion of the physical and the ideal becomes a confusion of fact and dream that the realist parts company with the romantic. That confusion produced *Alastor;* the fusion is attained in *Epipsychidion* — in the perfect moment that is a kind of eternity, in a supreme, sensuous beauty that for a moment realizes the Idea of the beautiful.

For this aesthetic victory over all that is ugly, there is need of a special preparation of mind — of that self-control and assured magnanimity of the individual by which egotistic hope and fear of change and death are somehow cast out. Only after that preparation has been made can the aesthetic moment, freed of anxiety in respect of its own repetition and perpetuation, achieve the perfection that outfaces time and change. The moral victory is the forerunner of the aesthetic victory. Both victories are attitudes — assured attitudes that are recoverable again and again at will; attitudes of the whole mind, of the emotions and the imagination purified of the petty and the ignoble by the reason; attitudes in which egotistical hope and fear are subdued.

Chapter Six

NOT A DREAM, BUT A VISION:
THE MYSTICAL VICTORY

Μη ὄναρ ἀλλ᾽ ὕπαρ
(Heliodorus)

Is not mysticism of the essence of all deep aesthetic experience? If mysticism is a visioned conviction of a super-sensuous, super-rational reality in which all things are somehow one without losing their disparateness, mysticism being thus a solution of the paradox of unity in variety, then each profound aesthetic moment is at least potentially mystical. For in that moment the mind is moved with a feeling of a metaphysical identity of unlike things. Robert Louis Stevenson cited the line,

And visited all night by troops of stars,

as an example of what poetry at its best can accomplish. Walter Pater is reported to have said: " Talking of Blake, I never repeat to myself, without a strange and almost terrifying sensation of isolation and long weariness, that couplet of his:

Ah, sunflower, weary of time,
Who countest the steps of the sun."

Both passages, by their imaginative animation of natural phenomena with intelligent intention, suggest a ' somehow ' identity of mind and matter, or an *anima mundi;* and the more intense the reader's response, the more powerful is this mystical suggestion. Indeed, it is the function of the imagination to synthesize experience, including such unlike experiences as mind and matter. Dr. Johnson, in one of his verbal broadsides, saluted this fact: " Imagination . . . has always endeavoured to baffle the logician, to perplex the confines of distinction, and burst the enclosures of regularity." Coleridge's theory of organic unity is a philosophical development of this uniting power of the imagination, in particular of the power or operation he calls the secondary imagination. Reference has already been made to statements by J. M. Baldwin, Bosanquet, and Dr. Masefield which also support the proposition. Shelley himself said that " poetry unveils the permanent analogy of things by images which participate in the life of truth." But for example and authority to support this theory of the mystical quality in aesthetic experience, each individual has only to remember his own most intense aesthetic moments, when, gazing perhaps from some Alpine peak, or reading a line of Shakespeare, or confronted with the Taj Mahal, or passing through some similar experience, he has had a quick, it may be evanescent, impression of a ' somehow ' oneness of all things, a sense of something religious and sublime. The student of poetry recognizes this intuition as the fundamental poetic truth, i.e., the momentary awareness of how all things *might be* one. For, as Aristotle said, poetic truth is a representation of things not as they are, but as they might or should be; and this mystical guess, or vision, is of how *all* things *might be* in reality.

At any rate, as we have just seen, Shelley gave a mystical interpretation of the deep aesthetic experience by which, in *Epipsychidion*, he conquered his distaste for death. That mystical statement is his explanation, I believe, of the feeling-tone of the aesthetic moment — not, indeed, of that one moment alone, but constructively of all the many similar moments he as a poet must have experienced. And now, quite in his characteristic way, he goes on to repeat, develop, more adequately realize, and perfect, in other compositions, the beauty and significance of an idea broached in a previous poem. In a poetic mysticism he is to combine and extend his previous victories, moral and aesthetic, over death. This is the fruit of a mysticism somehow sowed in him at birth.

I

" The *Adonais*, in spite of its mysticism, is the least imperfect of my compositions." So Shelley wrote in 1821. For over one hundred years critical tradition has echoed this judgment. But there are those who prefer to alter one phrase, reading not *in spite* of its mysticism, but *because* of its mysticism. For it is in the second and mystical part of the poem that a truly transcendent thought and expression are achieved. Nowhere else does Shelley trust so profoundly an Ideal Reality. The conception is bolder, the faith profounder, the mood sincerer, the accompanying music and imagery more severely beautiful, than in anything to be met with in all his previous work. Here is completed his progress from a febrile, spendthrift genius to a master of controlled vision. Austerity is added to power. Dante's soul awakes within him.

It is in an elegy that Shelley attains this height. His long pursuit of death is finished. At its close stands one of the half-dozen greatest elegies that have been written as yet on this midget planet.

Professor Woodberry better than any other critic has indicated the spiritual progress of the poem, the inter-relation of the groups of ideas, and the cultural significance of the impressive reversal of mood which coincides with the climax:

> The development of the poem, beginning with the poignancy of human grief rendered through images of beauty and the saddening of the things of earthly life however lovely, and then changing by subtle interpretations of the spirit evoking its own eternal nature in brooding over the dead form of what it loved, and ending at last in the triumphant reversion of its initial grief into joy in the presence of the eternal life foretasted in

fixed faith and enduring love even here, — this is the classic form of Christian elegy.

The elegy is in two unequal parts, dividing at the thirty-ninth Spenserian.

The first part, which gracefully borrows the exquisite imagery of the Alexandrian elegies of Bion and Moschus, has been reproached with classic coldness and a lack of human interest. We are told it little concerns the " average reader " (as though there were such a creature), with the implication that the only really human interest is that of the obvious and ordinary, and that the expression in elevated style of the distinctively human powers of reflection and idealization is not really human after all. This modern deification of the " average reader "! Is poetry to be manufactured for the moronic " average," like tenuous underwear and crime-club mysteries? But similar charges have been based on less Philistine grounds by Matthew Arnold, Mark Pattison, and even Mary Shelley. Arnold, regretting, rather incongruously, that Shelley did not think like other people and act like an angel, could only see him beating vain wings in the void. The " Winged Persuasions and Veiled Destinies " of Adonais must have been a case in point. As Professor A. C. Bradley has remarked, Arnold seems, at least when in controversy, " to have been ready to condemn as merely fanciful the imaginative expression of any idea that went beyond his own creed." Mark Pattison praised Milton's manlike figures of God and Christ at the expense of Shelley's " incarnated abstractions and spirit voices . . . airy nothings and creatures of pure fancy . . . who leave behind them no more distinct impression than that we have been in a dream peopled with ghosts." Yet all these luminous and airy nothings are such a symbolism as it has always been the custom of poets to use for the deepest speculations of the race. Mary, blind to the meaning of the *Witch* and fretfully dissatisfied with her husband's unbelievable trait which made him try to live his poetry and philosophy in the matter-of-fact world, often wished him more prosaic.

What, then, are the airy nuncios, or spiritual delegates, that pervade this threnody for the death of Keats, and leave both the Philistine and Matthew Arnold so cold? Many of them are voices for what Professor Woodberry has called " the saddening of the things of earthly life however lovely." They are the recollections, stirred by the death of one whose very soul was the worship and creation of beauty — the sad remembrances, of the descent of " all things wise and fair " to the grave. They are the tears that are a part of the essence of life. The tragic affinity of beauty and death, long since the haunting theme in Shelley's thought and verse, becomes musical in these mourners, classic bred, for the dead poet. Bion's weeping Loves and his Aphrodite become the Uranian Aphrodite, borrowed from the *Symposium*. They become figures of Keats's own dreams, his " passion-wingèd ministers of thought " that fed in the " living streams of his young spirit." The various company of fairies, Priapi, satyrs, Panes, and others, in Moschus's *Lament for Bion*, become the personified emotions and thoughts of poetic experience: Desires of the beautiful, Adorations of the ideal, Persuasions of words wingèd by enthusiasm, Destinies veiled by our ignorance or forgetfulness, Splendours and Glooms of sensitive hearts, " glimmering Incarnations of hopes and fears," Sorrow and her family of Sighs: all faint with the sense of death, " like a pageantry of mist upon an autumnal stream." All these mourn the stilled eloquence of the poet. If they be cold, inexpressive figurations of the most passionate and beautiful of human experiences fading and deliquescing in death; if, instead of them, we must have " living realities " clad in lugubrious black, keening the corpse, or the sentimental effusions of second-rate minds sunk in funereal gloom, or uncontrolled Ossianic hysteria — alas, great poetry is dead. In this modern mechanical age, Wordsworth, nearly a century ago, longed for the mythopoeic imagination that once had converted the multitudinous, ever-changing waves of the sea into a Proteus; that had seen the sea while it named the god. Have we to-day gone so far in the mechanical habit of mind that the analogies between humanity and the rest of nature must either be physically dissected or exposed as pathetic fallacy? Is there no eye to see or heart to feel beneath these personifications that elegy of the universal waning of mind and matter which Homer figures by Hades, or by the falling leaves of the forest? These nuncios are a congregation of the waning raptures of earthly life, sorrow for which is mitigated to a pensive sadness by beauty of imagery and music, and by a nobility of emotion approaching that of the ancient Greek funerary sculptures. This is such a congregation — in the very words of the poem —

> Where kingly Death
> Keeps his pale court in beauty and decay.

But why animadvert further upon those who ruin the beauty of this court of Death? Instead, let us be attentive awhile to the despair which runs beneath the smooth surface of this art. It is notable that though there is much of grief and sorrow in this elegy, and more of sadness, the effect is never weakened by cynicism. For that matter, cynicism almost never, in Shelley's poems, makes its gesture of personal, ineffective bitterness. Despair, even pessimism, speak in the *Adonais*. But not cynicism, the disgust with which a dissatisfied spirit poisons itself.

It is the finality of death that cages despair in the heart. The reiterated dirge of this part of the poem is a cry of finality, *He will awake no more, oh, never more;* and this dirge is the more impressive for being dramatically set over against the glad spring-theme of vital renewal, the glory of plasmic immortality. Keats had died close to spring-time, on the twenty-third of February, 1821. The poem was written in certain

weeks of the spring of the same year. With direct reference
to the season's vividness, Shelley cries:

> Ah, woe is me! Winter is come and gone,
> But grief returns with the revolving year;
> The airs and streams renew their joyous tone;
> The ants, the bees, the swallows, reappear;
> Fresh leaves and flowers deck the dead Season's bier;
> The amorous birds now pair in every brake,
> And build their mossy homes in field and brere,
> And the green lizard and the golden snake,
> Like unimprisoned flames, out of their trance awake.

The quickening life everywhere bursts into " the beauty and
joy of renewèd might." But, " *he* will awake no more, oh,
never more." This is the ancient, classical farewell, spoken so
poignantly and briefly by Catullus:

> *Nunquam ego te, vita frater amabilior,*
> *Aspiciam posthac.*

All that we loved of him, except for our grief is as though it
had not been; and grief itself, as Tennyson later deplored so
tragically, is mortal, too. By the immortality of the seed all
else reawakes: " nought we know dies." Yet the intensest life
of all, the fire of his spirit, is quenched. For a moment — even
while the unhappy antinomy provokes a disguised omen
of unconsumed spirit, which is the first dubious appearance
of the idea that in the second part of the poem is to become
the sure ground of spiritual victory — for a moment the disconcerting contrast between the periodic renewal of the life
of nature and the definite cessation of the life of the spirit,
plunges the poem into pessimism:

> Shall that alone which knows
> Be as a sword consumed before the sheath
> By sightless lightning? the intense atom glows
> A moment, then is quenched in a most cold repose. . . .

Whence are we, and why are we? of what scene
The actors or spectators? Great and mean
Meet massed in death, who lends what life must
    borrow.
As long as skies are blue and fields are green,
  Evening must usher night, night urge the morrow,
Month follow month with woe, and year wake year to
    sorrow.

Into this last weighty stanza is compressed the pagan, unmitigated tragedy of the finality of death for the human individual. Then the course of mourning is resumed. Mourning
frames the picture of despair.

But now an intenser grief is released, for with the repetition
of these ideas of mutability and death, which so continually
had been the burden of his own living, Shelley begins to
identify his own fate with that of Keats. The lyric cry becomes keener as it grows personal. But, true to Shelley's preoccupation with fundamental reality, it is a cry at once of
self and spirit, of a mind forever distraught by its attempt to
realize its vision of the eternal; the cry of one who

  Had gazed on Nature's naked loveliness,
  Actæon-like, and now he fled astray
  With feeble steps o'er the world's wilderness,
  And now his thoughts, along that rugged way,
Pursued, like raging hounds, their father and their prey.

This intrusion of Shelley's personality has been deemed an
unforgivable breach of elegiac etiquette, by some professori-
ally-minded critics. Alas, the biographical prepense in criticism can see nothing but autobiography in this picture of the
" pard-like spirit beautiful and swift," and then is decently
shocked by such concealed self-praise on the part of the chief
mourner! It is far better to forget the supposititious search
for the author behind the work; especially if the critic in the
search loses his power to view the personal contribution im-

personally for its artistic worth in relation to the dominant effect of the composition. Viewed in this truer and more catholic way, the advent of this " one frail Form, a phantom among men," has a very special effect in intensifying the saddening decay and death of the poetic loveliness that was Keats, and the sympathetic saddening of the lovely things of all earthly life. For the lament of this stranger among men, this " lost angel of a ruined Paradise," is the quintessence of spiritual grief. It is the witness of one supremely in love with natural beauty and the mind's beauty, to the rarity of the perfect union of those two in the poetic spirit, as in Keats, and to the yet greater rarity of contemporary appreciation of that union. By neglect, or misunderstanding, of its idealists the commonplace world spreads disaster about them, and their love becomes " a love in desolation masked." *Love in desolation masked:* its voice, with unforgettable personal anguish, tragically beautiful, makes the final moan for Adonais.

In the first part, then, there are sadness for the passing of all lovely things, sorrow for the passing of a poet whose spirit was one with their loveliness, grief for the disastrous fate which in a commonplace world overtakes the poet of pure beauty, and despair that the intensest life of all — this fire of the spirit — is quite quenched, while all other life goes on, changing, but not dying. So the Sadducees have spoken in every age; but with a special poignancy in classical antiquity. One recalls Homer, with his pensive figure of the falling leaves of the forest, which has already been quoted above more than once; or the patient close to that sublimely powerful account of the cremation of Patroclus, wherein the night-long tumult of the winds and waves and of the flames of the pyre on the headland, and the long vigil of the grieving Achilles, are succeeded by saffron dawn, the subsidence of the storm, and sweet sleep for Achilles, but dead ashes for the hapless Patroclus. Or one listens to Pindar's sad confession, darkening momentarily the living story of his victory-odes: " From Zeus there cometh no clear sign to men. . . . If any lift up his eye to look on things afar off, yet is he too weak to attain the bronze-paved dwelling of the Gods." Or one recalls Aeschylus moaning the blighted fates of men: " An oozy sponge blots out their fleeting prints and they are seen no more "; and Sophocles, lamenting the miserable race of mortals, like nothing but shadows, " drifting about, cumbering the earth." In the Greek Anthology, an epitaph for a poet recites: " Drenching my ashes with wine, you will but make mud of them." Lucretius declares that no mortal awakes " when once the cold pause of life has overtaken him." Then there is the stoic's stern concession that reality is but a series of fleeting impressions; culminating in the austere philosophical outlook of the age of Marcus Aurelius, " so completely disabused of the metaphysical ambition to pass beyond ' the flaming ramparts of the world.' " But closest, perhaps, to the prevailing emotion of this first part of the *Adonais* are those three sad lines in which Catullus speaks of human death as an eternal night, though suns may set to rise again:

> *Soles occidere et redire possunt:*
> *Nobis cum semel occidit brevis lux,*
> *Nox est perpetua una dormienda.*

But from this pagan dirge for the finality of human death, there arises suddenly, in the second part of the poem, a paean of human immortality. It may well be said that the new strain is born of the old, because it springs from this very idea of natural change, which in the dirge serves only to heighten by contrast the tragic effect of human death and personal pessimism.

First, hard upon the famous passage denouncing the Quarterly reviewer, comes the comforting reflection that now Keats has escaped from the cruelty of all the dull, malicious tribe represented by the reviewer; and on this mood of death's quiet release from pain the transition turns, in the last stanza of the first part:

> Nor let us weep that our delight is fled
> Far from these carrion kites that scream below;
> *He wakes or sleeps with the enduring dead;*
> Thou canst not soar where he is sitting now.
> Dust to the dust! but the pure spirit shall flow
> Back to the burning fountain whence it came,
> A portion of the Eternal, which must glow
> Through time and change, unquenchably the same.

In these lines, with their reminiscences of Milton, Dante, and Plato, the theme of change is converted almost unawares to an optimistic and joyful character. The comfort of escape, or release, in the first four verses, passes insensibly, in the following lines, into the Dantean figure of victorious absorption into the glowing light of the Eternal. Then, in the next, the thirty-ninth, stanza, the full meaning of the conversion suddenly breaks forth in a *sforzando* of music and imagery. In a subtly beautiful phrase, William Michael Rossetti calls this part a " paean of recantation." One can almost see Shelley's mind take this leap into mysticism, for the weak uncertainty of the words I have italicized, *He wakes or sleeps with the enduring dead*, produces all at once a startling revulsion, and a vehement intuition is released by the Dantean image, as he cries out in deep denial,

> Peace, peace! he is not dead, he doth not sleep.

From reconsideration has sprung vision. Now all the paraphernalia of despair are thrown to the winds, while idealism and mysticism speak forth with no uncertainty.

The next asseveration is the age-old paradox that life is death, death is life. Shelley's previous use of this paradox, from *Queen Mab* onwards to *Prometheus Unbound*, has already been reviewed in our commentary on the Earth Spirit's answer to Asia's tragic question, " Cease they to love . . .

who die? " (*Prometheus* III, iii, 109; see above, Chap. IV);
and reference has been made to three famous formulations of
the idea in antiquity, including the ironic twist with which
Plato cites Euripides' question, " Who knows if life be not
death and death life? " There is, also, the *vestra quae dicitur
vita mors est* of Cicero, and Virgil's hint of the idea in his
hae tibi mortis erant metae, and the related *quotidie morimur*
of Seneca, St. Augustine, and their many followers. Fundamentally, the paradox is a hasty transposition of two terms
consequent upon a realization of the untenability of their antithesis. When Hegelian dialectic, or modern science, or even
sheer emotional intensity, easily breaks down the popular
conception of either life or death, until one merges into the
other, then the mind, at first, involuntarily transposes the
meanings of the terms, and later, perhaps, resolves the antithesis into a higher factor.

Shelley takes both steps, one after the other. First, the
paradox serves to characterize vividly the meanness of worldly
living by transferring to it the ignoble connotations of death:

> *We* decay
> Like corpses in a charnel; fear and grief
> Convulse us and consume us day by day;
> And cold hopes swarm like worms within the living clay.

In the glow of his enthusiasm he has reverted to one of his
oldest fascinations, the charnel and the worm; but he has converted it now to an attack upon life itself, instead of upon
death. One feels that the revolution in his thought is so essential that at once his old *cliché* is turned inside out, as it were,
or completely reversed. All his staple ideas must be revolved
within this intenser light. Even the old anathema of tyranny
and bigotry suffers a sea-change into a thing of dream and
unreality:

> 'T is we, who, lost in stormy visions, keep
> With phantoms an unprofitable strife,

And in mad trance strike with our spirit's knife
Invulnerable nothings.

To such an unreality have dwindled the cordilleras of evil
that agonized Prometheus! All these Adonais has outsoared
in death, all the " envy and calumny and hate and pain." From
the " contagion of the world's slow stain " he is secure.
Browning, in *Pauline*, has a reminiscence of these lines —
" cunning, envy, falsehood, all world's wrong that spotted
me "; and there is a striking anticipation of the whole passage in the *Silvae* (II, 2) of Statius, which Shelley probably
had read:

> But he whom we weep is happy; he has outsoared
> gods and men, danger and hazard, and the pitfalls of our
> blind life; he is secure from fate. . . . We are a restless
> people and evil-starred.   (Tr., D. A. Slater)

But in the present poem this common enough idea of the escape that is in death is transformed, under the stress of a sudden idea, into the hasty paradox that life itself is death,
and that therefore Adonais has left death and entered into
life.

Had the poem ended here, it would have ended as flimsily
as *The Sensitive Plant;* for, however intense the mood and
beautiful the imagery which here have been lavished upon
the paradox, the thought itself is little more than a figure
of speech. It happens, however, that this rhetoric is only a
wingèd step to the synthesis of life and death in a higher concept. This higher and mystical persuasion is consummated in
the last four stanzas.

But it is reached through a beautiful climax of allied
themes, from the forty-first through the fifty-first stanza.
From a final reiteration of the paradox — *He lives, he wakes
— 'tis Death is dead, not he* — evolves a countermand of the
grief that had been evoked, as in the fourteenth stanza, from
natural objects. Before, morning was dim with grief, and the

winds, thunders, and ocean itself became pathetic figures. Now, they are adjured to cease their weeping for Adonais. Dawn turns her dewy tears to sunrise splendour. The lamentations of the natural powers are converted to a hymn of joyful resurrection. Therewith the sense of the ceaseless energy of nature again dominates the creative configuration, or *Gestalt*, of Shelley's mind, and the very rhythm of the forty-second Spenserian pulses in accord with the more energetic mood. Under the influence of this vitality, his mind rises to contemplate gladly and hopefully the order of the universe as the signature of a directing, spiritual power. The hypothesis of a spiritual universe becomes a conviction. The paradoxical figure is dropped. Adonais is said through death to be made one with that very mundane life which before had been called death. But now that life is veritable life. Both with the things of nature and with the spirit of nature his power is associated. His voice is heard alike in thunder and in the nightingale's song; his presence is to be felt and known in all appearances of light or dark, of animate and inanimate, of plant or stone. And the power which wields this world, sustaining it, kindling it, has withdrawn his being to its own.

> He is made one with Nature: there is heard
> His voice in all her music, from the moan
> Of thunder to the song of night's sweet bird;
> He is a presence to be felt and known
> In darkness and in light, from herb and stone,
> Spreading itself where'er that Power may move
> Which has withdrawn his being to its own;
> Which wields the world with never-wearied love,
> Sustains it from beneath, and kindles it above.

But now it seems advisable to pause a moment or two to discuss the philosophical implications which have accumulated thus far in the poem. It will become apparent, I hope, that from a rather confused philosophical idealism, Shelley turns at length, instinctively and aesthetically, as a romantic poet should, to a mystical fusion of mind and matter, the one and the many.

It would be a disservice to the poem to try to read between its lines a consistent philosophy. The moods aroused by a thought rather than discussions of it are the true substance of this as of most elegies. Yet I do not mean to contravene the general truth of Coleridge's observation, in his criticism of Shakespeare, that " no man was ever yet a great poet, without being at the same time a profound philosopher." But profound philosophy is not necessarily a systematic thing of the schools, and the deep thought of a poet is little concerned to restrict itself to one variety of a given type of philosophy. At any rate, in the present case, though an idealistic temper of mind pervades the second or constructive part of the poem, it is largely a waste of effort to try to refer all its sentiments to one variety of idealism. Instead, one should frankly admit that there are references to such widely differing phases of idealism and transcendental realism as are represented by Berkeley, Plato, Aristotle, and Spinoza. But I think it can be shown that the final mood of the poem, escaping the pitfalls of subjective idealism, is connected with the teachings of Aristotle and Spinoza.

Rossetti was content to illustrate the philosophical implications by rather indiscriminate references to Berkeley and Plato and to pantheism and theism.

Shelley's so-called Berkeleyism comes out uncertainly, not without contradictions, in the prose fragment, *On Life*, written perhaps as early as 1815; and Mrs. Shelley, in her note on the essay, asserts, erroneously, I believe, that he was a disciple of Berkeley. But so far as one can judge from the fragmentary, imperfectly developed essay *On Life*, Shelley's idealism in 1815 was subjective in tendency, whereas Berkeley's idealism, according to Professor Hocking, is not. Berkeley showed that colours, sounds, objects, and distance are mental experiences, having no independent matter-reality of their own. What we are in the habit of calling matter or nature, turns out, on analysis, to be only ideas, conscious experience. Material things, to retain the mechanistic assumption for a moment, could not possibly, merely of themselves, give rise to anything so entirely different from their own nature as sensations and ideas. But Berkeley does not assert that objective things are *illusions*, mere figments created solely in the mind of each individual; for when one opens his eyes he cannot choose what he will and will not see. However, since what one does ' see ' is mental and does not, and cannot, have an independent reality of material object, distance, etc., it follows that what he ' sees ' must be in its externality the product of another activity similar to his own mental activity, that is, the mind of God. ' Things,' so called, are really signs or symbols of God's mind. Our sensations are produced by God's infinite mind acting through these symbols upon our finite minds. There is ' something ' there, outside our minds. But it is not matter with an independent reality of its own; it is the ideas of God's mind. " What Berkeley seeks to show " says A. C. Fraser, " is, not that the world of the senses is unreal, but in what its reality consists." Professor Warner Fite explains that Berkeley " was less interested in denying the existence of things independent of our perception than in proving that they could not be *inert* and *unthinking* things." Berkeley himself complained that his readers had confounded him with the skeptics who doubt the existence of sensible things, whereas he is arguing only for the unreality of abstract unperceived matter:

> I question not the existence of anything we perceive by our senses. I do not deny the existence of the sensible things which Moses says were created by God. They existed from all eternity, in the Divine Intellect; and they became perceptible (i.e., were created) in the same manner and order as is described in Genesis. For I take

creation to belong to things only as they respect finite spirits; there being nothing new to God.

Of course, one wonders *how* God's mind acts upon man's mind, *how* finite minds originated and were determined, and whether ' God ' be not only another mentalism, made within one's own mind, like ' matter.' But this is not the place to argue with Berkeley. Here it is pertinent only to point out that Berkeley, like Descartes, is not a subjective, or egoistic, idealist; for he assumes that my experience is not the result solely of my own activity, but also of an external, divine reality coöperating with my own activity. Now Shelley's *On Life* takes a different turn. The individual perceiving mind is only a part of the one-mind; and therefore, Shelley implies, it partakes of the activity of the one-mind, viz., supplying the so-called things of matter, which really are ideas. Individual mind is not, then, acted upon, but is always contriving, " creating." By implication, at least, he denies the existence of sensible things. Things are outright illusions; the mind's regard of them as having an external reality of their own is an error, a dream in which most men spend their lives. For Berkeley the phrase, to be is to be perceived (*esse est percipi*), means that the reality in sensible things is a mental reality, that of God. But for Shelley it means that sensible things do not exist. They are illusions. Now Shelley's line of argument not only represents the popular misunderstanding of Berkeley, but is also characteristic of subjective idealism, i.e., of the belief that experience is the product solely of the ego. But the logical extreme of subjective idealism — that experience is solely the product of *each* ego, *solus ipse*, so that each individual is completely shut up within himself, unable to perceive even other minds or to prove they are real — which is called " solipsism," and which many regard as the *reductio ad absurdum* of subjective idealism, Shelley refuses. For he reasons that from the fact that every individual mind is really only a piece of mind-general it follows that, (a) the distinction between minds is a fallacy, comparable to the illusion of the existence of sensible things, and (b) that all " individual " minds " see " identically, because they are at one with each other. Differences are differences of degree, not of kind. Here, too, one would like to ask many questions: if the differences are of degree, as between larger and smaller pieces of the homogeneous one-mind, will not any piece, howsoever minute, carry in it all the powers of the whole, and therefore be unlimited? how does mind-general split up? if " sensible " things are the product of individual minds, are they not *ipso facto* the product of general-mind, and therefore have they not a constant reality of the sort Berkeley avers, so that sensible things are not illusions? if minds are in essence identical would they not all " see " one cow, the " ideal " cow? whence, then, *particular* cows? how do minds achieve the illusion of material reality? not by the conditioning influence of brutish matter, since matter does not exist? not by mind-general, since individual minds are pieces of it? are not the true alternatives for idealism, objective idealism and solipsism? But this is not the place to argue with Shelley, either. We are concerned, only, to expound the various idealistic backgrounds of a poem. But if Shelley ever really thought he was a disciple of Berkeley, he was a confused disciple, as I have tried to show.

The poem itself makes no use of Berkeley's idealism and no consistent use of the imperfect subjective idealism of the essay *On Life;* its references to the latter are brief, indeterminate, confused; and almost immediately it leaves the latter behind for other varieties of idealism. The references to the thought of the essay are in the thirty-ninth stanza. Adonais in dying has " awakened from the dream of life," while the living, victims of their " stormy visions," continue " an unprofitable strife with phantoms," in " mad trance " struggling with " invulnerable nothings." The quoted words assert clearly enough that sensible experience is an illusion by which the mind is fooled, and the further statement that the " spirit's knife " strikes at these illusions implies that the deepest power of individual mind is completely victimized by its own illusions. How else could they be created? So far the poem is in agreement with the subjective idealism of the essay, and in entire disagreement with Berkeleyism. But as soon as we take into account the assertion that by death Adonais is liberated from these illusions, the relation to the essay is confused. For if death destroys the illusion, something in the sensible experience, which is an illusion of mind, has limited mind, which then cannot be a true piece of mind-general. Mind limits itself and fools itself, but becomes unlimited by death, which itself must be one of its own illusions. One illusion destroys all the rest.

But Shelley is not versifying his essay on subjective idealism. He is embodying the emotion of victory which attends any idealistic synthesis of mind and matter, subject and object. He is dramatically incorporating the *raison d'être* of all idealism, the feeling that in mind lies the final victory over all that is ugly and painful. Now in the light of that victory all ugliness seems much like a bad dream. We are nearer the heart of the stanza when we regard its talk about illusion as a poetic figure for that bad dream, rather than as a part of a philosophical system. And, too, we are that much nearer to the psychological, therefore relative, meaning of idealism itself, of whatever system. Philosophy multiplies distinctions; poetry drives back to the essential intuition and mood which philosophy attempts rationally to dissect and justify.

The poem passes next, we have seen, to the assumption of a spiritual power that wields the universe. This concept, if it were joined with Berkeley's psychology of the individual, would fit well enough into Berkeley's system. But the conjunction is not made. Nor is the assumption conformable to the egoistic idealism of the essay, for the One Moving Power is set over against, or within, a material universe. Moreover, this idea of the One, in the poem, as we shall see, is essentially related to a philosophy of becoming, whereas the thought of the essay is essentially related to a philosophy of being. If one idea does permeate this poem, as it does most of the poems of this year, it is a doctrine of motion and change, which is scarcely in strict conformity with Plato's insistence upon immutability as characteristic of the real, or with his faith that a true philosophy liberates us from the illusion, or, at any rate, decadence, of change. Indeed, the famous forty-third stanza, upon which Mr. Kellett has commented most perspicuously, so strongly stresses change as a process of becoming that an affinity with characteristic ideas of Aristotle, Dante, and Spinoza cannot but be discerned.

A brief reminder of these characteristic ideas may be illuminating. Aristotle teaches that nature ($\phi\acute{\upsilon}\sigma\iota\varsigma$) is a force working in matter ($\H\upsilon\lambda\eta$), through forms ($\epsilon\H\iota\delta o\iota$), to produce the best possible forms. In its purpose to realize, say, the best possible form of what is known as an oak-tree, it is held back by various recalcitrancies of matter and circumstance — poor soil, poor seed, poor exposure, and the like. But in the universe at large, this teleological process forever prevails, and in spite of all failures imperturbably perseveres. The speculative conclusion of the process is the complete and perfect adjustment of matter and form in pure " substance," or God. Dante frequently recurs to the Aristotelian idea of God as the unchanged ultimate of change, the All-mover, whose glory, penetrating the universe, says Dante, reglows in some things more and less in others, according to their susceptibility to the divine. Spinoza's mystical theory of mind and body as parallel phenomena, two aspects of an indescribable reality, or substance, and his distinction between nature as thought in God (*natura naturans*) and as created form (*natura naturata*), different as it is fundamentally from Aristotelian theory, bears to it at least a superficial resemblance. Perhaps, how-

ever, the fundamental difference itself tends to disappear as
we realize fully the effect on Aristotle's theory of his constant warning that form and matter are only two ways of
looking at reality, for then his continuum of becoming is only
the one reality seen in a time-picture relative to our powers
of observation.

Be that as it may, these three trains of thought, all deriving
from thinkers with whom Shelley was acquainted, all positing
a spiritual universe (for even Spinoza's mechanics are divine), and all involving some attempt to harmonize the imperfections of the Many with the perfection of the One,
reach a poetic rendering in the following lines of the forty-
third stanza:

> . . . the one Spirit's plastic stress
> Sweeps through the dull sense world, *compelling there*
> *All new successions to the forms they wear,*
> *Torturing the unwilling dross that checks its flight*
> *To its own likeness, as each mass may bear,*
> And bursting in its beauty and its might
> From trees and beasts and men into the Heaven's light.

Surely this praise of the God-compelled procession of forms
does not belong to Plato's variety of philosophy. But in comparison with the importance of the basic conviction that the
universe is a spiritual fact, these differences in formulating
the faith are insignificant; and the poet, while mixing philosophic varieties, as tactfully avoids the pitfalls of particulari-
zation as he successfully emphasizes the point of agreement.
Thereby, with the assistance of metaphors that escape the
misleading narrowness of abstract definition, he remains true
to the essential, spiritual principle, and, in a way, is superior
to the philosophers themselves, who are apt to lose sight of
their fundamental agreement while dwelling on their differences. The poet is more faithful both to the underlying
intuition and to the concrete it would explain. Where the
philosopher by his long disquisition in the abstract cannot

but tend to put asunder thought and things, the poet reunites them; and by the incommensurable connotations of his imagery and his music stirs continuously and aesthetically in his reader a vivid but vague sense of that ineffable union which the philosopher dissipates in analysis. In that vivid aesthetic " sense " the poet turns to mysticism, i.e., to a visioned conviction of a super-sensuous, super-rational reality in which all things are somehow one. Therewith he is indeed at least a potential, perhaps the profoundest, philosopher; and for understanding him an acquaintance with philosophies is illuminating.

The present significance of all these implications is that Adonais, i. e., Keats, somehow lives on in this spiritual beauty, bearing a very real part in the " plastic stress." Moreover, by the testament of beauty in his works, wherein he added spirit to the physical sense of beauty, he has become forever a visible portion of the divinely revealing loveliness of life. There are, therefore, two phases to his immortality: that of participation in the spirit itself, and that of influence upon successive generations — an immortality of spirit and of the works of the spirit.

But it is an immortality of spirit, not of person. Again, there is a similarity to one of Spinoza's affirmations: that the human mind, but not the human personality, must persist somehow after the destruction of the body, because the essence of mind can be explained only as partaking of the nature of eternal, spiritual reality. " Some kind of consciousness or something better; that is the probability." The words are Maeterlinck's: they might as well have been Shelley's.

And here the mind that is so deeply wedded to its own meagre personality that it can by no means bear to contemplate the erasure of its momentary, worldly adventure, holds the poem defective, to say the least. Even such a lover of it as Francis Thompson is deeply distressed:

285

What desolation can it be that discerns comfort in this hope, whose wan countenance is as the countenance of a despair? What deepest depth of agony is it that finds consolation in this immortality: an immortality which thrusts you into death, the maw of Nature, that your dissolved elements may circulate through her veins? Yet such, the poet tells me, is my sole balm for the hurts of life. I am as the vocal breath floating from an organ. I too shall fade on the winds, a cadence soon forgotten. So I dissolve and die, and am lost in the ears of men: the particles of my being twine in newer melodies, and from my one death arise a hundred lives. Why, through the thin partition of this consolation Pantheism can hear the groans of its neighbour, Pessimism. Better almost the black resignation which the fatalist draws from his own hopelessness, from the fierce kisses of misery that hiss against his tears.

To Spinoza and, I believe, to Shelley, this indignation would appear the result of an eloquent confusion of personality with individual mind. It is a confusion, perhaps, of personality in its bondage to worldly desires, with deepest thought's approximate freedom from those desires, from the hopes and fears that are the slavish attendants of possessions; a confusion, perhaps, of the trials of intellectual development, viz., the details of worldly adventure, with the intellectual development, or realization, itself. At any rate, a fuller and clearer poetizing of the relation of personality to desire Shelley himself is presently to give us in *The Triumph of Life,* thus completing what here he has suggested.

Death (Stanza XLIV) now is called a low mist which cannot blot the universal spiritual brightness it may veil. The splendour of the spirit, like that of the stars, may be eclipsed; but it cannot be extinguished. For whenever a young spirit faces the mystery of life and death, struggling to escape the mortal lair of its lower desires, the teachings of the great dead come to life again in the inquiring mind, and move there " like

winds of light " on the murk and storm of puzzled effort. So
Keats has joined, as George Eliot would say,

> . . . the choir invisible
> Of those immortal dead who live again
> In minds made better by their presence: live
> In pulses stirred to generosity,
> In deeds of daring rectitude, in scorn
> For miserable aims that end with self,
> In thoughts sublime that pierce the night like stars,
> And with their mild persistence urge man's search
> To vaster issues.

This immortality of service is one of man's most ancient
friends in quelling the death-fear. Between George Eliot's
" choir invisible " and Homer's similar consolation for
Hector stretches a long series of these consolatories, stoically
offering a redemption in works to the *animula blandula,
vagula*. Perhaps there is nowhere a more beautiful poetizing
of this comfort, which is so opulent with age, as in these four
stanzas of the *Adonais*, beginning with the pealing lines of the
forty-third —

> He is a portion of the loveliness
> Which once he made more lovely —

and changing abruptly, daringly, to the figurative welcome
extended to Adonais by the invisible company, as they rise,
to do him honour,

> . . . from their thrones, built beyond mortal thought,
> Far in the Unapparent.

First, Chatterton, Sidney, and Lucan — doubly Keats's
brothers as poets who died young, " the inheritors of unful-
filled renown " — rise in welcome. Then —

> . . . many more, whose names on Earth are dark,
> But whose transmitted effluence cannot die
> So long as fire outlives the parent spark,

Rose, robed in dazzling immortality.
" Thou art become as one of us," they cry.

Thus the underlying idea, *I change but I cannot die*, has been converted into the ancient consolation of an immortality of works. And the figure of the welcoming poets, though it must not be taken literally, involves a conversion of the idea into a spiritual, not necessarily personal, immortality through absorption in the " One Spirit's plastic stress."

But now the gestation of these two ideas of the spirit's persistence stirs a deeper intuition of the nature of the human spirit. Ah, know thyself aright! cries the poet. What is this spirit that can expand to contemplate immensity, until it seems to " satiate the void circumference " of all the universes; and then, by turn, shrinks into ineffectiveness, one infinitesimal in the All? In its magnificent research it is kindled by a hope which lures it gladly to the brink of the grave. Then keep the heart light and the hope supreme, never yielding to the sense of impotence! Seek shelter, indeed, in the shadow of the tomb! " Die, if thou wouldst be that which thou dost seek! " " What Adonais is why fear we to become? "

Those cries of gladness, those exhortations to conquer death by living at the top of one's consciousness, pass over at once into the thought whose clear statement they emotionally anticipated. And what is it, this final statement? What but the clear demotion of the antithesis of life and death under a superior synthesis? The key-phrase changes. No longer is it: I change but I cannot die. It becomes: I live *and* I die, the many change and pass; but the One remains, and the individual in losing his worldly personality by becoming at one with the eternal achieves the perfection of self. Life and death, like thoughts and other things, are phases of one indescribable, mystical " substance." The similarity to Spinozism is obvious, and probably not accidental, since Shelley had begun reading Spinoza, at first with no great interest, as

early as 1810, and then, in 1820, with consuming interest, was
translating brief passages from his works and planning to
write his life. Yet the stanza (LII) which contains the final
formulation and which is now quoted is less a borrowing
from Spinoza than an effluence of Shelley's own mind:

> The One remains, the many change and pass;
> Heaven's light forever shines, Earth's shadows fly;
> Life, like a dome of many-coloured glass,
> Stains the white radiance of Eternity,
> Until Death tramples it to fragments. — Die,
> If thou wouldst be with that which thou dost seek!

This is faith, not demonstration; thoughtfulness matured to
inspiration, as Spinoza would say; poetic mysticism, not
philosophy. In this aesthetic ecstasy Lionel died. It is, surely,
a high dialectic of the imagination, by which the popular
antithesis of life and death is overcome. Victory over death,
alike over the fear of it and the problem of it, consists in
realizing that these weak terms, life and death, express only
our lowest common sense. Alike reflection and emotion, at
their highest, are done with these blind terms of the weak
spirit. Though it is difficult to tell " just what " a poet means,
for his meaning is so incommensurable in its music and emotion, so much more than " just what "; yet the declaration, at
once speculative and intuitive, of an inclusive synthesis is
here, to my mind, perfectly obvious. Moreover, whatever
may be the fullness of meaning and allusion and mood in the
passage, and however indescribable may be the state of mind
that can only faintly impart itself in the mystical assumption
of a One, two significant but simple conclusions concerning
the meaning of these lines are inescapable. First, they register
a faith in a universe that is benevolent toward the individual
— neither hostile nor neutral. Second, they present a clear
case of the mind's elevation of the essence of being, from both
the life and the death of the many, into a generalization it

pronounces infinite in the sense that mind can go no further. I have borrowed Professor Santayana's terminology in the previous sentence, because it seems to me entirely adequate, peculiarly fitted, to the circumstance.

The exultant faith that death transfigures life, ascending, as on two steps of fire, the ideas of influential and of spiritual persistence, now reaches the ecstatic conviction that mortality and immortality, like life and death, are unsatisfactory and misleading terms. Both pairs of words name incomplete, shortsighted ways of looking at experience. They are only flimsy subjectivities. Here is the poetic completion of that annihilation of the meagre, worldly-minded personality that we commented upon, in the third Chapter, in our study of the essay, *On Life*.

This synthesis of life and death is the product of despair; a hope created out of the wreck of hope. Coleridge has said that hope and despair meet in the porch of death. They have met in this poem on death. Shelley's despair was the result of his attempt to square his conduct with his idealism, to harmonize the hubbub of the mundane with a celestial song. Again and again in that struggle he approached this synthesis that reconciles life and death by transcending their antithesis. But never before has he expressed so whole-heartedly his trust in the mystical reality, for always an intense personal disturbance has confused his vision. His extraordinary sensitiveness to beauty has impulsively rebelled against all the ugliness of life he has symbolized in death. But as his suffering has increased, the faith has become ever more necessary. His despair during the years 1819 and 1820, poignantly figured in this very poem, especially in stanzas thirty-one to thirty-four, is at last freed from the confusion of personal disturbance by the objectification of his own history in the sorrows of Keats. As a result of this detachment, despair has powerfully projected its antitype — hope. With greater care and artifice than in any previous poem, as he himself has testified, he has once

again assembled in a poem his paraphernalia of joys and sufferings and ideas, and the realized issue of them all is a profounder conviction of the reality of a mystical essence than
he has ever before achieved. This synthesis was inevitable; it
is always inevitable if the idealist does not deny and abjure
his idealism.

So now, once more, and at the very close of the poem,
Shelley appears in his own person, much to the scandalizing
of the literal commentator. But he appears in order to give
complete testimony to the reality of the faith he has confessed. And such is his intensity of expression that his first-
person address becomes the confession of every idealist. The
sympathetic reader, indeed, identifies himself with the poet,
and finds not a singular ineptitude, but only a greater vividness, as for all men, in this personal conclusion. Is Shelley's
heart, after all, any the less representative because we know
so much about it? Is he not spokesman for us all — for the
idealists, at any rate? Prophet and poet in one (we remember that the Old Testament uses the word " prophet " for
" poet," thus implying the mental depth of all poetry
worthy of the name), he speaks for his faith in the person of
humanity itself, *in persona non propria sed humana*. His utterance has, in truth, the effect of rapt prophecy, of some
special psychic experience, as of the mystic in his moment of
ineffable insight — as of Dante, whose influence is stamped
here, at the close of Shelley's own vision. *Raptus est suprema
gradus contemplationis*, said St. Augustine. To that height of
contemplation Shelley is caught up in the two stanzas which
close the poem.

> That light whose smile kindles the Universe,
> That Beauty in which all things work and move,
> That Benediction which the eclipsing Curse
> Of birth can quench not, that sustaining Love
> Which, through the web of being blindly wove
> By man and beast and earth and air and sea,

Burns bright or dim, as each are mirrors of
The fire for which all thirst, now beams on me,
Consuming the last clouds of cold mortality.

The breath whose might I have invoked in song
Descends on me; my spirit's bark is driven
Far from the shore, far from the trembling throng
Whose sails were never to the tempest given.
The massy earth and spherèd skies are riven!
I am borne darkly, fearfully, afar!
Whilst, burning through the inmost veil of Heaven,
The soul of Adonais, like a star,
Beacons from the abode where the Eternal are.

These words are the words of mystical contemplation —
not of a dream, but of a vision. The words are at once figurative and literal. Figurative, because something beyond language, like Dante's God or Spinoza's Substance, is put into
enigmatic language; literal, because the things of sense —
light and breath, man, beast, and earth, beauty and love, life
and death — which are freighted with spiritual meaning, are,
by this faith, in essence themselves spiritual. Nor are these
words in any way new in their meaning; many of them not
new even in their juxtaposition: so closely has Dante been
followed (as for instance in that figure of the driven boat,
which is taken from the opening *terzine* of the second canto
of the *Paradiso*). Of old, such words and their ecstatic joy
have been the language of the prophet. *Rapitur anima, cum
coelestia contemplatur, et contemplando jucundatur.* One
cannot but be reminded of those clauses of perfect cadence
which are said in the Office of the Dead at the close of all the
Psalms — in place of the " Glory be to the Father " — so
that they become the refrain of joy and peace and light for
the multitudinous dead: *Requiem aeternam dona eis Domine,
et lux perpetua luceat eis.*
     This faith, or vision, then, is the answer alike to the fatal

problem in *Alastor* and to that despairing question of the twentieth stanza of *Adonais:*

> Nought we know dies: shall that alone which knows
> Be as a sword consumed before the sheath
> By sightless lightning?

Symbol of the answer — what a happy reversion to the subject of the elegy! — is the soul of Adonais, as are the souls, too, of all the beloved dead. And the answer itself, like their souls, is a *beacon*, that is, a light that lights one homeward: an expression of that complete at-homeness and eternal rest the mind senses when it reaches this conviction. The philosopher, said Plato, in the *Phaedo*, has a lifelong struggle with the mundane, even with his lower desires; and therefore he should welcome the release which comes with death: he has, indeed, been all the while in pursuit of death. And all the while, Shelley's long pursuit of death has been lighting *him* homewards, " to the abode where the eternal are."

Bagehot, in one of his less happy phrases, calls Shelley a poet of " peculiar removed essences." And it is commonly said that Shelley lacked a strong sense of actuality and fact, such, for instance, as one finds in the poems of Clough or Meredith; or that he easily confused fact and idea, things as they are and as we would like them to be, where Clough and Meredith and Hardy were dogged with a failure to reconcile the visible and the invisible. As for the " removed essences," they are those of love and beauty and the ideal, which always have been the characteristic concern of the human mind, and are " peculiar " and " removed " only in the fact that persistent intensity in the contemplation of them is not a trait of common sense. Yet rarer is the power, but not therefore less significant, to clothe the intenser pursuit of these mental realities in symbols, or figures, drawn from the reciprocal manifestations of non-human and human nature — from this complete imaginative adjustment of outer life to the intensest inner life. But the principle of that adjustment, the animation of things by thought, the adding of spirit to sense, is that poetic animism which always has produced poetic, as distinct from common-sense, truth. It is Shelley's eminence in this poetic power that constitutes the rarity of his work, rather than any peculiarity in his subjects.

The unsympathetic reader, failing again and again to discern in these figures an expression of the eager, subjective life that has been led by all persistent thinkers, sees in them only a curious felicity in the fanciful, or an incongruous exaggeration of the actual, or a wilfully blind confusion of dream and fact. For him the *Witch* is a human woman, *in extremis* of romantic beauty; *Prometheus* is a capital story gone wrong; Asia is love etherealized beyond conveniency of courtship; everywhere the scene is unnecessarily confused with Desires, Adorations, veiled Destinies, and Demogorgons; and in *Adonais*, after a dull flight of the usual Dreams, Fantasies, and moonlight wings, the culmination of romantic unreality is reached in the plastic stress of something half-way between pantheism and deism. But once Shelley's mythopoeic power is understood in its relation to the intensest human moods, these personifications are seen to be " the passion-wingèd ministers of thought." The difficulty in Shelley is not that he is less a poet than many, but more than most: less concerned to picture the combinations of men in outer action, as Browning observed; more concerned to express their intensest inner action in such terms as suggest the hidden analogies between mind and matter, thought and things.

II

Reading *Adonais* stirs old memories of other songs of desolation and consolation, and perhaps we shall better evaluate Shelley's capacity for this kind of writing if we give way for a while to those memories.

Not a Dream, but a Vision: The Mystical Victory

One thinks wonderingly of that medieval gem of faith and mysticism, the *Pearl*. Ever since Richard Morris, in 1864, published his prose rendering of *Pearl*, his interpretation of it as an elegy on the death of a poet's infant daughter has been very generally accepted, notably by Ten Brink, Sir Israel Gollancz, and Professor Carleton Brown. But many parts of the poem are brought into line with this interpretation only with difficulty. It seems to me that Sister M. Madeleva's explanation, in her *Pearl, A Study of Spiritual Dryness*, is to be preferred. She regards the poem as a piece of spiritual autobiography in which the author, in all probability a young religious, describes a state of spiritual dryness, aridity, or interior desolation, his various experiences while in that state, the consequences of it, and the restoration of perfect peace of soul. The pearl itself I think of as a symbol of a complex conception. It is a symbol of a state of spiritual happiness — the peace that passeth understanding — temporarily lost; it is a symbol, also, of that state visioned in its heavenly perfection; and, finally, it signifies a particular soul moving toward eternal bliss. The young religious has lost his precious mood of religious exaltation, his "perle plesaunte." He lost the pearl, he laments, in a garden: not in a graveyard, but in an herb-garden of sensuous delight. In the weariness of his vain search for the lost gem he falls asleep, to dream of a beautiful young girl, in whom he thinks he recognizes his pearl. She tells him that the pearl is not lost, and chides him for desiring its sensible possession. To his increasing wonder and ecstatic delight she explains to him her marriage to the spotless Lamb, a state of spiritual oneness with the divine; descants for his comfort on the meaning of Paul's gospel that we are all members of Jesus Christ; retells the parable of the labourers in the Vineyard, revealing its bearing on the efficacy of grace, so that the young religious may have good hope despite his tragic mood; and concludes by showing him a vision of the New Jerusalem as described in the Apocalypse. He sees that noble city of the soul's supreme expectation as John the Apostle saw it: a burgh of burning gold, burnished like gleaming glass, set on glorious gems, with twelve steps, twelve foundations, every slab a jewel. Suddenly the City is filled with maidens, all gowned and crowned alike, arrayed in white raiment and pearls; and on the breast of each is bound " the blissful pearl, with great delight." Along the golden streets, in hundreds of thousands, but all of one order, they march. Then the Christ passes before them, and his robe is fair as pearls. Their delight is excellent. Legions of angels scatter incense. The poet's own pearl is in ecstasy. But he himself cannot, as yet, set foot in that New Jerusalem. First he must pass, like Everyman, through dreary death. Thereupon the poet awoke from his dream and, committing himself fully to the grace of God, was again at peace.

If this quaint and lovely poem, wherein, with true pre-Raphaelite grace and animism, every region of the spirit is sensuous, be not an elegy for a little daughter, it is, nevertheless, intrinsically, an elegy for the loss of a precious reality; and such an elegy as carries consolation to the afflicted in this mundane existence by pointing to death as the gate to a spiritual and perfect life. It is an example of that uncomplex Christian elegy which always ends divinely. The sincere, bright flame of its faith burns quietly, inextinguishably — the very taper-light of the medieval soul. Its faith derives not from reason, but from an undoubted, historical, matter-of-fact revelation. In it is no debate, no loss of belief in a spiritual universe; only a temporary aridity of a believing soul that is quickly refreshed by a new poetizing of the revelation. It is a story of a personal renascence of Christian impressibility.

How far it is from the debate of cultures — classic, Christian, and modern — in *Adonais!* Reading it to-day is like passing from a modern, pragmatical university into a quiet church where the trustful pray. It is an idyl of primitive faith. It is unlearned, unsophisticated. Yet, emotionally, it is what most elegy is: the story of desolation and consolation. By complexity of culture — by the classical renaissance, Christian apologetics, modern philosophy, and modern science — elegy develops, at last, an *Adonais,* a new poetizing, learned and sophisticated, of an idealistic consolation. Both poems, indeed, end in visions of reality. The reality may be, is, stated differently. Is that so very important? Both statements, or both realities, are only ways of looking at things, after all, the medieval one only a little more figurative than the other. Their pretension to absolute truth fails. Their poetic truth is relative: it remains — two earnest figures of how things may, or might, be.

How far, too, it is in its idyllic sensitiveness and beauty, from Bunyan's feverish fear of Vanity Fair, headlong retreat from the worldly life, and anguished pursuit of the heavenly life! But in purpose and recompense the *Pearl* and *Pilgrim's Progress* are identical. " To escape from the City of Destruction and to reach the Celestial City," said Professor Dowden, " is Christian's one concern; all his recompense for the countless trials of the way lies upon the other side of the river of death."

Gray's elegy is another kind of story altogether, for in it there is no desolation — only " the passing tribute of a sigh." The sequestered life of the hamlet fades gently into death, like the lying down of a flower. Then, for the body, the undisturbed repose of the consecrated grave, under yew-tree and elm, near the twittering of swallows; for the soul, the rest in the bosom of its Father and its God! Here the life of the body and the soul are simplified, and the one melts imperceptibly into the other. No debate; but pensive medication of the mind. No stir of effort, not even of vision. Evening shadows and sounds, life at rest, and eternal peace: a poem of humility and contentment. Little or nothing is lost; the soul passes reverently into eternity. One is reminded of Sir Thomas Browne's description of a peaceful death:

" His soft departure, which was scarce an expiration "; or of Vaughan's " Dear, beauteous death, the Jewel of the Just." And so perfectly does the music of the words convey us into the mood of the poet that we do not pause to question his assumptions, or remark the infinity of Jenniness appropriated to each village Jenny. In a way, it is one of the most sensuous and least intellectual of all elegies; although every line has its thought, its pointed commonplace. Its function has always been to liberate men, momentarily, from fervid living, and to reconcile them with death in the abstract. To that extent it helps to elucidate a difficult world. It has made the country churchyard a universal idyl of peace in life and death. It holds a solemn stillness for troubled minds, entrancing them for the time it takes to read the poem; and leaving them forever after a little different, for the memory of it. To it *Adonais* is strange, foreign, exotic, tumultuous.

But *In Memoriam* is the elegy of grief, almost of anguish, *par excellence*. Nowhere else in English, perhaps in any, poetry is there anything really comparable with it, if we take the whole of it into view: the anguish, so primal that it belongs equally to a Maori of old New Zealand and to a sensitive mind that has fallen heir to a culture accumulated through four thousand years; the tragic questioning of man's blind circumstance, the pondering of the mystery — always in poignant reference to an inconsolable grief; and the final, pensive victory over sorrow by a faith born of a love that instinctively refuses annihilation of itself and the beloved. Brief things of exquisite grief we have: none more powerful, in bitter constraint, than those few perfect lines of Catullus for his brother, quoted above; none more lovely than some from Pugliesi, Dante, and Petrarch; few more intense than Christine de Pisan's longing to lie in the grave with her father; none more feminine than Alice Meynell's *To the Beloved Dead;* none more deeply steeped in despair than Rossetti's four Willowwood sonnets. But where else is there such lengthening and modulation of intense grief as are in *In Memoriam?*

One is tempted to say that as an elegy *In Memoriam* is everything that *Adonais* is not. In *In Memoriam*, the grief, if not wildly passionate or passionately dumb, is acute and personal, for the loss of an exceedingly precious friend. There is a heavy, heavy weight of tribulation, a resultant sense of the emptiness of life; like the stark vacancy of a house whose beloved master lies dead, and one feels that in the depth of the silence is a room where grief itself sits, grim and inconsolable. The expression is simple and immediate, the imagery comparatively sparse and realistic, the metre and rhyme hypnotically insistent, the construction lyrical and disjunctive. All the marks of common grief are here, to be recognized instantly by every reader, phrased to make an immediate appeal: the stillness of the house, the closed door, the empty room, the burial in the home-ground amid the well-known engraved names, the sacred rest of the graves of the dead family; the old haunts now deserted, the effect of time on grief, the abiding sorrow, the agonized prayer to God; days of dark doubt, succeeded by a compensating faith in the goodness of the inscrutable God and by a comfortable belief in personal immortality and joyful reunion beyond the grave; remembrance of the dead at Christmas, on the anniversary of his death, and on his birthday; the wonder whether the dead are cognizant of the living; the sad conviction that it is better to have loved and lost than not to have loved at all; the sublimation of a mundane friendship into a more perfect, spiritual communion; the tragic recognition of the inevitability of death, yet the realization that it would not seem at all strange to meet the lost one, alive, in his usual activity; the awareness that such grief as this is the portion of all men —

> Never morning wore
> To evening, but some heart did break.

299

Those two lines, with their sheer simplicity, their homely truth yet intensity of personal appeal, their grave, steady cadence, are as representative of *In Memoriam* as they are foreign to *Adonais*. But what more telling contrast is there than that between the stanza-forms chosen for the poems: Shelley's Spenserians with their intricate music, the gorgeous pictorial power, the impressive magnificence of idea and mood and phrase; and Tennyson's concise, unadorned quatrains, with their threnodic closes?

Because of these traits, *In Memoriam* makes both a wider and more immediate appeal than does *Adonais*. It is popular and personal in a way Shelley's elegy never will or can be. It easily " enters in at lowly doors." As Andrew Lang, A. C. Bradley, and nearly every commentator have noticed, it is almost unique among the greatest elegies for its sympathy, familiarity, and directly consolatory power. Lang's reaction is that of most readers:

> Another, we feel, has trodden our dark and stony path, has been shadowed by the shapes of dread which haunt our valley of tribulation: a mind almost infinitely greater than ours has been our fellow-sufferer. . . . It is the sympathy and example, I think, not the speculations, mystical or scientific, which make *In Memoriam*, in more than name, a book of consolation.

The very sentimentality of the poem, such as its references to the father pledging his gallant son even while on some distant field a shot stills the dear one's life, to the mother praying for the safety of her sailor-boy while his weighted hammock-shroud sinks in the waves, to the golden-haired dove setting a ringlet aright for her lover while he is killed by falling from his horse — this very sentimentality, at the antipodes of Shelley's treatment of death, makes for popular acceptance. It is little wonder that the ordinary reader, passing from the admired *In Memoriam* to *Adonais,* finds the latter cold, puzzling, remote.

A simple God and a sentimental people find each other rather easily in *In Memoriam,* to their mutual satisfaction, no doubt. Yet, after all this has been said, and even after the philosophical innocence of the speculative part of the poem has been noted, it remains to point out that in several points it is similar to the *Adonais,* though these similarities are so differently managed that they only heighten the contrast. In both poems, so long as the attention is fixed upon things which die, sorrow is supreme; but with the direction of the mind toward the vitality of nature, the victory over sorrow is attained. But in *In Memoriam* this change is gradual: an insensible decrease in the vividness of grief, a gentle spiritualization of the lover's love and of the object of his love, and a slow rise through returning hope to a belief in a benevolent universe, " as the dead friend ceases to be a silent voice and becomes a living soul "; whereas in the *Adonais* the change is dramatic and apocalyptic: a continuous and tragic debate, in the first part, between the renewal of life in nature and the definitive failure of the human being, is suddenly resolved, by a realization of the impropriety of the antithesis, into a convinced affirmation of the indestructible essence of being in all things, human and non-human. In nature, with its obscene struggle of fang and tooth, Tennyson finds no warrant for optimism, but the reverse; in mutability, Shelley, much as he has rebelled against its ugliness, at last perceives the very signature of a greater reality that includes the lower realities of life and death. Again, both poems progress to a faith in immortality and to a conception of the relation of the individual to a spiritual power. Tennyson reaches these ends by faith alone — his heart protests against the finality of death, demanding a continuance of love after death, and in his best and noblest emotional moments he experiences an immediate certainty of survival; he assumes a personal survival and reunion because only so can his heart be satisfied, because without them life seems to him senseless and futile. His last word is that these certainties we can

> By faith, and faith alone, embrace,
> Believing where we cannot prove.

But Shelley, working upwards positivistically through the immortality of works, and scientifically through the indestructibility of the life-plasm, rationally affirms a persistence in an indescribable but surely transcendentally satisfying reality, without committing himself to the naïvely comforting faith in an everlasting persistence of the individual as known by name on earth. He rises above the desire for a particular form to a glad reconciliation with the ever-changing accomplishment of being. He substitutes the joy of being in general for that of being in particular. Finally, both poets experience a special psychic state, with a unique feeling-tone and meaning, which leads to a mystical pronouncement of their belief. But Tennyson glances at this state of mind in the midst of his elegy (Poem xcv), immediately expresses his doubt of its validity, and then places his certainty, in the weakened terms of a pious faith, as the apologetic prologue of his poem; whereas Shelley, rising steadily and surely through positivistic and rational concepts, attains at last a trance-like state in which mystical certainty is not only added to his speculations but is made the ecstatic yet intelligent culmination of the entire poem, without any aftermath of doubt or rejection or apology.

For all its imperfections, therefore, and in spite of its undeniable inferiority to *In Memoriam* as an intimate, easily recognizable example of acute, personal grief and sympathy, the *Adonais* is, for me, the more stimulating as a poem and the more satisfying as a rational coming-to-grips with the problem of death. To-day, to the post-war critical mind,

Not a Dream, but a Vision: The Mystical Victory

Tennyson's sentimentality and his argument from the higher emotions must seem singularly naïve. Shelley's rational idealism, imaginatively illuminated, is on stronger ground. But I can readily and sympathetically understand that one of the worst preparations for reading the *Adonais* is a consuming appreciation of *In Memoriam*.

When *Lycidas* and *Adonais* are put side by side, another temptation arises — to say that the latter contains much that the former has and much more besides. Both are built on the same general play of inherited ideas and forms: the classical allusions to grief, under figures of weeping natural forms (*sunt lacrimae rerum*), under mourning abstractions and mythological personifications; the bitter indictment of nature for permitting the death of the beloved; a moral indignation expressed in a protest against unsympathetic persons; the tragic sense of the finality of death; the change, somewhere beyond the middle of the poem, to the modern comfort of immortality; the picture of heavenly spirits welcoming the newly dead to their undying company; the association of the liberated soul with the environment of the living. Even the ordering of these elements is much the same in the two poems. Again, neither poem has the intensity of personal grief that makes *In Memoriam* impressive. Moreover, the Doric restraint of Milton's mode is not unrepresented in the first part of *Adonais*, and there are definite similarities in imagery. And, by a natural, reflective transition, both poets ponder their own fate, in conjunction with that of the departed.

But here the extrinsic similarity ceases, and the intrinsic differences, far more important, begin. *Lycidas*, in comparison with the deep psychic movement of *Adonais*, is a formal, academic exercise — a " consolatory writ with studied argument "; Milton writes coldly, in undisturbed agreement first with the classical, then with the Christian tradition. Doubt of inherited dogma never stirs his reason to salient effort. There is no originative mind-work on fundamentals of ex-

perience and faith. But, as grief for Hallam plunged Tennyson into tragic questioning of the fate of the individual, so
intense sympathy with the grievous life of peoples and the
representative fate of an individual stimulated Shelley to
examine to his utmost power the popular antithesis of life
and death. Milton knew little grief and no doubt; perceived
no human unsolved problem. There is no tragedy in *Lycidas*.
The assumption of personal immortality is complete, the
kinds and the ways of it are known like a lesson in anthro-
pology. There is, therefore, no discovery in *Lycidas*, no
grief-born faith or apocalyptic introspection. The Christian
affirmative,

> Weep no more, woful shepherds, weep no more,
> For Lycidas, your sorrow, is not dead,

is not projected out of the classical negative, either emotionally or intellectually; the former stands over against the latter
in a designed but not rationalized contrast. The Christian
faith is not forged in the poem itself, out of elements of an
intense, human sympathy, but is of a sudden imported into
it from without, as a revelation whose glory long since has
been taken for granted. *Adonais* possesses both emotional and
intellectual fervour; *Lycidas* is fervid only in the denunciation
of the selfish pastor. Great as is the contrast in variety and
richness of imagery between the two poems, they differ in
nothing else so much as in the amount and ardour of fundamental brain-work. *Lycidas*, in its climax, neatly assumes
what *Adonais* at its close comes perilously near to demon-
strating. For Milton, the spiritual life is a calm, remote fact.
With Shelley, each sympathetic reader, entranced, seems almost himself to have entered the larger life. But Milton, his
elegiac part played, twitches his cloak upon his shoulder and
marches off scene to the next engagement.

Shelley, in his *Defence of Poetry*, wrote:

Not a Dream, but a Vision: The Mystical Victory

Poetry reproduces the common universe of which we are portions and percipients, and it purges from our inward sight the film of familiarity which obscures from us the wonders of our being. . . . A poet participates in the eternal, the infinite, the one.

The *Adonais* as a whole, and particularly in its close, is the very picture and living example of what Shelley describes in this definition. *Lycidas*, a poem of occasion, written by request, is not.

And now, what may be a more important distinction may be examined. These three poems, *In Memoriam*, *Lycidas*, *Adonais*, are alike in that each gathers its reflections into a conclusion of immortality. Tennyson argues the point; Milton does not: both affirm the Christian idyll of the persistence of the individual through that eternity which to other minds is but a fiction of ignorance. Therein they are in definite opposition to the elegiac tradition of Homer, Plato, Bion, Moschus, Catullus, and the *Greek Anthology*. Again, Tennyson's arguments from love, from an ephemeral inner conviction, and from his personal way of determining what is significant in life, are not rational, as we have seen; and Milton's assumption rests on a doubtful theistic revelation. Therein Tennyson and Milton go yet further apart from that apogee of clear-headedness, the ancient elegy. In antiquity, so often the self-dependent home of an unconfused mind, one finds the best, that is, the classic, utterances on the primitive problem of death. Primitively conceived, death is the greatest reminder of the forever untold treasury of life, of the known joy symbolized by the sun of this life, as well as of the irremediable and inevitable loss of all this gladness. The classic mind of Greece and Rome placed an intellectual control over the emotional expostulation with the unavoidable fate. Every Greek funerary monument is carved in that tradition. In literature, the tradition runs from Homer to Statius and Ausonius, except where it is infected, as in Pindar or Cicero, with the sentimentalism of the mysteries. The anguish of departure was powerfully brought under the control of minds definitely aware of their inability to demonstrate an after-existence. Ignorance was true and clear. The classic result of that splendid confession of ignorance was an elegy, or elegiac oration, permeated with proud sadness, without surrender to a childish grievance against fate. So spoke Homer and Thucydides, Catullus and Virgil; and Pindar, too, at times, howeversomuch his imagination was energized by the splendour of human achievement, of the skilled body flashing in the midday sun at the Olympian and Nemean games. In this respect, classical elegy has an affinity with the fatalism of that Greek tragedy from which, as Sir William Watson has so fitly said, " a certain tonic and astringent philosophy of life may be extracted."

Now Milton endeavoured to write in this classic tradition. Tennyson did not. But what did Milton accomplish? The clear self-knowledge of the classic endeavour? Its stern heroism in the face of ignorance and death? Its sad beauty, gracefully shrouding despair, too heroic to complain? No, only an imitation of the outer habiliments of the classic mode: a thing of shreds and patches, illogically imposed upon a Christian desire and dream. Neither purely antique, nor yet purely modern, *Lycidas* falls between the two. The measure of its fall is its uninspired commentary upon the futile, the minute, the mundane, which disfigures it. Deep neither in grief nor insight, neither in emotion nor in recognition of the human frontier, neither assuaging grief nor fortifying the soul, it achieves an undoubted eminence, partly by its now silvery, now solemn music, partly by some almost unsurpassable imagery both of the minute and the vast, partly by the force of a pseudo-classical tradition. It is a compromise, better a confusion, of tendencies, classic and Christian. It has the air of both. It is welcomed as somehow harmonizing them, though in reality it is but a superficial construction with neither romantic, infinite dream, nor classic confession of the limits of happiness.

In Memoriam, making no pretension to understand or imitate this classic mode, stands firmly upon the single ground of desire and dream, or faith. It is, fundamentally, a poem of a personally rediscovered deism, however untheological its arguments may be. But because it nowhere definitely rejects the belief in an historical revelation of God and immortality, it has by its readers been uncritically assimilated to theism. And with Christian theists it has always been popular; under whatever suspicion of self-interest its persuasion of personal immortality may suffer in the eyes of a later, critical denial. But what it lacks in argumentation, it makes up in sympathy. It assuages grief. It comforts and supports, even if it does not strongly fortify, the soul. Therein its title to significance is perfectly clear and quite undeniable.

Adonais, like *Lycidas*, imitates the classic mode, but it penetrates the thought as well as imitates the form. The finality of death fashions the fair imagery of sorrow, adding strength to grace and deepening the Virgilian "sense of tears in mortal things." Superficial formality and decorum, "festooning the porch of things," are as foreign to *Adonais* as to the *Ode on a Grecian Urn*. Yet the consenting detachment from anguish, the strong reconciliation with blind fate, are significantly absent. Throughout the first part a deep impatience with the negative conclusion is discernible, and directly out of the struggle against it is born the affirmation of the second part. A dogma of personal immortality is not suddenly set in question-begging contrast, as in *Lycidas*. The affirmation does not evade, it completes, the problem raised by the antithesis of life and death. Nor is the affirmation that of Christian desire and dream, supported by the suspicious argument from the affections, as in *In Memoriam*. Instead, it is that poetic rendering of the dialectic liberation from the popular antithesis, which has been noticed above. It is neither deistic nor theistic nor pantheistic: the absence of the term " God " is as characteristic of *Adonais* as its frequent recurrence is of *In Memoriam*. It is not theological, but philosophical: a monism that discovers reasonably a higher synthesis in a substantial ground of mind and matter; an objective idealism that resolves mind and matter, or the Many, into an indescribable reality, or the One. Its affirmation of immortality, therefore, cannot be in the naïve terms of personality; but only in the tactful and honest terms of the indestructible essence of being. Then it concludes with an imaginative rendering, or vision, of what the mind has conceived. As such, its thought and its poetry are more far-reaching than the achievement of either *Lycidas* or *In Memoriam*. Its thought and poetry, penetrating and repeating the classical elegiac mode, harmonizes the antique, heroic confession of ignorance with the highest reaches of modern reason. Neither in English elegy before its time nor in English elegy after its time is there any comparable achievement.

Browning's tyrannical optimism concerning the personal immortality of the soul has made him the favourite poet of Christian apologists. Mr. Leslie D. Weatherhead, for instance, writing with a studied Christian *tendenz* on *The After-World of the Poets*, first points out how Wordsworth and Shelley contributed to the Christian thesis by raising objections to it, how Tennyson contributed to it by exploring and overcoming the unchristian fear of death, and how Arnold, Clough, and Swinburne collaborated with it by suggesting stimulating doubts! Then he thankfully puts Browning at the head of them all in a final chapter unhappily headed " The Climax of Development." But even Mr. Weatherhead reminds us that Browning's ideas on the subject are not all of a piece, and that it was after 1850, under the influence of Miss Barrett's somewhat discriminating faith, that he spoke most fluently and forcibly of personal persistence. However, even in the midst of this period of assertive optimism, Browning paused, at the age of sixty-five, in *La Saisiaz* (1877), thoroughly to reconsider the grounds of his conviction. Since it is a question of forthright, clear consideration, he makes a fine rational gesture of forthwith rejecting all emotional attitudes and imaginative conjectures of the poets, all symbolic reading of the beauty and ugliness of nature and death, all ingenious assumptions of the theologians. " The mere opinions of men," says Mr. Weatherhead, " are scrutinized with acid severity." But, alas! for Mr. Weatherhead, Browning, suspiciously careful to insist that his argument is with himself alone, finds that his " conviction " is only one man's hopeful opinion, after all.

Miss Ann Egerton-Smith died suddenly, September 14, 1877, of heart-failure. After the funeral, Browning climbed Mt. Salève to explore his soul once again, to wrestle once more with the arch-fiend, Death. Now let's be sure of ourselves on this matter, he seems to say with an assumption of colloquial directness. We have consigned Miss Egerton-Smith's body peacefully to a lovely earth-bed. But where is her soul? Let's try to find out, as clearly as possible! And, to be perfectly fair, let's not put any words into the mouth of God! Let's not take anything for granted, not even the Christian revelation! Let's be perfectly rational, at whatever cost! We may be a poet ourself, but let's not be poetic; let's be rational!

Well, first, what are the fundamental facts? That's easy. There's the fact of one's self, and the fact perceived outside one's self. I know, therefore I am; call me a soul, if you like. One fact! I know something outside myself; thus there is the world of things and human beings. Another fact! There must be a cause of me and of them; call the cause, if you like, God. Another fact! (What a quaint epistemology! What a short way with Plato, Descartes, Spinoza, Berkeley, Hume, and Locke; with mysticism, determinism, realism, and subjective and objective idealism, including holism and solipsism! But, we must remember, forsooth, not to object, for the argument is with himself alone, after all). But, now, let's on with our pure and complete rationalism. If these be all the " facts " — self as soul, not-self as things, and cause fundamental as God — then it's hard to be certain that the cause is really benevolent, for in my own experience there is more sorrow than joy, more grief than gladness. And I, I am sure, am not an unrepresentative human being, though I'm enough of a solipsist to realize I can argue only from my own experience. Indeed, judging from my own experience of myself and of others (this solipsist again admits there *are* others), it is hard not to think the world is ruled by blind, indifferent chance. For if we assume the world is not ruled by a God of caprice and chance, but by a benevolent, omnipotent God, then why are right and wrong at strife in His world? No, I cannot reconcile divine wisdom with a world distraught, with evil triumphant over good, with power failing daily in its benevolent aim — except in one way: that there is a blissful end to all this present failure, a second life the beauty of which is exalted by the ugliness of this. If I'm barred from conceiving this life as a probation for another, there is no way of reconciling man to God. Life is so imperfect, there must be perfection beyond death. Incidentally, it is tacitly (all too tacitly!) assumed that *personal* persistence is the only possible off-set to the hardness of the probation. Where is the triumph if it is not a personal triumph — with endless gratification to be had from endlessly remembering the former pains suffered for an infinitesimal moment on that midget of a planet? But, alas! probation and the second-life are only surmises, not facts. Reason, then, leads me only to a hope, a rational hope, of personal immortality. In that hope, let me fight and conquer, manfully! Here, then, is the conclusion of this all-to-be-trusted reason as set forth by the poet for himself alone in this argumentative elegy, *La Saisiaz.*

Not a Dream, but a Vision: The Mystical Victory

If this argument be either good poetry or good reason, then Shelley and Keats and Shakespeare never sang, and Hume and Berkeley never reasoned. Elsewhere in *La Saisiaz* there are powerful poetry and quick, ironic reasoning. By the way, Mr. Weatherhead misses the irony! But the main argument begs the question of what a " fact " is, begs the question of what " self " is, begs the question of what " right " and " wrong " are, is singularly naïve in its epistemology, makes much of an incomplete and confused solipsism, tacitly assumes that personal immortality is the only possible immortality, or the only one worth talking about, eschews theology and adopts the theological, juridical argument from the imperfection of this life, used by Kant and Butler, and rejects the emotional-imaginative attitudes of the poets only to come to rest in an attitude of hope for personal immortality, though there is nothing in the argument that necessarily leads exclusively to the *personal* quantity. But it satisfied Browning! That is the only virtue he claims for it. I cannot claim much else for it, except, pragmatically, that it has been found " wholesome " and " wonderfully subtle and profound " by many devoted readers. But even they, including Mr. Weatherhead, turn more happily to their poet's less reticent faith in a benevolent God and in personal immortality, as it is to be found in Pippa's song, *Rabbi Ben Ezra*, *Abt Vogler*, *Prospice*, and the *Epilogue* to *Asolando*.

From these niggard reasons stiffly shut up in crackling rhythms, I prefer to turn to the poetic splendours of the *Adonais*, where symbolic image and deep feeling and subtle music, each penetrating each, seem to body forth by their very fusion the mystery of spirit in sense:

Glory about thee, without thee; and thou fulfillest thy
    doom,
Making Him broken gleams and a stifled splendour and
    gloom.

Other elegies of something less than the first rank do not equal the scope of *Adonais*. Arnold, in his elegiac mood, is less philosophical than Shelley, less assured of a splendid essential reality that compensates us for the agony of change, less ready to give up the simple faith in an unadulterated individualism beyond the grave. For his comfort he falls back, a little like Browning, but not with the latter's cocksureness, on the intoxication of heroic effort. In *The Scholar-Gypsy*, *Thyrsis*, the *Stanzas* for Edward Quillinan, but most clearly in *Rugby Chapel*, comfort, and a not full-hearted assurance of survival, are derived from the courageous unworldliness of the strong soul. From the futile strivings of the crowd he reserves the significance of the indomitable searcher for the good life. But this significance he is not content, like Homer and Aeschylus and Sophocles and Virgil, to view as an immortality of works, or influence. He craves a personal survival as indispensable to a moral universe. A quotation or two will illustrate these points. First, the picture of futility, from *Rugby Chapel:*

> What is the course of the life
> Of mortal men on the earth?
> Most men eddy about
> Here and there, eat and drink,
> Chatter and love and hate,
> Gather and squander, are raised
> Aloft, are hurled in the dust,
> Striving blindly, achieving
> Nothing; and then they die, —
> Perish; and no one asks
> Who or what they have been,
> More than he asks what waves,
> In the moonlit solitudes mild
> Of the inmost ocean, have swelled,
> Foamed for a moment, and gone.

Not a Dream, but a Vision: The Mystical Victory

Then, from the same source, the contrast of the strong soul, and the desire that it itself, let alone its works, may never be lost:

> O strong soul, by what shore
> Tarriest thou now? For that force,
> Surely, has not been left vain!
> Somewhere, surely, afar,
> In the sounding labour-house vast
> Of being, is practised that strength,
> Zealous, beneficent, firm!

Finally, the sonnet *Immortality*, which sums up these contrasting ideas:

> Foiled by our fellow-men, depressed, outworn,
> We leave the brutal world to take its way,
> And, *Patience! in another life*, we say,
> *The world shall be thrust down, and we upborne.*
>
> And will not, then, the immortal armies scorn
> The world's poor, routed leavings? or will they
> Who failed under the heat of this life's day
> Support the fervours of the heavenly morn?
>
> No, no! the energy of life may be
> Kept on after the grave, but not begun;
> And he who flagged not in the earthly strife,
>
> From strength to strength advancing, — only he,
> His soul well-knit, and all his battles won,
> Mounts, and that hardly, to eternal life.

Swinburne, in his elegiac masterpiece, dedicated like *Adonais* to the memory of a brother poet, chaunts the praises of death and oblivion. In other poems, *Hertha, Thalassius, A Nympholept, The Palace of Pan*, he sings, with a kind of musical mysticism, the spirit that abides " loftier than life and serener than death." But in this elegy he is, like James Thom-

313

son, in love with the " restful rapture of the inviolate grave."
No euphrasy of faith or reason frees his mind from that
overpowering bewitchment by biological materialism which
atheistic science spelled for a while against the romantics of
the later nineteenth century. A quarter of a century after the
publication of *In Memoriam*, a half-century after *Adonais*,
appeared this most sombrely lovely of English elegies, with
the tragic title, *Ave atque Vale*, a tribute to Baudelaire. The
mood dramatically and intentionally befits the author of *Les
Fleurs du Mal*, who himself has been called an *élégiaque
macabre*. After a singularly acute characterization and eulogy
of Baudelaire's genius for " the fervid languid glories," the
" sin without shape and pleasure without speech," Swinburne
turns in a less neurotic mood to the contemplation of death.
The classic acquiescence in finality is delivered as sadly as by
Catullus:

> There is no help for these things; none to mend,
> And none to mar; not all our songs, O friend,
> Will make death clear or make life durable.

But the last four words, *or make life durable*, carry us to a
position the very opposite of the classic regret for life. The
ancient elegy, characteristically, was pessimistic in respect of
death, not of life also. Swinburne's pessimism, here at any
rate, embraces both. First, the pursuit of death is futile:

> What ails us gazing where all seen is hollow?
> Yet with some fancy, yet with some desire,
> Dreams pursue death as winds a flying fire,
> Our dreams pursue our dead and do not find.
> Still, and more swift than they, the thin flame dies,
> Still the foiled earnest ear is deaf, and blind
> Are still the eluded eyes.

Does not the quotation read like an answer to Tennyson? We
recall that Tennyson said that *In Memoriam* was really too
hopeful, more than he was himself. Mr. Nicholson thinks

Not a Dream, but a Vision: The Mystical Victory

Tennyson sublimated his fear of death by dwelling upon the beliefs he desired to feel. But, second, the annihilation that is in death is welcomed, after the insult of existence:

> O sleepless heart and sombre soul unsleeping,
>   That were athirst for sleep and no more life
>   And no more love, for peace and no more strife!
> Now the dim gods of death have in their keeping
>   Spirit and body and all the springs of song,
>   Is it well now where love can do no wrong,
> Where stingless pleasure has no foam or fang
>   Behind the unopening closure of her lips?
>   Is it not well where soul from body slips
> And flesh from bone divides without a pang
>   As dew from flower-bell drips?

This rapture in the sensuousness of death, so instinctive an expression of a mind too much fettered to the obscenities of the struggle for existence, so different from the adolescent longing of Keats, is the antipodes alike of the Homeric praise of life, the Tennysonian praise of the after-life, and the Shelleyan reconciliation of life and death in the essence of being. Tennyson confessed that he could never found a belief in a beneficent God upon what could be observed in nature or natural science; so he built upon his desires and intuitions. Swinburne, finding no ground either in the outer or the inner nature, in matter or mind, utterly renouncing the Tennysonian formula, took the obvious way out: the adoration of an extinction where, at long last, the soul, i.e., the mind, "slips from the body" into nothingness. Giving up the gleam and the dream and the argument, he here praises death as the deliverer from consciousness. The eloquent denial of immortality in the third book of Lucretius of course comes to mind. But where Lucretius is scornful of the will to live and the fear to die, Swinburne is ecstatic in the contemplation of the great escape.

In poem after poem, and particularly in *The Garden of*

Proserpine, he is eloquent on extinction. Yet occasionally, as in the lines in memory of Landor and concluding quintet of those on Marston, in *After Sunset* and *Past Days,* he erects a pensive " If " before the belief in an after-life. But the one comfort for the living in their bereavement is the immortality of works. So of Baudelaire he takes his leave thus:

> Not thee, O never thee, in all time's changes,
> > Not thee, but this the sound of thy sad soul,
> > The shadow of thy swift spirit, this shut scroll
> I lay my hand on, and not death estranges
> > My spirit from communion of thy song. . . .

> For thee, O now a silent soul, my brother,
> > Take at my hands this garland, and farewell.

The last two verses are entirely Catullan, like the title itself:

> *Accipe fraterno multum manantia fletu,*
> > *Atque in perpetuum, frater, ave atque vale.*

But the poem is not yet finished. Swinburne's own signature comes last:

> Content thee, howso'er, whose days are done;
> > There lies not any troublous thing before,
> > Nor sight nor sound to war against thee more,
> For whom all winds are quiet as the sun,
> > All waters as the shore.

What a contrast is this elegiac *diminuendo* to the burning beacon of *Adonais!* Nor is it as though Shelley, dead before Darwinism startled the superstitious, were unaware of the red struggle of fang and claw. His intense awareness of all the evil done under the sun, his preternatural susceptibility to all that was ugly, death included, made for him as great a problem of pain to be faced as Darwinism was for Arnold or Swinburne or Clough or Meredith. Moreover, he had to pass through French materialistic philosophy. But he was born

with the gift to see invisibles. Always, underneath his aesthetic and humane revulsion from the ugliness of life, there
was the ineradicable intuition of the essence of being. But he
did not base his faith in feeling alone; nor find hypnotic
refuge in that

> . . . peace that grows by Lethe, scentless flower,
> There in white languors to decline and cease.

The lines just quoted are from one of the most tranquil
and sincere elegies of the nineteenth century, appearing in the
first year of the last decade, Sir William Watson's *Wordsworth's Grave*. Written in the quatrain consecrated by
Gray's *Elegy*, with much of the serene movement of that
measure, but lacking the intimate and popular quality of
Gray's poem; missing out the graceful, devious music of
Lycidas; not pretending to the scope and variety of thought
in *In Memoriam;* eschewing the voluptuous serenade with
which Swinburne greeted death; having nothing of the sublime passion and imaginative grandeur of *Adonais:* it yet has,
as I have observed elsewhere, something of its own to say to
minds distraught by a fevered century, and it says it clearly,
unmistakably. The same message, if one may continue to
dare assume that poets have messages, informs Watson's elegy
for Tennyson, *Lachrymae Musarum*. It comprises a restate-
ment of Wordsworth's faith in a beneficently spiritual universe. Like Tennyson, but with less misgiving, Wordsworth
based his faith in a special mystic state of mind — that state
which Shelley actually enters as he closes his metaphysical
speculation, that state with which Dante closes the *Paradiso*.
But Watson stresses not the burning exultation of that mystic
experience, as did Shelley; but the profound peace, too deep
for words, with which Wordsworth, never doubting, recol-
lected it. The vagrant soul, at last wearily wise, must needs
return to this peace, says Watson, and therefore to Wordsworth —

To him and to the powers that with him dwell: —
　Inflowings that divulged not whence they came;
And that secluded spirit unknowable,
　The mystery that we make darker with a name;

The Somewhat which we name but cannot know,
　Ev'n as we name a star and only see
His quenchless flashings forth, which ever show
　And ever hide him, and which are not he.

One-hundred and two-hundred inch telescopes, spectrum analysis, and the theory of relativity have indeed taught us, in the mean time, much more about the star; but the truth of the figure, being itself relative, remains. It is the truth poetized in *Adonais*, though here it is stated in the reverse mood. But the *Adonais* gives or implies a philosophical basis for the mystical persuasion; adding, as none of these other elegies does, reason to introspection.

III

From *Adonais*, Shelley's last great poem on the spiritual, we go to his last improvisation on the political, renascence of mankind, *Hellas*. This tribute to the Greek struggle for independence, composed hurriedly in the autumn of 1821, a few months after *Adonais*, is a lyric drama of liberty and death, forming a sort of political counterpart to the philosophical handling of life and death in the elegy. It is a tragedy of political desolation — the failure of the Greek cause — mitigated by the consolatory hope of the eventual triumph of freedom. Throughout, from the Prologue to the last semi-choruses and the concluding stanza, peals a tragic antiphony of good and evil, liberty and tyranny, life and death. The Prologue inaugurates the antithesis in a dispute between Christ and Satan. The main story, with the triumph first of the Greeks, then of the tyrant, exemplifies the contrast. The semi-choruses, intoned against the victors' jubilant cries for blood-vengeance, bewail the failure of the rebels. The final lyric begins with a promise of an age of freedom and love, and ends with a lament on the return of hate and death.

Similar as the poem is in many ways to *The Revolt of Islam* — in the Levantine setting, in the alternation of victory and defeat, in the prophecy of the final victory of freedom, in a representative rather than historical purpose — it is in other ways very different. It is not the expression of a young, strong, fanatic man, completely fascinated by a social ideal, dreaming of an early and complete political regeneration as the *summum bonum* for the individual as well as for society. Its social idealism is less strenuous. Ideology no longer fires the impetuous, unwearied emotions of an untried youth to the white heat that can heedlessly incinerate each human failure as though it were no more than a mere incident in an ideal progress. Instead, an older heart, mortally acquainted with grief, all of whose ardent loves and hopes have been beguiled by impetuosity to the grave, does full homage to the tragedy of the individual. In this later, wiser, and sadder poem, the personal drama of struggle and failure is constantly present; speaks in verse after verse, and informs the antiphonal construction; and is to be read everywhere between the lines. At last Shelley's idealism is more scrupulous of the individual. No longer content to compensate the defeated eleutherarchs with the mere anticipation of a perfected world-order, or with an entrance into a symbolic abode of fame, he now finds for liberty's martyrs a more immediate blessing.

This more immediate felicity has its roots in a speculative idea, which is fittingly broached in the Prologue in Heaven. " Dominations " meet in Heaven to debate the fate of Greece. We are taken behind the human stage, to have sight of controlling powers. Of course, what we find are only personifications, or abstractions, of the two groups of antagonists, in the forms of Christ and Satan debating before God. But here, in this high and secret play of the two opposed forces, if anywhere, a satisfactory way through and out from the struggle must be indicated for the individual who in it is sacrificed.

An effect of infinity makes the problem immense. Fragment as the Prologue is, nowhere else has Shelley so splendidly compassed vastness in a description. With a comprehensive power rivalling Milton's, though with very different devices of style and matter, and with less prodigious words than he has formerly used for such a scale, he brings infinity before us. From the abyss the Herald of Eternity summons the Sons of God to the roofless senate-house whose floor is Chaos. There they sit,

> Pavilioned on the radiance or the gloom
> Of mortal thought.

In passing, one notes again the special quality of Shelley's poetic power — the imaginative embodiment of the abstract; here, in particular, the embodiment is of his rationalized theology, for these pavilioned Powers are clearly only the ideal projections of man's abstractions upon infinity. But this unsuperstitious recognition of how anthropomorphic gods are made, strengthens, rather than weakens, the effect, for the poetry of vastness progresses without any dubious aid of superstitious belief or any tacit demand for a temporary, willing suspension of disbelief. For a simple empirical vastness, dear to naïve religion, is substituted the subjective vastness of ideas. Unalloyed imaginative enjoyment accrues to the reader. But the objective vastness is not lacking:

> The curtain of the Universe
> Is rent and shattered,
> The splendour-wingèd worlds disperse
> Like wild doves scattered. . . .

Not a Dream, but a Vision: The Mystical Victory

> Like a thousand dawns on a single night
> The splendours rise and spread.

Two of the symbolic splendours, Christ and Satan, then contend for the earthly doom of Greece. Christ champions Greece, reverently calling his own spirit " a burning morrow of Plato's sacred light." Satan, the spirit of time and space, deriding the " mockery-King crowned with a wreath of thorns," confidently claims all human enterprise as his to ruin with failure, suffering, scorn, and death. Christ replies,

> True greatness asks not space, true excellence
> Lives in the Spirit of all things that live.

This is the speculative gospel for the martyr: the true victory is in the spirit — not in the outer kingdom in space and time, and therefore subject to ruin and death; but in the inner kingdom, not subject to death. Again, the realized, undauntable beauty of individual mind swallows up defeat and pain and death.

The philosophy that is the ground of this gospel, at first glance may seem that of *Adonais*. It is, on the contrary, that philosophy of subjective idealism to which Shelley had held in his prose fragment, *On Life,* and which, to the best of my understanding, he had rejected in *Adonais* in favour of a poetic mysticism, as I have explained above. Indeed, Shelley's favourite type of endless suffering, Ahasuerus, the Wandering Jew, erstwhile antagonist, or at least victim, of Christ, is now called from afar to explain the metaphysics of this new gospel. To the Islamic tyrant, desirous of knowing his hidden fate, Ahasuerus discloses the illusory character of the phenomenal world of change. The whole of suns and worlds, earth and ocean, men and beasts and flowers, with all their changes and cessations, and space and time themselves, are figments of the mind, which is their cradle and their grave. Thought alone subsists, only that which knows itself to be. It follows, therefore, that the sagacious mind, realizing itself in itself, is not deceived into desiring the illusory mutants of time and space and circumstance. True excellence is in the mind that knows itself. For the initiated mind there is no failure, no martyrdom, no death, no slavery to the tyrant, no sacrifice of itself.

Now there is much to comment upon in this teaching, but I shall limit myself to a mere indication of each of some six critical difficulties. The doctrine is a recession, without assigned reason, from the more advanced monism in which the *Adonais* culminates. The doctrine itself, whether in the poem or in the essay, *On Life,* is confused, escaping solipsism only at the price of self-contradiction, as I have already suggested in discussing the Essay; and in the poem no adjustment is made between " the One, the unborn and the undying " and the illusory phenomena of " matter." There is a further contradiction in the statement that thought is " what that which it regards appears " (l. 798), for there it is assumed that there is a somewhat which thought does regard, whereas elsewhere it is plainly said that all matter is illusion. So there is an indiscriminate mixture of philosophies in the poem. What is more important, the doctrine of illusion destroys the significance of the poem as a tribute to the Greek struggle for freedom by making both the struggle and its object and its failure and its success so many illusions; and also renders nugatory the antithesis of good and evil out of which is built the antiphonal, lyric construction of the poem. Finally, the doctrine is not carried through the poem, but is dropped in favour of this very antithesis which it destroys.

Because of these closely interrelated difficulties, however felicitous may be the imaginative achievement of some parts of the poem taken separately, I cannot regard the poem taken as a whole as one of Shelley's greater works. It is indeed, as he confessed, an improvisation, bearing many signs of the haste with which it was composed. He seems to have had too easy and indiscriminate resource to many of his older ideas and phrases. Although the poem is drawn out from the fundamental theme of this year, which appears somehow in each of the year's more remarkable compositions ("I change but I cannot die"; cf. l. 34, "Life may change, but it may fly not"), it shows the least significant management of that thesis. This idea leads naturally to a philosophy of becoming, and the political thesis of *Hellas* is indeed one of progress; but its philosophical core is one of being and illusion. Perhaps the theory of illusion was hurriedly introduced to explain the prophetic power of Ahasuerus, for his clairvoyance of the future depends on the assumption that time, like space and matter, is an illusion; the present, past, and future have no real difference, any more than Me and Thee, and are therefore all equally open to the sagacious mind. However, one really significant aspect I do discern, and that is the emphasis upon the havoc wreaked upon the intellectual life by the individual's — Mahmud's — *desire* for the things of the senses. This Buddhistic theme of the confusion arising from desire is taken up again and further developed, of course in association with death, in Shelley's last and most significant fragment, *The Triumph of Life.*

IV

. . . I the most
Adore thee present or lament thee lost.

The fatal year of 1822 opens with a fragment, *The Zucca,* written in January, which is an epitome of the early story of Shelley's heart. As such, it interweaves the two principal threads of his intellectual life — beauty and death; reveals his characteristically aesthetic approach to his problems; and incorporates his salient ideas in an appropriate symbolism of life, death, and reinvigoration. These three phases of the poem correspond to the three chief habits involved in his way of looking at life, his *Weltanschauung.*

The Pursuit of Death

The Zucca falls into two parts, with the division at the close of the fifth *ottava rima*. Part I is another address to Intellectual Beauty. It is not a mere *réchauffé* of the *Hymn* of 1816, though it is an elegy nearly related to the elegiac part of that ode. It is a lament for the loss of his pearl, i.e., the loss of his ecstatic sense of spiritual beauty. Like the Middle English *Pearl*, as interpreted by Sister M. Madeleva, it springs from that aridity or emptiness of the heart which is the ever-recurring interval between moments of mystic contemplation. It opens with death. Summer is dead, autumn is expiring, winter laughs upon a cold and cloudless land. The poet, " desiring more in the world than any can understand," viz., spiritual beauty, weeps its loss typified in the seasonal failure of the beauty of nature which,

> . . . like sea retiring,
> Had left the earth bare as the wave-worn sand
> Of my lorn heart. . . .

In this animistic simile, he esemplastically, if not by pathetic fallacy, connects his state of mind with a state of nature, his interior desolation with an exterior analogy. He proceeds sadly to contrast his enduring desolation with that reinvigorated natural life whose glowing immortality is not divided by death. Earth-life changes, but it cannot die. It ever renews itself in joy. His desolation persists. All his life he has loved — not the individual merely, though that too — but the perfect Idea of beauty and love. H. S. Salt appositely quotes from a letter to Hogg, written as early as 1811: " Do I love the person, the embodied identity, if I may be allowed the expression? No; I love what is superior, what is excellent, or what I conceive to be so." Though he has felt this perfect beauty everywhere, veiled but not hidden

> In winds, and trees, and streams, and all things common,
> In music and the sweet unconscious tone
> Of animals, and voices which are human,

324

Meant to express some feelings of their own;
In the soft motions and rare smile of woman,
In flowers and leaves, and in the grass fresh-shown,
Or dying in the autumn,

yet nowhere can he grasp it finally, rest in it absolutely. Forever it escapes him, and its loss leaves the noblest things vacant and cold as " a corpse after the spirit's flight." This is the old lament, the reverse of the joy of possession in *Epipsychidion*, which we have heard in the second stanza of the *Hymn to Intellectual Beauty*,

Why dost thou pass away, and leave our state,
This dim vast vale of tears, vacant and desolate?

It is Shelley's perennial problem, arising from his deep sensitiveness to beauty: his inability to reconcile himself with the death of beauty. It is that aesthetic regret for the death of loveliness which makes and pervades his poetry and chiefly stimulates his philosophy. And this first part concludes with a line that of all his lines most perfectly confesses this problem of aesthetic sensitiveness. It is addressed to the Idea of beauty:

. . . I the most
Adore thee present or lament thee lost.

Part II forsakes the pattern of the *Hymn*. In place of the ecstatic dedication to the service of spiritual beauty it substitutes an image of comfort, by another animistic symbol. Of a day, lamenting thus, like a troubadour singing his plaint for a love far-removed, the poet comes upon a zucca, frost-nipt, near death, like " one who loved beyond his nature's law, and in despair had cast him down to die." The zucca is taken home, and under tender care is revived, becoming beautiful and strong. The parable of comfort is plain. So might the poet himself, finding strength in ministering tenderness, like that of his *Magnetic Lady*, forget his pain.

It is a weak ending. The whole poem is a throwback to his

purely Platonic days. To that philosophy of being, which makes all sensible experience a falling away from perfection, and so encourages an impatient love-longing for something unattainable save in ephemeral ecstasy, the poet who rose higher in *Adonais* has sunk backwards. One cannot constantly maintain one's position on the spiritual mountain-top. That invigorating philosophy of becoming, of ever greater forms to be achieved — true projection of the naturalistic process, " I change but I cannot die " — which in *Adonais* was exultantly and mystically converted to the Spinozistic monism of the indescribable substance, is here overlooked. Moreover, the full analogy of the spiritual to the natural process is neglected, even though the latter is outlined. Instead of vigorous pursuit we drop back to dejection and to dependence upon others. This little elegy ends with no high consolation drawn from heroic self-dependence, but with the very, very human desire for understanding, for tender companionship. Impatience to possess the absolute is the foible of the Platonist, much more so of the mystical Neo-platonist. Both must be reminded of the patience recommended by Jellaludin:

> Draw Him not impatiently to thee, lest He fly as an arrow
>   from the bow.
> His Name will flee, the while thou mouldest thy lips for
>   speech:
> He will flee from thee, so that if thou paint His picture,
> The picture will flee from the tablet, and His features
>   from the soul.

Upon this short poem I have commented at length for two reasons. It so well sums up the earlier, Platonic period of Shelley's thought and emotion that an interpretation of it serves as a reminder of much that has been said before, and such a reminder is proper at a point where the story of his last, and one of his most powerful, poems is to be told. Again, it well illustrates the gloomy side of his life, never far to seek, which so often in the briefer lyrics finds an expression it is denied in more extended efforts. *The Zucca* is another of those little chantries of dejection and agonized prayer which surround the shining spires of his greater building. There are several such in this year — some dozen — in which his despair of love, health, the world, and achievement escapes into utterance. His ill health, with its paroxysms of pain, was still with him. In the home there was some irritation, natural enough, that unduly depressed his sensitive spirit. Mr. H. J. Massingham, in his recent work on Trelawny, has told again the story of the tension between Mary and Shelley. Besides, the scorn of the world followed him. There seemed little hope of attaining eminence in his art. His younger raptures seemed falling away. His hopes of regenerating society had been left far behind. These things oppressed him continually. Not continuously, to be sure. Shelley's was not a melancholy temperament. In these very lyrics there are compensating moods — of gratitude to Jane Williams for her tender friendship, of simple holiday pleasures, and deeper joys suggested by natural beauty — " sweet oracles of the woods," as he calls the last. There were many happy days near Lerici. But these alternations of mood are not those of a lightly mercurial temperament. There is too much of disappointment and grief in the total for that. The authentic antithesis to the dejection generates, as usual, a long poem, to the making of which he girds up his powers, putting aside every-day oppressions. This long poem, upon which he was yet working at the time of his death, is called, by an irony of fate, *The Triumph of Life*.

It was Mary Shelley's misfortune to preface two of Shelley's most beautiful and significant poems with deprecatory references to their lack of human interest. What she said of *The Witch of Atlas* has been quoted above. Of *The Triumph of Life* she wrote:

Whether the subject [Charles I., about whom Shelley had begun a play] proved more difficult than he anticipated, or whether in fact he could not bend his mind away from the broodings and wanderings of thought, divested from human interest, which he best loved, I cannot tell; but he proceeded slowly, and threw it aside for one of the most mystical of his poems, *The Triumph of Life.*

If the poetic incorporation of one of the most ancient and widely-spread of philosophical ideas in an undeniably beautiful form amounts to a mental meandering devoid of human interest, Mrs. Shelley speaks truly.

There is an ancient Vedantic saying that life is a succession of incarnations (*samsara*) caused by desire; and that by getting rid of desire the rotation of *samsara* may be halted and the soul returned into the First Cause, the inmost being of nature, *Brahman*. Brahman is identical with the inmost being of the individual soul, called *Atman*. So long as desire triumphs, the *Atman* is caught in the wide-spread net of bondage to the sensuous. Desire is life's triumph over the *Atman*.

Before Garnett had the ill luck to discover four colourless additional lines, which still leave the poem a fragment, *The Triumph of Life* closed with the dramatic question: " ' Then what is life? ' I cried." The answer, judging from the context, should be, " Desire." The triumph of life over the individual is the triumph of desire.

So far as I know, Shelley never read any Vedantic literature; but the recognition of the incarcerating effect of desire is not peculiar to the Vedanta. In Brahmanism, and later, Buddhism, we find the classic philosophies of desire. But reflection the world over easily discovers that desire for things shackles the spirit, weakens benevolence, kills metaphysics. When the mind generalizes the petty hubbub of life, as in Piers Ploughman's field of folk, or in Bunyan's or Thackeray's Vanity Fair, it perceives pygmies enslaved by their worldly desires to delusions of greatness. Therefore, withdrawal from the world has always been a formula for spiritual liberation. Perhaps Shelley's attention was directed toward the enslaving effect of desire by the story of St. Cyprian's infatuation for Justina, found in Calderon's *Magico Prodigioso*, which he was reading and translating early in this year. But in all his previous poems, his scorn of worldliness notwithstanding, there is a singular obtuseness in respect of the philosophical implications of this idea. The reason is patent. He was not by temperament a recluse. He forever craved intellectual and emotional companionship. His vision was of a regenerated, genial society, not of a perfected psychic solitary. Therefore his expostulation with selfishness has been political rather than metaphysical. In *Hellas*, we have seen, there is some anticipation of the philosophic use to which he was to put this spiritual commonplace in this last composition. But the best text for the new disquisition is a line in *Adonais:* " the contagion of the world's slow stain." William Michael Rossetti, we remember, long since observed that this line states the main subject of the *Triumph*.

Perhaps the scorn he suffered from the world, and a certain, always innate, now steadily growing worldliness on Mary's part, were driving Shelley at this time to idealize seclusion. One remembers the dream of seclusion toward the close of *Epipsychidion*, in its suggestion of escape from an unsympathetic world quite different from the usual bower-theme of a bliss attained within a perfected society. Be circumstances what they were, in these ringing tercets, many of them gaining something, in spite of their enjambement, from the marvellous gravity of Dante's *terzine*, is Shelley's first considerable poetic realization of the ancient philosophy of desire.

He is not concerned with ascetic practice as a practical means to attain a remote Kingdom of Heaven. The religious expediency of the Christian eremites of Egypt is erratic, outlandish barbarism beside the tense beauty of this poem. Here is no calculation of means to render man oblivious to beautiful things, or even to ugliness; nor any attempt by threats to frighten the hedonist. The implied teaching is a serene ethics, inculcating an ungreedy love and a generous rivalry in all beautiful effort. It is greed that falsifies the spirit, substituting mediocrity for excellence, triumphing over the humane ideal.

The machinery of the poem owes much to the first of Petrarch's *Trionfi*. Like Petrarch, Shelley imagines himself stretched on the grass, wakeful with unhappy thoughts of his past, then falling asleep, and dreaming of a triumphal car surrounded by an endless human crowd. As in Petrarch's vision, the car moves in a blinding light, a mysterious figure is enthroned upon it, and someone by the wayside proceeds to explain the symbol to the poet. Yet other resemblances have been pointed out by Professor Bradley. The meaning of the symbol in the two poems is, of course, quite different; for Petrarch contemplates only the triumph of love, especially youthful love, over man; not of life itself over spirit.

The car is the car of life. The light it emits is icy cold, like the freezing eagerness of selfish desire; it obscures the sun itself, as greed obscures good. The figure within, deformed and darkly veiled, crouching in the shadow of a tomb, is, according to some commentators, the Soul; but surely Bradley is right in calling it " the conqueror Life " — represented, I would add, as a Death. A four-faced charioteer, blindfolded, guides the car. Unable to see in any direction, eyes banded by desires, ignorant of the deeper life of the spirit, like the religious bigot and the political tyrant, the charioteer guides the car awry. Nevertheless, it proceeds solemnly, majestically; and one is reminded of the regal calm of Jupiter in *Prometheus Unbound* — " one that does, not suffers wrong." The world's mighty conquerors and its ribald crowd follow the triumphal car as victims, vanquished by life. All are there, save

> . . . the sacred few who could not tame
> Their spirits to the conquerors, but, as soon
> As they had touched the world with living flame,

> Fled back like eagles to their native noon.

Amazed at this sad pageantry, the poet would ask the meaning of this scene where all is amiss. A voice answers, " Life! " It is the voice of Rousseau, the Apostle of Nature: a soul so worn and warped by its immoderate worship of the heart's desires and fears and hates that it has the semblance of the distortion death produces in nature — a figure gnarled like an ancient root twisting from a hillside, the thin, discoloured hair hanging limply and widely like withered grass, mere empty holes where once the eyes had burned. It is the figure of a heavenly soul stained with desire, victim of the world's slow corruption. Rousseau becomes interpreter. He points out certain forms that are chained fast to the car of life, men who for all their greatness in deeds and thoughts never learned perfect control of desire, or who were hurried down the stream of life, temporarily forgetful of the spiritual mystery their material achievements could not repress. There are Napoleon and Plato, Alexander and Caesar, Aristotle and Bacon, and the great bards of antiquity who " quelled the passions which they sung," and Fathers of the Church " who rose like shadows between man and God," eclipsing what they worshipped; but neither Socrates nor Christ, for they attained complete self-mastery. But the poet is deathly weary of this perpetual flow of souls conquered by life, and his heart is sick with wonder as to the meaning of it all. The confusion, the futile misery of it! With the Preacher, he cries, " What is man that thou art mindful of him? " Whence comes the soul, whither does it go? What is the reason, the plan of it all? Rousseau gives Shelley's own answer to these First Questions:

> *Whence* I am, I partly seem to know,

> And *how* and by what paths I have been brought
> To this dread pass, methinks even thou mayst guess.
> *Why* this should be, my mind can compass not;

> Whither the conqueror [Life] hurries me, still less.

Then, with details reminiscent of Dante, follows another of Shelley's myths of the mystery of being, narrated by Rousseau. The condition of the soul before birth, or between incarnations, is figured as a sweet oblivion in a Lethean valley, like Spenser's Garden of Adonis,

> . . . the first seminary
> Of all things that are borne to live and dye
> According to their kynds.

In this seminary Rousseau's own soul had at length awaked, and seen a gentle light diviner than the sun, and heard magic sounds woven into one oblivious melody. The sun, symbol of ultimate good, threaded the forests with emerald fire. But in the heart of the sun, as it amidst the blaze of its own glory, was a Shape of intenser light, soul of its soul — another feminine incarnation of the Idea of beauty. This Shape, advancing through the silver music of invisible rain and in the midst of rainbows, like one in dreams treading lily-paven lakes through a silver mist, made all things seem unreal in comparison with her own intensity of beauty. Step by step she trampled beneath her sweet, entrancing feet all common memories and thoughts, even as the revelation of the One annihilates commonplace particularities. To her, as coming from the nameless, inconceivable realm of essential being — from the very cave of Demogorgon — and bringing thence the spell whereby particularity both is made and again, in vision, unmade, Rousseau himself had addressed Shelley's recent ques-

tion: "Show whence I came, and where I am, and why."
Whereupon she gave him to drink of her cup of nepenthe.
Straightway from his mind was erased all memory of that
sweet Lethean valley, as a wave removes a track upon the sand,
and he found himself gazing at the vision of the car of life,
though all the while he was dimly conscious of the unseen
presence keeping its obscure tenor beside his path, even as
Shelley was haunted always by the shadowy presence.

The cold-bright car, attended by its rout of victims, moved
across the grove. Then the air became grey with phantoms.
Dim shapes hovered in confusion: some were like eagles on
the wing, others quaintly danced upon sunny streams; some
were cradled in royal ermine, or like vultures sat on the
crowns of pontiffs; or chattering like restless apes, or humble
like tamed falcons, perched on vulgar hands; others, like
evening clouds of gnats and marsh-flies, thronged about the
heads of lawyers and statesmen, priests and theorists; and
some fell, like discoloured snow, on the hearts of young
lovers, and were melted by the gentle ardour they extinguished. At long last, Rousseau became aware of the origin
of all these forms which stained the track of life. From each
figure about the car, from every firmest limb and fairest face,
these phantoms, superficially like the *simulacra* of Lucretius
(IV. 99), fell incessantly, the while the beauty of each figure
waned slowly and care took its place. In the eyes where at
first hope had shone, now

> *Desire*, like a lioness bereft
>
> Of her last cub, glared ere it died; each one
> Of that great crowd sent forth incessantly
> These shadows, numerous as the dead leaves blown
>
> In autumn evening from a poplar tree.

With these phantoms of desire all the world was filled. Mask
after mask, they fell from every countenance, until, long be-

fore the close of the day, every soul which in the morning
had waked in the oblivious valley with a heavenly joy, grew
weary of the ghastly performance, and fell, Rousseau among
them, by the wayside and were nursed by the food of opinion. Those fell soonest from whom most shadows had passed.

"Then, what is life?" cries the poet. The context implies
the answer I have written above: Life is desire, and the
triumph of life is the triumph of the lower desires over the
spirit, over the higher desires. At last the dæmon-of-the-
world idea, which in Chapter II we have traced in the
bookish *Mab* and *Dæmon* fragments, and in Chapter IV in
the half-true Jupiter-theme of the *Prometheus*, has united
with this profounder realization of the human adventure as a
pursuit and purgation of desire, to produce Shelley's best
reading of life and death.

The beauty of this poem, particularly the beauty of the
myth of the oblivious valley, is of the type the poet has made
so peculiarly his own that it is called by his name, Shelleyan.
The well-known elements are here: the metaphysical Idea
and its emotional aura, the embodiment of both in a profusion
of figures drawn from nature and mysterious dream, the
subtle analogies of poetic experience and natural forms, the
scintillation of light and colour, the eager movement, the music as of the essence of beauty — the whole effect that of adding spirit to sense, or, better, revealing the spirit in sense.

But one characteristic element is lacking — death. Desire
has taken the place of death! Death is no longer the symbol,
always illogical however impulsively natural, of the ugliness
of life. From a symbol of the ugly we are taken to the cause
of the ugly — the lower desires. And one may well question
how, after the victorious end of the pursuit of death, in
Adonais, in a synthesis that annihilated its worn-out antithesis
to life and beauty, Shelley could continue to use it in its old
form in any major poetic effort. In this major fragment, at
any rate, he has turned away from it. There is less about

death in *The Triumph of Life* than in any other of Shelley's
greater poems. Turning away from death, he has answered
the question, " What most of all obscures for men that spiritual synthesis of experience, that high realization of the
becoming-process, that indescribable vision of a ' substance '
of which matter and mind are but forms? " The obscuring
cause is the lower desires.

Therein he is in partial agreement with those classic Eastern
philosophies of which mention has been made; as was Anatole
France when of human tragedy he ironically remarked:
" Desire nothing and evil-doing will be done away with."
The Buddhist says that desire binds us to the wheel of life;
Shelley avers that desire chains us to the triumphal car of life,
which drags its slaves behind it as in the triumph of a Roman
emperor.

But the agreement is only partial, after all; for in a very
fundamental respect Shelley's teaching is not in complete accord with some, at least, of the Oriental philosophies of desire. By every implication of the fragment it is evident that
by desires Shelley means only the lower desires, whereas the
Buddhist finds all desire retardative. But Shelley would sub-
scribe Aristotle's doctrine that it is by desire the universe is
ruled — by the universal appetite for the lower goods, by the
human desires for higher goods, by the highest desire for
the essence of being, which rules the philosopher. Perhaps the
completed poem would have drawn such distinctions clearly.
Such distinctions and such a conclusion would accord with
the high desire for spiritual reality which informs the
Adonais.

The myth of the Lethean valley, the awakening of the
soul there as the sun floods in, the projection of the Shape
from the heart of the sun, the soul's draught of nepenthe, and
the presence therewith of the car of life, with all its effort of
phantom desires, the while the individual retains some dim
intuition of the hidden presence of the mysterious, ultimate

Shape — all this is an attempt, not to explain, but symbolically to poetize the relation of the Many to the One. The problem of that relationship is the rock on which so many philosophies split, even Aristotle's, but notably Plato's and Spinoza's and Berkeley's. But it is interesting to remember, in view of Shelley's approach to Vedantic ways of thinking, that Samkara, in his commentary on the *Vedanta Sutra*, boldly affirms that we cannot conceive the relation between the Many and the One. However, in one of the *Upanishads* we find a parallel to the intuitive awareness of the Shape, or ultimate reality, viz., the teaching that though ultimate reality cannot be defined, it may be grasped through intuition, but this intuition is not communicable. It is supreme knowledge, quite different from inferential knowledge. It is the knowledge vouchsafed to Shelley as he wrote the concluding lines of *Adonais*. It is the knowledge vouchsafed to Plotinus and the mystics in general, who are so very certain about what no one who is not a mystic can be in the least certain. It is that alleged super-sensory, super-rational knowledge, or momentary mystical awareness, in which, it is said, the paradox of unity in variety is solved without the sacrifice of either term to the other. But quite aside from the question of the final validity of this knowledge is the undeniable fact that the possession of it has always made for a triumph over life and death. To that victory both *Adonais* and the *Triumph of Life* bear witness.

In another direction Shelley's thought seems to be making a final advance to one of the most liberating of moral ideas — an advance the earlier stages and anticipations of which we have seen in the beginning of *Julian and Maddalo* and the end of *Prometheus Unbound*. From the insistence upon the supreme good that lies in self-mastery, such as that of the free souls, Socrates and Jesus, it is to be inferred that Salvation is an achievement of the individual rather than of society. The Kingdom of God is not to be a realistic perfected community, but is a state of individual mind achieved continually, not in some far off time. For his socialistic panacea, Shelley is substituting the liberation of the individual through mastery of the lower desires — the ultimate *rationale* of all effort, the ethical justification of all idealism. The poem, indeed, is cast in the terms of Shelley's old political theorizing: it is shot through with an antipathy to the desires of bigots and tyrants; it is conceived in life-terms that are applicable to that antipathy. But instead of proceeding to denunciation of tyranny and bigotry, of a special class of tyrants and bigots, and anticipating a City of God to be realized by the destruction of a class of human beings, he is concerned with each individual's liberation through self-mastery. At the same moment, then, that he has exchanged his imperfect symbol of death for the principle of desire, he has coördinated his political theory with his philosophy of salvation for the individual.

Adonais and the *Triumph* are companion, or supplementary, poems. They both strike out higher syntheses and in doing that overcome the old complaint against death. In *Adonais* the synthesis of life and death in an indescribable end or " substance " is the more pronounced; in the *Triumph* the synthesis of society and the individual in the progressive liberation of the latter is the more pronounced. The pursuit of death is ended. The victory is complete — moral, aesthetic, and mystical. " The last enemy that shall be destroyed is death."

Therewith, on July 8, 1822, Shelley entered his own death. In the " Ariel " he sailed out into a sea-fog. The weather grew sultry. For twenty minutes a furious storm raged. That was the end.

The last days at Casa Magni had been crowded with premonitions and visions, and Jane Williams is reported to have said " He is seeking what we all avoid, death."

INDEX